YARN · THREAD · STRING

— MAKING, MANUFACTURING *and* CREATING —

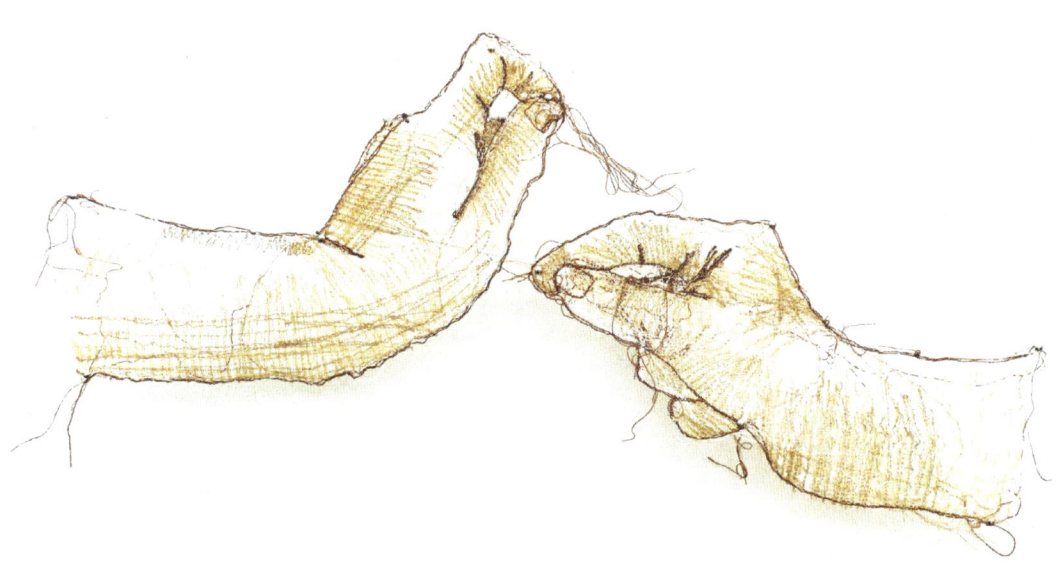

ROVING TEXTILES, AMANDA McCAVOUR

WRITING & DESIGN

Janine Vangool

COPYEDITING

Correy Baldwin

©2021 UPPERCASE publishing inc

This book may not be reproduced in any manner without written permission. You are welcome to share photos of this book in your life on Instagram: #encyclopediaofinspiration @uppercasemag

Art and photography copyright belongs to the artists.

PRINTED IN CANADA BY THE PROLIFIC GROUP

BLUE SKY FIBERS

Yarn keeps us warm,
thread reveals who we are
and string ties us together.

UPPERCASE PUBLISHING INC

201B – 908, 17th Avenue SW
Calgary, Alberta, Canada T2T 0A3

Contents

A. ZARINAH NURI	8
AIMEE BETTS	14
AMANDA MCCAVOUR	22
ANDREA REVOY	30
ANNA HUSEMANN	36
BETZ WHITE	44
BLUE SKY FIBERS	52
BRIGGS & LITTLE	60
BROOKLYN TWEED	66
BUREAU BAGGERMAN	74
CARMEN BOHN	80
CAROLINA REIS	86
COCOKNITS	92
CRAFTING THE HARVEST	98
CUSTOM WOOLEN MILLS	104
DREW MCKEVITT	112
ELIZABETH ASHDOWN	122
FIBREVOLUTION	132
FRECKLE & KNOT	142
HANNAH BURNWORTH	148
HEMPTIQUE	156
HUSTON TEXTILE CO.	162
ITO YARN	170

JEREMY R. BROOKS *178*	SAYAN CHANDA *342*
JUNE CASHMERE *184*	SECOND ASCENT DESIGNS *352*
KELLY WRIGHT *192*	SECRET WOOL SOCIETY *358*
KIM MCCOLLUM *200*	SHAWN O'HAGAN *366*
LIZ SOFIELD *208*	SHENEQUA *374*
MAINE THREAD COMPANY *214*	SIMONE ELIZABETH SAUNDERS *382*
MARINA DEMPSTER *220*	SIMONE POST *390*
MATA AHO COLLECTIVE *228*	TEMARICIOUS *400*
MILLPOST MERINO *234*	THE ENDERY *408*
MODERN MACRAMÉ *244*	THE WONDERMAKERS COLLECTIVE *412*
NADIA NIZAMUDIN *250*	TIM EADS *420*
NADINE FLAGEL *258*	TUIJA HEIKKINEN *428*
NATALIE CICCORICCO *268*	ULLA-STINA WIKANDER *436*
NINE LIVES TWINE *274*	UNRAVELLED YARNS *444*
PAPERPHINE *280*	WE GATHER *448*
PICHINKU FIBERS *286*	WEAVER HOUSE *458*
PURL SOHO *292*	WHITEHALL STUDIO *468*
RACHEL PARKER *300*	WILD FIBERS *476*
ROVING TEXTILES *308*	WILDWESTDYE *484*
RUTH MILLER *314*	WONDERFIL SPECIALTY THREADS *490*
RUTH WOODS *324*	OTHER UPPERCASE ENCYCLOPEDIAS *496*
SABRINA SACHIKO NIEBLER *334*	

A. Zarinah Nuri

Drawing from textures and patterns found in nature and the "intuitive forms found in the magic of my dreams," A. Zarinah Nuri, currently based in Providence, Rhode Island, designs woven textiles and surface patterns. "Anything that crosses my path can become the conceptual source of rich and innovative art and design," she says. "Ultimately, I seek to convey the mystery and music of life. Through my work, I hope to inspire viewers to conjure up their own connection to the enchantment of everyday life."

"I come from a family of makers—from sewers to graphic designers to quilters," says Zarinah. "Watching the women and men in my family make things created an almost intuitive sensibility towards the elements of cloth in all its forms. I remember having a bead loom that I had to dress with string as an 11 year old. I find it amazing that thread, yarn and string are these deceivingly simple elements that can construct garments, tapestries, cloth, jewellery. I really just love feeling the texture of yarn in all its various forms—cotton, wool, silk and the man-made!"

Her work is deeply influenced by travels in her early years: "I remember sights, sounds, colours and textures from West Africa and India. I still hold memories of open-air markets, women and men dressed in fabrics that swirled with graphic strokes, patterns and bright colours. My work often starts out as mistakes and big messes that form from taking chances, revising and ultimately recovering into new possibilities."

Zarinah recently graduated from Thomas Jefferson University in Philadelphia, where she worked on floor looms and jacquard looms, exploring various yarns and materials, and dyeing and printmaking methods. "Currently, I am starting to think about how

"I love pattern, the play of lines, textures and colours. One thing I really like about producing textiles is that a diverse approach makes my heart sing. It's funny, most people say, ooh I can tell you made that, but I often feel like the things I make don't connect, that I don't have a signature style—which I like! It keeps life interesting and always in the realm of creating new things and material exploration."

I want to build a business. My first step is imagining how the handmade can be at the forefront of the mainstream. I eventually want to offer my soft goods to the interior design markets, boutique hotels and museum stores."

The coronavirus pandemic has been a trying time and a reason for reflection. "Sometimes the smallest touches of light, like the light that comes through my window in the afternoon, sparks an energy that can carry me through some excruciatingly tough moments. Mostly I hope that this image of an afternoon light leads to a brighter future, perhaps one that is more unifying and less divisive."

It is important to Zarinah that a connection to the hand of the maker is evident in her creative endeavours. Bringing beauty into the world is the highest calling of art: "Life can be so beautiful," she says, "Enjoy it as you can." ❋

afutureunitingall.com
@afutureunitingall

"I often have what I call anxiety of the hands—I just need to make things. Making is a form of expression that soothes my soul."

STUDIO PLANS

Right now, I have a room where I work alone—my studio is a work in progress, so to speak. I have some shelves where I store fibre and am super excited to be in a process of acquiring a loom to further woven play and support myself beyond my day job!

BEAUTIFUL OBJECTS FOR THE HOME

Aimee Betts

As a mixed-media textile designer, Aimee Betts makes handcrafted objects and one-off commissioned art pieces. Aimee balances her creative practice with a part-time job as a "stitch and fabric practice leader" in the art department at Goldsmiths, University of London. After a decade in the hustle and bustle of the city, Aimee and her husband and daughter have recently relocated to Berkshire, England. "We are adjusting to a slower pace of life after a decade of living in a fast urban environment."

Aimee was one of six siblings, growing up in social housing in 1980s Leicestershire. "As a child I was

"The ideal project for me is one that is challenging and engaging, and flexes my creativity. I enjoy the complex and layered discussions that creativity provokes."

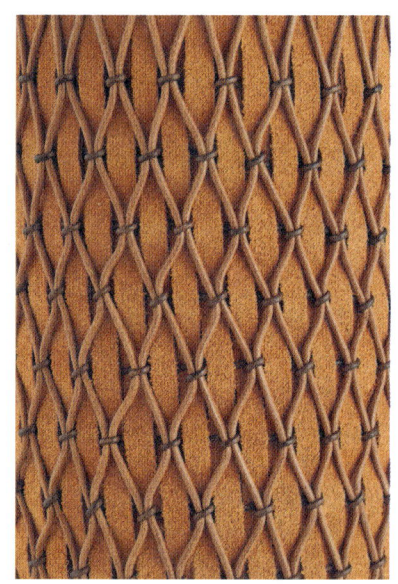

known for drawing," she says. "I loved the freedom the expression gave me, and I still vividly remember the raw flow of energy that mark making gave me." A first-generation university student, Aimee says the experience was a real privilege. "I was very lucky to study a BA in multimedia textiles at Loughborough University, and later an MA in mixed-media textiles at the Royal College of Art."

Loughborough, a small market town, had a notable lack of good fabric or haberdashery shops, which led Aimee into hardware shops during her studies there. "I found myself working with sheet materials, such as paper, card, heavy-weight Vilene used to make handbags, fusible vinyl, plastic and recycled materials," she says. She made ends meet by working multiple waitressing and bar jobs and earning bursaries. "I have always had a strong work ethic, and have enjoyed working multiple roles and wearing many hats. So far I have managed to avoid working the nine-to-five existence."

Later, while freelancing for a textile design studio, Aimee was introduced to textile sample-making: "I discovered that embroidery and fabric manipulation was a commercial pathway, and I wanted to learn more about this discipline. With the support from my boss, I applied to do an MA at the Royal College of Art." Following graduation, Aimee attended a three-month design residency in Gujarat, India, which exposed her to artisanal embroidery, appliqué and block printing. "When I returned, I was a bit lost. I knew I wanted to start my own business, but I wasn't really sure how to go about this. I signed up to do the Crafts Council UK Hothouse program, which offers mentoring and support for emerging makers. The program helped me to acknowledge my goals, and within a year I set up my first studio, got a part-time job as a stitch technician at Chelsea College of Arts and began making work for the New Craftsmen gallery. This allowed me to shift my focus onto creating work for interiors."

"With a lot of my work I am applying a decoration onto a surface. It can be very difficult to combine the two components, so a lot of consideration goes into the materiality of the work. I believe decoration should add value to an object or surface. If the object or surface looks better without the decorative elements, then the idea isn't working."

COLLABORATION

I often collaborate with other makers and outsource production when I'm designing with processes that aren't my skill set. For example, I work with a woodworker who hand turns my lamp bases and handles on a lathe, and a metalworker to create the frames for my mirrors. These then provide a base for me to apply my techniques.

The form and function of the object tends to dictate the materials and techniques that I use. I want the outcome to be fit for purpose and durable. For example, for the Ricasso Mirror collection, I use a vegetable-tanned leather cord and a looping technique, which is suitable for the tubular form of the frame. If I'm making cushions, I source the best vintage linen and hand-dyed velvet I can find and I use a wide range of hand and digital embroidery techniques.

"This was a really special time for me, as I felt completely immersed in London's vibrant craft and textile scene. I loved the balance of working with students in an educational environment and developing my own practice. Having a creative pursuit has allowed me to embrace opportunities and be open to learning new things."

Aimee's work generally falls into two categories: three-dimensional functional objects and soft goods like fabric, cushions and throws. One particular specialty is her use of braiding in her handles, mirrors and lamps. "This is a braiding style comprised of leather ribbon, waxed cotton cord and hemp cord," she explains. "The idea began after a research trip to the Wallace Collection in London, where I saw historic European sword handles. I was drawn to the decorative and functional qualities of the handles, and the contrast between the fine metallic threads that are used to form an impressive grip surface."

"The techniques I use draw on the traditions of embroidery, knotting and braiding, as well as incorporating newer technologies such as digital embroidery," says Aimee. "I enjoy marrying fast and slow processes, to get the balance of a handmade object that is commercially viable." ✻

MAKER MOTIVATIONS

I am motivated to create beautiful original objects for the home, using hand-crafted skills and processes. As a maker I believe that being involved in craft making and exploring the philosophy can genuinely enrich and improve a person's quality of life — whether it is as a collector, maker or enthusiast.

Increasingly I have been thinking more about the slow movement and my own association with it. As a consumer of mass-produced products it is often difficult to make informed choices. I feel that I am able to control some of the decision making behind the sourcing and production in my own practice.

What I hope people see in my work is that there has been a deep consideration of the materials and techniques that have been chosen. I am motivated to create emotionally durable objects that are cherished.

AT HOME AND AT WORK

My workspace is a medium-sized room at the back of the house behind the kitchen that's separate from the rest of the house. Working from home enables me to balance my creative practice with the domestic duties of family life.

I have a range of embroidery hoops and tables of various sizes, a Domestic sewing machine, a Princess pleater and a Lilliput circular knitting machine. The tallor bobbins of threads are stored on narrow shelves, smaller bobbins are kept on a thread rack, embroidery threads are stowed in a sewing box and a Bisley drawer set, and I use large clear plastic boxes to store cones of yarns and leather cords. I also have a pegboard system for reels of cords and sewing paraphernalia.

At work in the Stitch and Fabric Department at Goldsmiths University I have access to a digital embroidery machine, a walking foot machine, industrial sewing machines, industrial overlockers and a tufting machine.

I work with freelance makers who are often former students, who assist me for my larger projects and commissions.

aimeebetts.com
@aimeebetts

AIMEE BETTS

DRAWING WITH THREAD

Amanda McCavour

The floating, delicate works of Amanda McCavour are made by washing a portion of the work away. Stitching by machine, Amanda creates thread drawings and large-scale embroidered installations. "By sewing into fabric that dissolves in water, I can build up stitched lines on a temporary surface," she explains. "The crossing threads create strength so that when the fabric is dissolved, the thread drawing can hold together without a base. With only the thread remaining, these images appear as though they would be easily unravelled, despite the work's ravelled strength. I am interested in thread's assumed vulnerability, its ability to unravel and its strength when it is sewn together."

Amanda's discovery of this technique dates to a 2006 drawing course at York University in Toronto in which her professor simply defined drawing as line. Within this loose interpretation, she began to experiment with sewn lines, using thread as a method to give line more of a physical presence. She wanted to make a drawing that existed only out of thread, with no base. This shift in materials—from lines made on paper to embroidery—was a significant turning point in her artistic practice.

"Stitch is used in my artwork to explore various concepts such as connections to home, the fibres of the body and more formal considerations of thread's accumulative presence," Amanda explains. "I explore embroidery's duality—its subtle quality versus its accumulative presence, and its structural possibilities versus its fragility. My work speaks to themes of memory, environment, colour and line."

Initially, her embroideries were quite small, but as her skill in this technique grew, so did the scale of her work. "Shifting the scale of my pieces to a larger scale

"I want my works to bring viewers into a playful, imaginative, dream-like space filled with line, colour and texture. In these pieces, viewers are invited to walk through paths that I create in the installation works."

"I'm often inspired by things that are related to memory and looking back. This is a common theme I can see throughout my room installation pieces, the more abstract dream spaces and some pieces inspired by botany. It is important to me that the subjects relate to the material of thread somehow—either its delicacy or its transparency."

moved my ideas into a different space, and this began with an idea of home and place," she says. In fact, she created a thread-rendering of the kitchen in a previously rented apartment. "Making this piece required me to revisit, remember and recreate a space formerly known as my home. Part shrine, part monument, part memorial, the thread drawings act as a tribute to a room that once was. This project was the first of a series of three installations based on my homes that were always made after I had left them."

Her work often takes over gallery spaces to create lace-like, immersive environments with delicate thread landscapes, spirographic constructions and colourful florals. ✢

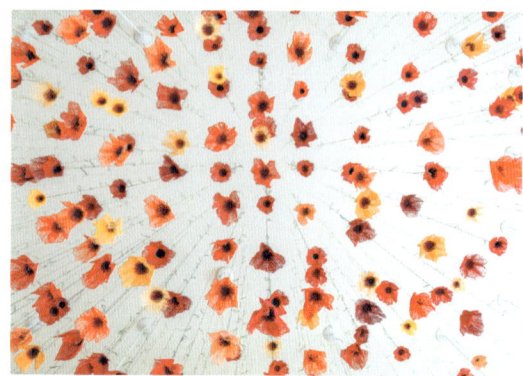

PREFERRED THREAD

I specifically like polyester thread because of the range of colours available. I love bright, saturated and neon colours and the effect created by many slight lines of thread together.

THE DESIRABLE CHARACTERISTICS OF THREAD

TRANSPARENCY

I like thread's fine nature. Creating images and installations out of embroidered parts allows me to create ephemeral and transparent pieces that are both in a space and also seemingly on the verge of not being there. These works are lace-like, with the ground of the work removed. You see the thread and the spaces between the thread. They are relatively light, allowing them to move slightly with the air currents in the room, which adds to the installation pieces.

STRENGTH

Another thing that I think is really interesting about fibre is how strong it is. Although the work appears to be quite delicate, it actually has a lot of strength that is created through the intersecting sewn lines. The ravelled strength of the work is quite surprising.

FLEXIBILITY

For practical reasons, I like how I can roll and pack up pieces made from fibre. Almost like breathing in and out, these pieces can expand to fill whole rooms and then contract to fit in a small Rubbermaid bin that gets stored underneath my sewing table.

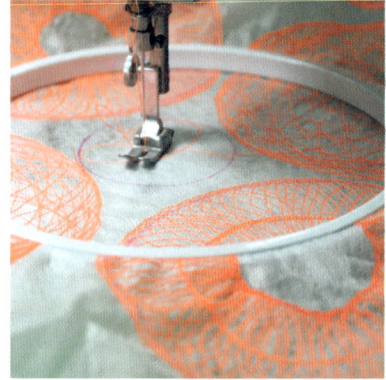

CREATIVE PROCESS

My designs start with drawing and research. I'm often sketching on paper before I start stitching. I like to look at books and take photos as part of my research, often collecting these images and keeping them on my studio wall. I don't keep a sketchbook but I do have binders of drawings and sketches that I keep. I draw things small and large to explore scale and I use different colours.

Then I move to the testing phase of my process, where I stitch things at the sewing machine. This testing phase is exciting because often I have to change my drawings to fit the process and the structural challenges of working with the water-soluble fabric.

Once I've tested things and finalized the design, I move on to the production phase of the project, where often I'm making many of one unit or moving to a larger scale. This phase can often take months (or years), so I often manage a couple of different projects at a time to keep things from getting too monotonous.

The next part of the project is finishing: cutting threads, pressing pieces and packing them for installation.

amandamccavour.com
@amandamccavour

SPACE TO CREATE

My studio is about a three-minute walk from where I live. The space is small, around 10 feet by 14 feet, which some people find hard to believe, since my work is often quite big.

My white walls are filled with colourful objects. I have a pegboard with my spools of thread arranged as a colourful gradient. On the walls, I've created boards where I have sketches and material samples for the projects I'm currently working on. These boards are a place to test out colours and textures, and to sometimes step away to think and reflect.

I have three different kinds of sewing machines that I use on a regular basis and they are out on the tables for easy access. Under my tables is storage for the large installation pieces, which I store in Rubbermaid bins. (Surprisingly, the installations pack down very small.)

BLUE MOON STUDIO

Andrea Revoy

Andrea Revoy works from her home in Creston, British Columbia, Canada. "I am fortunate that my studio is in the middle of a cherry orchard surrounded by mountains," she says. From this idyllic setting, Andrea imagines and crafts ceramic figures that are often coiffed and adorned with colourful yarns that she dyes and spins. "My current ceramic focus is primarily hand building sculptures with a bit of tile work thrown into the mix. I am attracted to colours, patterns, textures and flowers, and I love making whimsical, crazy things that have a quirky edge to them."

Andrea thrives with this multidisciplinary approach to making art. "Whether I am working with clay or wool, my work consists of many different methods and techniques to achieve the results I desire," she says. "Quality workmanship, attention to detail and a sense of humour are at the core of all my work."

Creating doll-like figures has been a lifelong interest: from a young age, Andrea would spend countless hours sewing doll clothes and making knit rugs and furnishings for their houses. And though she didn't learn to spin fibre until her thirties, she quickly became infatuated. "I was totally hooked and was spinning all the time—crazy big yarns with long locks, glitter, textures, silk, whatever I could spin into the yarn. I went through a *lot* of fibre and started to source my own fleeces for processing. This led to dyeing my own wool and growing an enormous stash. The problem was I had so much weird yarn and no one knew what to do with it when I tried to sell it. I decided to add this crazy yarn to my ceramic sculptures. I could make it as big and bright as I wanted and it would always have a use!" ✳

"I like to tell a story with my work, whether real or imagined, that makes people laugh. Life is too short to be too serious and my work reflects this."

"Seeing people laugh at my work or hearing how it has made them feel when seeing it is really gratifying both to me and to that person. I also love hearing what they *think* it means or what they see and how it can be so different than what I intended it to be."

FAVOURITE FIBRES

I love a blend I get of 60% merino, 20% silk and 20% yak. It is amazingly soft, has a natural streaky brown colour, and felts and spins super nice. This fibre blend makes an incredible yarn that has a soft sheen from the silk, some bounce from the merino, and softness and colour from the yak. Because of the brown streaks, when dyed the colour is a more muted tone and is quite lovely.

ANDREA REVOY

"I have this innate need to always be doing something. I think this need to create and make things started at a young age and has evolved into a mindset or daily practice for me. I use these skills to energize as well as to calm my mind."

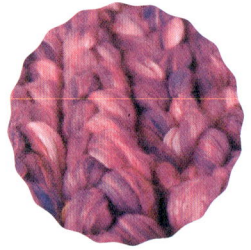

OPEN TO INSPIRATION

I try to stay open in heart and mind to suggestions coming from the world around me. Time goes so fast and we miss so much happening in our small circle surrounding us; I try not to miss the good bits. It is easy to get sucked into the black hole of social media and the Internet so I try to limit what I see and do there, as to not overload myself with excess stuff. I find this can stifle my creativity. When I really need inspiration, it comes flowing in if I am open to it. I know this sounds kooky but I really believe that if you open yourself up to the universe, the universe will provide what you need.

bluemoonstudio.ca
@bluemoonpotsandfibre

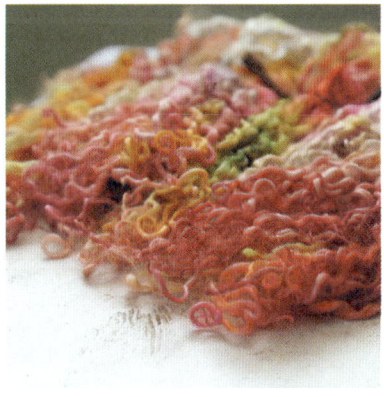

TWO STUDIOS

I have two studio spaces. The dirty studio is a converted two-car garage attached to my house; half of this space is dedicated to ceramics and half for dyeing fibre. My other studio is a clean space in my basement where I do my finishing work and store all the wool. I struggled with time management to work in both mediums for years and I have come up with a way that works great for me. I work one or two weeks in ceramics and then I work one week in fibre, which, along with dyeing, will include all the webstore work as well, where I sell fibre and supplies.

Anna Husemann

Based in Hamburg, Germany, textile designer Anna Husemann specializes in experimental knitting. During her bachelor's studies in textile design, she explored weaving, knitting, screen printing, embroidery and pattern design. She selected machine knitting for her design master program. "During my textile design studies, I worked in a non-commercial way by creating experimental samples and uncommon surfaces," she says. Anna started her business, PLYSH, in order to make these experiments wearable. A recent product, for example, is a backpack with interchange-

"My motivation is to slow down today's fast-moving consumer society by creating bold and colourful as well as environmentally friendly individual pieces. I try to think as sustainably as possible in every step of the design and production process."

able covers so that a variety of knitted surfaces can be displayed. "I am currently working on a collection of colourful hats knitted out of hand-dyed local merino wool. I am still at the beginning of my own label and it is slow but steady progress."

Anna's work focuses on the interaction between colour, shape and material to create haptic contrasts and vibrant surfaces, bridging textile art and textile design. "I try to interpret the traditional craft of knitting in a modern, abstract way—to take a step back from small repetitive motifs in order to achieve an expressive, pictorial character."

Her preferred knitting technique is intarsia, which allows her to incorporate multiple colours in her work. "Even on the knitting machine, it is a very hand-manipulated process, and knitting intarsia by hand means you need a lot of patience for untangling the balls for all the fields of colour," Anna says. "It is all worth it because intarsia can create a spontaneity and irregularity that I like to work with." Anna enjoys creating interesting work through pattern and colour by using monochromatic colours or slightly odd colour combinations. "When I design a new product, I spend hours thinking about colour combinations and material choices, as for me this is the most important part," she explains. The shapes are inspired by organic forms created by hand-cut paper collages.

"I often start new projects with a series of handmade paper collages that capture moods as well as colours and shapes. The analogous cutting results in irregular shapes, which are set in relation to each other by overlays and negative forms. These illustrations serve as a template for knitting motifs. I translate them into textiles by filling these shapes with various materials." ✽

FAMILY CRAFTS

I grew up in a family of creative women. My great-grandmother and my grandmother were both seamstresses and my mother is a passionate knitter. When I was a child, they made me handmade dresses and toys, and I learned to knit even before school. Craft binds us all together.

FAVOURITE FIBRE

I prefer to work with 100% sheep's wool. Besides all the impressive characteristics wool comes with, I just love how it feels while wearing it. I try to integrate more and more local sheep wool into my projects. It is important for me to only work with natural fibres. In every step of the product development, from designing to shipping, I try to think of a way to avoid or replace plastic.

As a maker, I want to be responsible for the materials I work with. I try to always use natural materials, recycled yarns and paper, search for local fibres and use up as many leftover yarns as possible. What I like about working with leftover yarns is that the design process is affected by the amount of yarn that is left, and the shapes may have to be adjusted during the knitting process.

WORKSPACE

As I have just recently started my own business, I am still developing my workspace. I share the studio with my partner, who is a communication designer, but I more and more take up the room. I have two domestic knitting machines with which I make most of my products. What I also use a lot is my sewing machine and a spool knitting machine for making i-cords. I have a huge stash of leftover yarns that are sorted by colour.

I try to work as much outside on the balcony doing admin stuff, designing and knitting, or sewing by hand. We have a little cat and she is my diligent assistant—whatever I am working on she wants to be part of it, sit on it or play with it.

BETZ WHITE DESIGNS

Betz White

Growing up in the 1970s, Betz White remembers macramé, sand painting and papier-mâché. "There were always craft projects happening around our kitchen table," she says. "My mom sewed a lot of our clothes and my dad was super handy with home projects. With their encouragement, I think I believed I could make anything! And that felt like a superpower."

"This really ignited my creativity in ways that helped me problem solve and discover new paths. This is a silly example, but when I was about 10 years old, the TV show *Happy Days* was a huge hit. I wanted a Fonzie T-shirt more than anything! Back in those days, unless they had them at Sears (they didn't) and unless I had the money (I didn't), chances were slim to none that I was getting one. But I had a copy of *Dynamite* magazine with a picture of Fonzie on the cover!" With decoupage ingenuity, Betz got to work. "That may have been the start of my DIY adventures."

Betz pursued her creative interests and majored in art and then fashion design in college. Having learned to knit as a child, in college she learned how to use a hand-operated knitting machine. "It's a similar concept to a loom, only for knitting, not weaving. I was wooed by its apparent speed yet challenged by the learning curve. I loved it so much I bought a used one after graduation with my rent money."

Betz worked for an apparel company, designing children's clothing, but after becoming a mother and juggling both roles for a few years, she decided to stay home with the children and freelance. "I began to play with fibre again, mostly upcycling felted wool sweaters, and started a craft blog in 2006. Things took off quickly from there and I soon found myself doing my first craft show, starting an Etsy shop, writing my first

"A lot of my ideas jump off from a previous project or idea. When inspiration strikes, often it's a new way to approach something or a different use of a material or technique. This discovery process is one of my favourite parts of design work."

"I believe in thoughtful design, skilled craftsmanship and the creative spark inside each one of us."

book and appearing on the *Martha Stewart Show*. It was a busy, exciting time! I hadn't felt that creative since design school and it was very fulfilling. I learned that I had enough skill, experience and motivation to creative-problem-solve my way through starting and running a small business, even if it was a bit by accident!"

Betz allows her interests to determine the course of her business. "I'm focused on teaching various stitching and fibre crafts via patterns, kits, books and workshops ranging from sewn accessories to felt ornaments, embroidery, patchwork and more. In addition, I explore a variety of fibre techniques for personal projects as well as offer one-of-a-kind handcrafted items for sale on my website." She has also rekindled an interest in machine knitting and has created knit

CROSS-TRAINING

My work has spanned a wide variety of craft disciplines over the years. I love being open to crafts that are new to me or revisiting old ones, especially when yarn and fibre are involved. Honestly, that's where some of my best ideas happen, when I'm "creative cross-training." If I'm ever feeling stuck or uninspired, I find that changing gears (projects, techniques) does the trick. Working with my hands always feels therapeutic. The repetitive nature of creating stitch after stitch calms the mind and opens me up to fresh ideas.

patterned pillows, scarves and bags. A yarn-bombing commission for a local yarn shop has been a fun assignment. "Over the past few years, I've knit and wrapped a six-lamppost installation, created a seven-foot striped stocking for a holiday window display and completely embellished a bicycle with knitted segments and pom-poms from fender to fender! Creating public art has been a surprisingly enjoyable endeavour that's really exercised my creative muscles."

Betz loves to explore new materials and techniques. "Learning inspires me!" she declares. "I'm a curious person and a designer at heart, always looking for a new technique, a new combination of materials or just a new perspective." Pairing punch needle with vintage wood vessels to create unique pieces is just one example of the vibrant and playful aesthetic that runs through all of her creative endeavours. Whether designing a product or teaching others, Betz believes that creating is an expression of love: "Love for yourself and those who you may make for." Learning a skill is empowering and confidence building, she says. "My goal is to ignite the creativity of others and to give them that 'superpower' feeling I had as a kid." ✼

FAVOURITE FIBRE

I'm a wool fan, through and through! My passion for wool began with felting and continues through my knitting, punch needle, rug braiding and crewelwork. To me, nothing beats the qualities of wool: its long-lasting durability, stain resistance and incredible texture and beauty. Colour variegation, heathers, tweeds, etc., add extra dimension and depth that make yarns irresistible to me.

betzwhite.com
@betz_white

STUDIO UPSTAIRS

My current studio is in a spare upstairs bedroom in our home. I have plenty of space for my sewing machine, work tables, inspiration wall and futon couch for daydreaming or power napping. For storage, I have a vintage armoire for books and projects-in-work plus two big closets with shelving for materials. Yarn is kept in bins and in a clear shoe organizer that hangs on the back of my door. I work alone and have a large window to the park behind my house, which I love for feeling connected to the outside world.

BETZ WHITE

ALPACA AND MORE

Blue Sky Fibers

A curious preoccupation with alpacas led Linda Niemeyer to buy one, shortly after she graduated from college, some 20 years ago. "Blue Sky Fibers started as a pet project, of sorts," she says. Soon, she found herself with a lot of yarn on hand, which she took to a nearby yarn store that was willing to buy and sell it. "And the rest, as they say, is history."

Based in East Bethel, Minnesota, Blue Sky Fibers is a yarn and pattern wholesale company known for its beautifully crafted and sustainably sourced fibres.

"Ever since the beginning, with a small herd of alpacas in the backyard, the commitment has been there to make yarn in the best way possible. From its beginning in nature, to carding, spinning and dying, Blue Sky Fibers remains true to our values of making beautiful yarn that inspires the creative community. While our exclusive offerings have grown beyond alpaca to include wool, organic cotton, silk and cashmere, the desire for getting makers excited about natural fibres and knitting hasn't changed one bit. It all winds back to the yarn, ensuring that every precious, handmade hank is lovingly filled with endless inspiration."

They partner with mills in the USA, Peru and Italy. "We have been travelling to Peru for the last 20 years," says Linda. "The textures and colours of the fabulous landscape, where llamas, alpacas and sheep graze on the immense plateaus, have inspired spinners, dyers, weavers and knitters for hundreds if not thousands of years, as well as us. From this inspiration, the development stage occurs, with mood boards, fibre and colour trends, and the intent to create the next consciously crafted fibre. Thoughtfully constructed fibre samples arrive in different weights, blends and twists. Each hank of yarn is studied and knit with to know exactly

"From its beginning in nature, to carding, spinning and dying, Blue Sky Fibers remains true to our values of making beautiful yarn that inspires the creative community. While our exclusive offerings have grown beyond alpaca to include wool, organic cotton, silk and cashmere, the desire for getting makers excited about natural fibres and knitting hasn't changed one bit."

what the end result will be for knitters. Then, when the final hank has been designed, the perfect nature-inspired colour palette is created. From there, the final stage of development is working with designers to create a thoughtful and cohesive collection of patterns."

The company is dedicated to making sure its products are "consciously crafted." Linda and her Blue Sky family care. "We care about the whole process: from the ideation stage, to the herders and their animals, to producing natural fibres with low-impact dyes with mills that help the people in their respective communities. Finally, it extends to the service of local yarn stores and to their end consumers, who create something truly beautiful with this exceptional-quality product." ❋

"Our twists, blends and colours create specialty fibres you can't find anywhere else. Each yarn has distinct characteristics: warmth, softness, texture and luxuriousness. Every hank brings unique qualities to both the knitting experience and to the finished pieces."

blueskyfibers.com
@blueskyfibers

ONE COMPANY, TWO BRANDS

Blue Sky Fibers has two brands: Blue Sky Fibers and Spud & Chloë.

Blue Sky Fibers is a selection of all-natural fibres, unique blends and textures, including luxurious baby alpaca, premium wool, silk, cashmere and organic cotton, with 17 yarn lines and over 200 colours.

Spud & Chloë is family friendly and machine washable, using super-wash wool, silk and organic cotton fibres with four yarn lines and over 60 playful colours.

CANADA'S OLDEST MILL

Briggs & Little Woolen Mills

MIKE, JOHN AND CARL LITTLE

With a history stretching back to 1857, Briggs & Little Woolen Mills is located in York Mills, New Brunswick, and is Canada's oldest woolen mill. "We believe the woolen mill was started out of necessity," says Leah Little, who maintains the corporate side of the business. Her husband's ancestor, Roy Little, purchased the mill in the 1890s. "In the 1800s, there was a saw mill, grist mill and woolen mill all located within five kilometres of each other. These businesses not only provided employment for the local residents but also provided essential materials. The wool yarns have always been offered at a modest price and many farmers would shear their sheep and trade the wool for yarn."

"The process of making wool yarn is simple but complex. Our machinery is antiquated but well maintained and it all functions at one speed. No slowing down or speeding up the process!"

Following Roy Little's ownership, the business was then bought by Mathew Briggs and Howard Little in 1916, giving the company the name it holds to this day. The mill was then passed down through subsequent generations, and by 2014 was under the ownership of father and son John and Mike Little. John fully retired in 2020, after working 50 years at the family business. The mill can also celebrate a century of the Little bloodline—there are currently two generations at the mill: Leah's husband, Mike, and their sons John-Michael and Carl.

Briggs & Little Woolen Mills purchases 90% of their raw wool from the Canadian Co-operative Wool Growers, located in Carleton Place, Ontario. "The remaining 10% of the wool we purchase is from local farmers," says Leah. Their inventory of pure wool yarns include eight weights, with colour ranges of up to 47 shades. "Our wool spun and roving unspun yarns are suitable for hand knitting, machine knitting, crocheting, macramé, weaving, rug hooking, punch needles, needle felting and so much more!"

The manufacturing process at Briggs & Little has only changed minimally in its long history, producing consistently functional, high-quality and durable products. "In the office and shipping department, we are fairly modern," says Leah, "but in the woolen mill we are very antiquated! Many pieces of our machinery were constructed by Davis and Furber, dating back as far as 1944, and one of our newer models is a 1976!"

"Our mission is to maintain a high level of quality wool yarns that meet or exceed our customers' needs and expectations," says Leah. The company motto is befitting of yarn that will be part of slow handcrafts such as knitting and rug hooking: "Your time deserves quality." ✼

"Briggs & Little is the oldest vertical woolen mill in Canada. We produce quality wool yarns at an affordable price. With our wide variety of weights and colours, you can create just about any yarn project that your mind can design."

RAW WOOL

UNWASHED WOOL

WOOL WASHING

WASHED WOOL

WASHED WOOL

WOOL DRYER

PICKER ROOM

PICKER ROOM

"THE HOUSE"

"THE HOUSE"

CARDING MACHINE WEIGH PAN

CARDING MACHINE

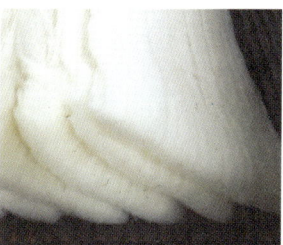

CARDED WOOL

SPINNING FRAME BOBBINS

REELER

REELER BUNCHES

BUTTERFLY SKEINS

5LB BUNDLES

PROCESSING

The raw wool is washed twice in a mild detergent, rinsed, then sent to the dryer.

After going through the wool dryer, it is blown to the picker room, where it is pickered to remove more of the chaff that remains after being washed. We do not use harsh chemicals to "burn out" the chaff, so some remains after the cleaning process.

The pickered wools is then blown to a holding room, which we refer to as the "house," located near the carding machine.

The next step is carding, which creates a beautiful unspun wool. At this point the wool is either made into roving (five strands, unspun) or sent on for further processing into a spun yarn.

The next step to create yarn is with the spinning frame. This process spins the yarn to create a more durable product. If we are creating a multi-ply yarn, it will now go to the twister, which twists the yarn strands together to create a single strand with multiple plies.

Now it's created into a skein of yarn at the reeler. The reeler machine is programmed to give the correct yardage for each weight of yarn made. It rotates the yarn around a frame to create an open skein, then is tied off, weighed and sent to the final station, which we call skeining and pressing. Each skein of yarn is hand twisted into a butterfly skein, pressed into a bundle of 20 and then hand labelled. It's now ready to be placed in storage or packaged and shipped to our customers.

briggsandlittle.com
@briggslittle

JARED FLOOD & LUIGI BOCCIA

Brooklyn Tweed

Jared Flood began his career in the fibre arts as a knitting designer; Brooklyn Tweed was the blog that he began in 2005. He founded the company Brooklyn Tweed in 2010 with its first yarn, Shelter, a two-ply worsted-weight yarn that is now available in 45 different beautifully mottled, heathered colours. "Shelter is woollen spun, meaning the fibres remain in a lofty jumble that traps air and offers remarkable warmth and lightness," he says.

Jared is the company's creative director and photographer, and Luigi Boccia is co-owner and manager of operations. "Since Shelter," says Jared, "we have added five more yarns to our core yarn offerings, as well as released three single-batch, ranch-specific yarns, and have published more than 600 knitting patterns."

"The crisp, minimalist design of our branding, yarn wraps and pattern layouts help to give the rustic and classic beauty of our yarns and patterns room to shine."

Brooklyn Tweed creates yarns produced domestically in America. "We develop and manufacture breed-specific wool yarns that support domestic textile production. This means designing, sourcing, dyeing and spinning our yarns 100% within the USA." Partnering with American ranches, spinning mills and dyehouses helps in keeping the textile industry alive and allows them to create yarns that highlight the unique qualities of specific sheep breeds while carrying on domestic wool production traditions.

"For example, the wool we spin into Shelter, Loft and Quarry comes from Targhee-Columbia sheep in Wyoming, while Arbor's wool is from Targhee sheep in Montana and South Dakota, and Peerie's wool is from Merino sheep in Utah and Nevada," explains Jared, discussing Brooklyn Tweed's different lines. "Dapple's wool content comes from Merino sheep in Colorado and its organic cotton comes from Texas." With the production chain for each of their yarns being unique, there is a lot of complexity for Luigi and

FROM SHEEP TO SKEIN

In making our yarns we aim to honour and carry on domestic wool production traditions. Each mill that we partner with has different types of equipment depending on their history and technical expertise. The equipment varies in age and type of product that the mill spins. Some of our woollen spun yarns are made on very old equipment. It varies from mill to mill.

While the technology has evolved over the decades, the basic process for turning wool fibre into finished yarn remains similar: clean the wool, pull the fibres apart from each other a bit, draft the wool to create a long strand and insert some twist for strength. These strands can be singular or combined for multi-ply yarns. There are many ways to create yarn but these basic steps apply to all.

the team to manage. It isn't straightforward from a geographical or logistical perspective: "Our inaugural yarn, Shelter, is a great example of our yarn's production journey. After the Targhee-Columbia wool is sheared from sheep at our partner ranches in Montana and South Dakota, it is scoured at Bollman Industries in San Angelo, Texas. It is then fleece-dyed at G. J. Littlewood & Son in Philadelphia, Pennsylvania, and woollen spun at Harrisville Designs in Harrisville, New Hampshire, before coming to our headquarters in Portland, Oregon, for distribution to our wholesale and retail customers."

In addition to their Portland office and warehouse, Brooklyn Tweed has a nearby studio space for photo and video shoots. Their website is an excellent resource for tutorials and videos, encouraging knitters to improve their skills while being inspired by the potential of Brooklyn Tweed yarns and the company's stylish patterns. ✤

HEADQUARTERS

Brooklyn Tweed's headquarters is located in Portland, Oregon, and consists of our office and warehouse. We have a small core team that typically works on-site, as well as a remote tech editing team. Our office is filled with plants and natural light, and of course lots of yarn, swatches and samples. We also have a studio space nearby for photo and video shoots.

brooklyntweed.com
@brooklyntweed

MICHELLE BAGGERMAN

Bureau Baggerman

Based in Eindhoven in the Netherlands, Michelle Baggerman is a design researcher with a love for sustainable materials, an interest in craft and technology, and a fascination with textiles. "I take an intuitive and inquisitive approach and see every project as a chance for exploration," she says. "I use the design process to create knowledge rather than products. The values of past practices and old techniques inspire my work as well as my taste for science (and science fiction) and a concern for sustainable development. My projects arise from unlikely intersections of old and new that provide approaches to a better future."

Michelle is currently teaching in the Reframing Textiles program at her alma mater, Design Academy Eindhoven. Her graduation project from 2009, entitled Precious Waste, laid the foundation for her professional pursuits. "It was the first time I used my design approach as a form of research, although I didn't know what to call it at the time. Now over 10 years later, the story I told through Precious Waste still continues to inspire people. It has been the catalyst for many projects that followed."

Investigating how plastic bags could be reused, Michelle's goal with Previous Waste was to "alter plastic shopping bags in a way that would extend the life cycle of the material, to improve its negative qualities and preserve its positive qualities."

"The mass-produced plastic shopping bag is a cheap and disposable product, meant to be used no more than a few times before it starts tearing and becomes useless. Of course plastic can be recycled, which is good in principle because it is not exhausting natural resources, but the process of recycling itself isn't very environmentally friendly. Recycling

"My professional interest in fibre and textiles is like a self-fulfilling prophecy: I'm really fascinated by textiles, so I'm always absorbing everything textile-related that I come across. When I start a new design research project and I'm looking for inspiration, I often end up finding it in some kind of textile practice. I can't seem to avoid it, so I embraced it and made it my main focus."

plastic takes lots of energy, heat and chemicals, and causes harmful emissions, and the recycled material is always of a poorer quality than the virgin material. Better would be to extend the use of a product for as long as possible before recycling, but these plastic bags were made for short-term use and need to be discarded quickly."

By hand, Michelle spun the plastic into fine yarn. "The resulting fabric forms a big contrast with the cheap, mass-produced bags it is made of. The plastic shopping bag is transformed by pure hand work into a beautiful and strong material that's suitable for making new bags with a much longer life span, or a wide range of other purposes. No chemicals, no heat or even electricity needed. When this textile is eventually worn out it can still be recycled in the conventional way, because it is not mixed with any other material, and can then be made into a new product once again."

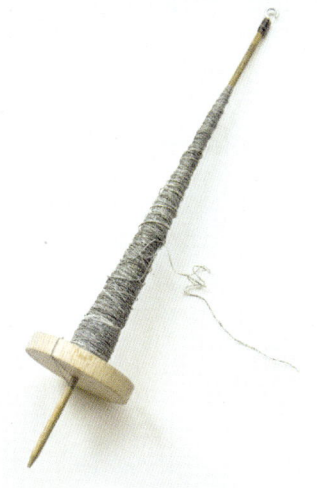

Michelle follows a similar approach with her design work now, through cycles of research, making and reflecting. "The tacit aspects of making, of actively experiencing materials through handling, exploring and shaping them, inspire questions and ideas that I wouldn't have had if I was only thinking with my brain," she says. "Fibre and yarn lends itself to this very well, because you don't need specialized tools or expensive materials to get started."

By constructing and deconstructing by hand, Michelle finds new paths. "There's always something unexpected I come across, something overlooked or underused, which I then zoom in on and create a concept around. This is also the point where I seek collaboration and try to find experts to learn from (for instance at production companies or research labs), to go beyond the basic experiments I can do on my own."

Motivated by sustainability and responsibility, Michelle believes that designers are in the position

MATERIAL FASCINATIONS

Materials fascinate me. The more versatile a material, the larger its spectrum of possible design applications, hence my love for textiles. From fibre to yarn to cloth, the raw material can keep transforming, allowing endless possibilities. That a fibre can ultimately become an antibacterial bandage as well as a warm coat or a tough rope is genuinely exciting to me.

This excitement started at a young age when I found a textile craft encyclopedia among my mum's books. I was amazed by the variety of things one could make with just some yarn, needles and hooks, and wanted to try all the instructions myself. My interest grew from there, and I still have a soft spot for vintage craft books.

to give shape to the future. "Creating value for me comes from closely observing something and finding something new in it, something useful. This can be value to the environment (something is nurturing), psychological value (something is satisfying), educational value (something generates an insight) and so on. Pure economic value is never a sufficient reason to make something. Design decisions can affect entire supply chains and should be made with mindful optimism that can be found in an awareness of responsibility. I hope to spread this kind of awareness through my work and inspire others to explore theirs, too." ✻

bureaubaggerman.nl
@bureaubaggerman

INDUSTRIAL STUDIO

Home base is my studio in an old industrial building full of artists' and designers' studios and workshops. It's pretty run down and out of date, but it's a wonderful place, although having only one power outlet in my studio is challenging sometimes. It has high ceilings and large windows facing a small courtyard. The view is dominated by a large tree, so I can usually see and hear some birds.

My space isn't that big, but I've managed to fit in a desk for myself and another one for an intern or guest, a sitting area with a small couch and a bookcase, and then a weaving loom, a spinning wheel and a lot of plants. The walls are covered in soft board, so I can pin anything to them. I've put up some of my textiles, and I always put up stuff from ongoing projects, some art and other visual things that inspire me. Every now and then I take it all down and start afresh.

IN THE PLY

Carmen Bohn

Calling herself the CYO (chief yarn officer), entrepreneur and fibre artist Carmen Bohn is the owner of In the Ply, a business in which she offers workshops and supplies, and sells her creative work in Ottawa, Ontario, Canada. She is also opening Ply Studio, a creative arts studio. "It will have a full slate of creative programming for artists and aspiring creatives," she says. "I also sell weaving looms, fibre packs, handspun yarn and other fibre inputs to create tapestries and other fibre art."

Her self-professed "fibre addiction" began with knitting, somewhat reluctantly: "I fully resisted until

"I'm a constant learner and love to learn a new craft, technique or style of doing something. I believe that making things by hand makes us feel better— a form of meditation, wellness. I am also motivated to make things with a deeper meaning."

a friend dragged me to our local yarn shop." She persevered through the frustration of learning the complexities of knitting, and a few months later, Carmen was infatuated.

"A few years later, a similar resistance emerged for spinning yarn," she explains. She was offered an old Louet spinning wheel, but the object sat unused. "It lived for many years in the corner of my living room until one day I decided it was time to learn how to use it. I took a drop spindle class through my local spinners' guild. I began to understand twist and tension. I set up my spinning wheel and got to work. I was immediately hooked."

She started spinning so much yarn that she could not possibly use it all herself. "I took some nice pictures and created some online listings, went to some fibre and craft shows, made a website," Carmen says. "From knitting and spinning, my fibre interests have spread into many other pursuits, including freeform crochet, weaving, felting, embroidery, etc. And because I am a learning designer in my day job, it was a natural progression to start teaching others how to weave, crochet, spin and enjoy fibre as much as I do."

Working in fibre allows Carmen to explore her colourful, textured and bold aesthetic. "My personality is reflected in what I produce," she explains. She loves items that have a story, that are unique and not "run of the mill." "I am interested in creating and promoting local, sustainable, handmade, one-of-a-kind, artisanal items. My weavings use reclaimed fibre and fabric to tell a story, and this is my signature style." The desire to keep things different means that Carmen doesn't often try to exactly reproduce a tapestry or a knitted or crocheted item.

Some 15 years after learning to knit and a decade since learning to spin, Carmen can attest to the power of these crafts. "Fibre has changed my life, my outlook, my temperament, my creative pursuits." ✻

LIFE LOVES

I have spent my life in a love affair with most things creative and artsy. Like many children, I had crayons, markers, scissors and paint in hand most of the time. My parents encouraged my siblings and I to use our imagination to make things. My dad further inspired me to reuse and fix things rather than throw them away. From him I learned that everything has a second, third or tenth life waiting for it. So, I have always saved old magazines, egg cartons, single-use plastics and interesting fabrics because they might make an interesting art project. Now, I enjoy the process of creating interesting yarns and one-of-a-kind fibre art using everything from beloved garments to bread tags. I think my dad would be proud, if he were alive today to see his influence sparking magic on my spinning wheels and weaving looms.

FAVOURITE FIBRES

Mohair locks! They stand out in anything I create, adding visual and aesthetic interest to my pieces. They are fun to photograph, giving a focal point to a work. They are soft and silky, wild and fluffy, neon or pastel. I like letting mohair locks stick out at weird angles from my pieces, especially if they are neon pink!

CARMEN BOHN

MAKING ART YARNS

My process for creating yarn starts with acquiring and preparing fleece and fibre for spinning into yarn. I am drawn to bold colours and interesting textures when it comes to my inputs. I buy interesting and beautiful art batts (big, fluffy clouds of "carded" fibre) or create my own on a drum carder (a machine that prepares fibres by combing them into a batt). I spin these fibres into novelty art yarns on one of my spinning wheels. I like thick and thin yarns, as well as ones with bobbles, tons of texture and interesting add-ins like pom-poms and unusual beads. After spinning the yarn, I remove it from the bobbin, wash it, hang it to dry, measure it, photograph it and sometimes offer it up for sale. But I mainly use it myself to create interesting tapestries or include it in my fibre packs for weaving workshops.

I use a Majacraft Aura spinning wheel and a variety of fleece and fibre inputs such as mohair, cashmere, alpaca, angora and other animal fibres (also stellina, tinsel, old craft supplies and vintage secondhand dresses) to spin novelty art yarns (primarily). I try to source as much of my fleece and fibre as possible from local and sustainable farms in the Ottawa Valley. My yarns appeal to those looking for something different to create a unique and inspired item or piece of art.

UNLIMITED THREADS

Carolina Reis

Carolina Reis sees being an artist as a responsibility. "In everything I do," she explains, "I want to contribute to a better world, make people happy and care for the environment. I am passionate about design, textiles, illustration and using my creativity to inspire and develop a more responsible relationship with nature, which is our life-sustaining system."

"Being an artist is not a choice for me, it is a necessity," she says. It is a difficult path, but a necessary one. "I have no choice. If I didn't materialize all the creativity that grew in me, my spirit would slowly die."

Originally trained in graphic design, Carolina worked with digital tools, spending her time on digital illustration, video and 3D animation. "I still like to work with technology, but I felt increasingly disconnected from my body and touch. To balance this, I started making things with my hands and it brought me great satisfaction." Having learned to sew, crochet and knit from her mother and aunts, she found it natural to turn to textiles.

"Now, as an artist, I intentionally pursue working with textiles," she says. "This helps me to reconnect with our physical materiality." Carolina creates installations of intricately entwined threads, conceptual videos and small stitched work; all these approaches are intimate and personal. "I work with threads in different kinds of ways. I knit them to create three-dimensional soft sculptures. I use them to embroider on canvas and make visual pictures that can be hung on the wall. I try to use natural fibres as much as possible, because one day, everything I make will go back to nature, and I want it to be able to disintegrate without doing harm to the environment."

"I am inspired by the properties of thread, how to use it to connect, how you can assemble it in so many different shapes. Fine strings assembled in different combinations create a negative space that reverberates."

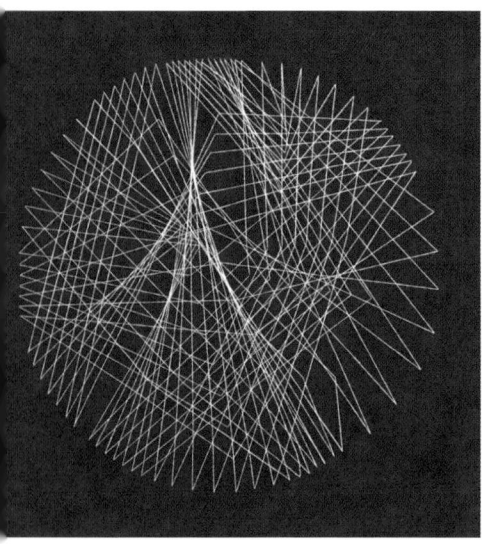

Carolina has also studied fashion design, where she learned about the properties of materials and the origins of various fibres. "Thread became increasingly more important to me, in terms of how it is made and where it comes from," she says. "Meanwhile, I was also very interested in the parallels in textile terminology and the virtual world." For example, communication-related technologies borrow a lot of vocabulary from textiles: "We connect to the 'network,' we browse the 'web' and we read 'threads' of news." Webs, nets, meshes, weaves and networks become intangible concepts, but with each new intertwined loop, Carolina builds new tactile and visual stories.

"Abstract ideas or concepts nourish my practice," she says. "I am fascinated with the omnipresent virtual communications and intangible connections we use daily to interact. In an attempt to make this very real but invisible aspect of our life visible and tangible, I turn to thread—that ancient technology that is at the origin of so many things that we make and use. Thread connects two pieces of fabric or skin. When it is interlaced or woven in particular structures, it becomes very strong."

She searches for authenticity and sustainability of the materials, with raw colours and textures. "The use of intertwined lines with contrasting backgrounds, often black and white, is one of the predominant styles in my work," Carolina explains. "For the moment, I am mostly working with threads that give me unlimited play with lines. However, this stems from the fact that I am very much working and exploring the idea of networks."

"I believe that if we keep in touch with our past and keep our traditions alive, we are more able to build a sustainable future." ✳

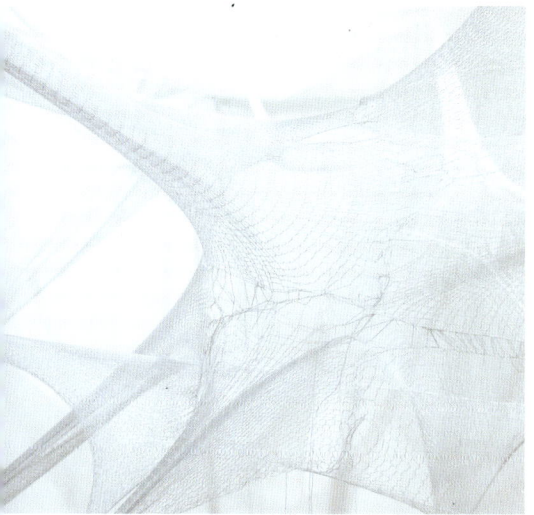

"Most of my work starts with an idea, something I want to express from my heart, and the most appropriate material arises from that idea."

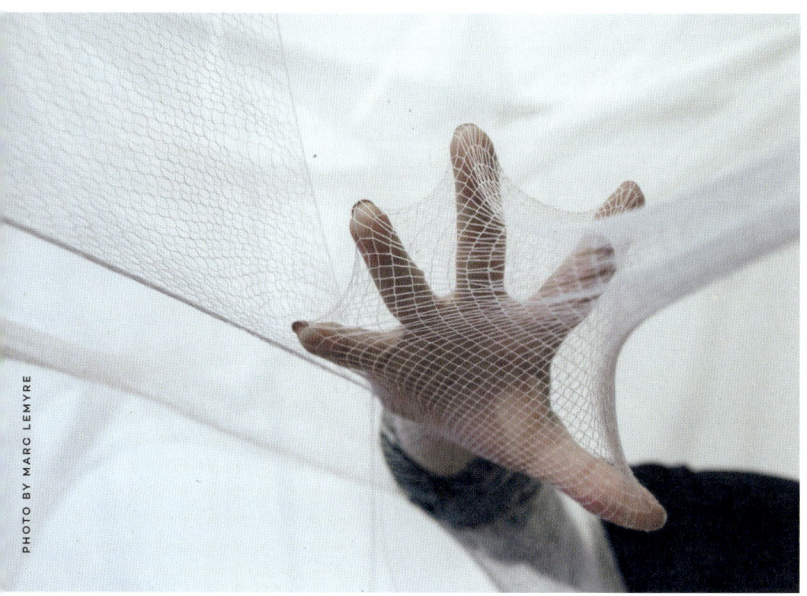

PHOTO BY MARC LEMYRE

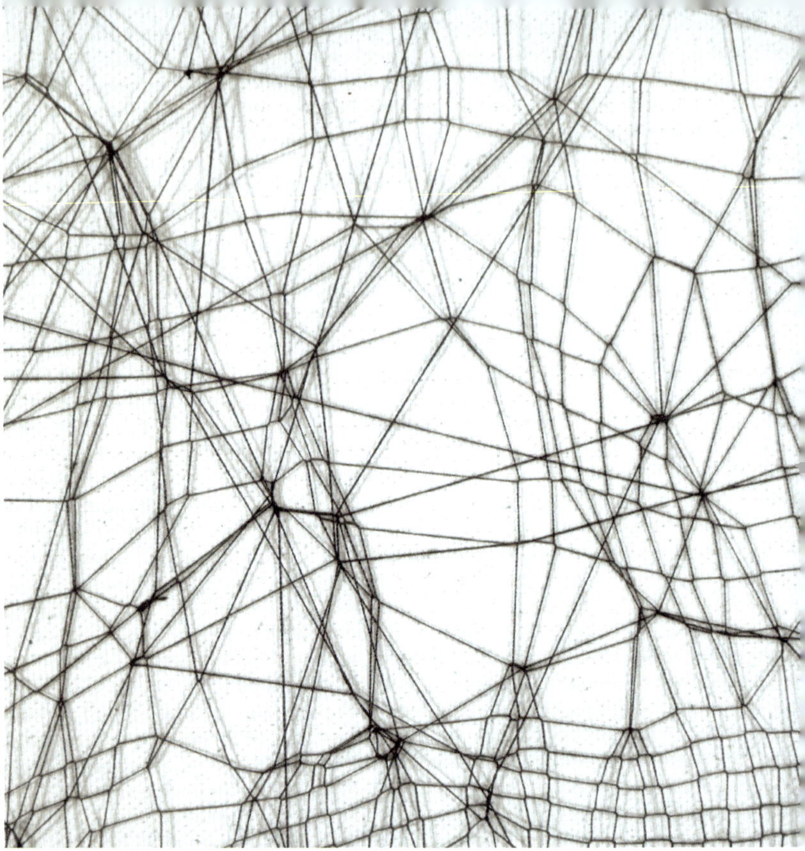

FAVOURITE FIBRES

I like cotton embroidery thread, vintage sewing thread, fine mercerized cotton, as well as raw untreated and undyed yarn and thread.

"Looking at the sky and its constant change of colours and shapes inspires me. I am fascinated by the intricate ramifications and networks of branches in the winter trees set against white skies and snow."

carolinareis.com
@carolinareisdesign

visible men

CREATING AT HOME

My studio and working areas are in several areas of my home. I have a knitting and sewing station in the corner of my living room. I also have a desk in a small sunny part of the house. I often end up working in various parts of the house depending on the scale of the work that I am doing. Sometimes it takes over and expands into a great part of the living room. I would like to move my studio space out of my home eventually, but since I have been working a day job, it is much more efficient to be able to work whenever I have some time throughout the week, including evenings.

KNITTING NECESSITIES

Cocoknits

Julie Weisenberger learned to knit while studying abroad in Salzburg, Austria. She didn't learn to knit at the university, but from a local yarn shop—which goes to show that you never know when or where you might learn something life changing. "My business grew organically out of what I was interested in, and maybe a bit of not pressuring myself about creating a formal business," says Julie. "It began when I was just out of college and had several jobs, but was always designing and knitting for myself on the side." She sold her hand-knit designs, and interest from shop owners grew. Soon she was employing other knitters, in Ireland, to make her designs, which sold to Nordstrom, Henri Bendel and boutiques across the United States.

That first business ran its course. "Manufacturing in China became popular and so the business was no longer viable," explains Julie. "Which is okay because that's when I switched to designing for hand-knitters." Always teaching others to knit, Julie paid close attention to her students: women of all shapes, sizes and ages. "I was really paying attention to what they were comfortable wearing and what worked and didn't, and why. It has been humbling and rewarding work to design things that make women with 'normal' bodies feel good about wearing what they knit. At the same time, more and more knitters wanted fewer or no seams, which makes perfect sense to me! This led to developing my own system of seamless, top-down sweater patterns that we now call the Cocoknits Method."

The Cocoknits Method streamlines the process of creating a sweater with a unique fit. "With the Cocoknits Method, a knitter starts at the top with a simple construction that creates shoulders with a 3D shape, using techniques from English tailoring,

"Cocoknits is very focused on the maker's experience—we want to provide patterns and tools to bring delight to the creative process. If we have brought joy to a maker, our job is done!"

"Making beautiful and useful things is deeply satisfying. Not limited to knitting, our Making page includes other fun ideas, as well. We're always imagining new ways of creating and crafting."

almost like turning the heel of a sock. The size is adjustable at each section, so the knitter can create a completely customized garment to their exact specifications. The seamless yoke increases are tracked on a simple worksheet that breaks the sweater construction into sections and follows along with six rainbow-coloured stitch markers. Whether it's the shoulder construction or the ease of the worksheet, almost everyone falls in love, and I never tire of that!"

While teaching knitting, Julie grew frustrated with the lack of quality tools for knitters, particularly tools with a sophisticated palette that were sustainably produced. She set out to redesign common knitting tools such as stitch markers, stoppers and counters, and along the way designed a few new tools to aid modern knitters. "The pattern designing and tool designing are so intertwined that really both are our signature," she says. "What Cocoknits is most recognized for are our stitch markers—they are French nylon-coated steel and cling to the magnetic

"The design of every aspect of Cocoknits products and patterns is so important! We've tried to create a brand that is simple but sophisticated, with an emphasis on quality that will last."

Maker's Keep, and I originally made them in six rainbow colours to specifically go with the system of the Cocoknits Method."

Fibre artists have a heightened awareness of the provenance of their materials. And this consideration of environmental impact and sustainability is carried through to the design of Cocoknits tools. "Our tools are designed to last; we are committed to using high-quality materials," says Julie. "Many of our products are recyclable and all of our packaging is recyclable or reusable. We strive for continuous improvement in this area. For example, one of our newest tools, the Needle Gauge, is made with PLA (polylactic acid), an alternative to plastic that is made from fermented plant material, and is 100% biodegradable."

Decades after she first learned to knit, Julie and Cocoknits continue to develop and grow. "Over the years I've continued developing new tools and improved versions of classics—Cocoknits has grown to 30 products—and we're not done yet! Cocoknits is now a mighty team of six women who manage all different parts of the business. We're all knitters and makers, and love helping to make people's creative time more enjoyable."

Their products are available direct online, but also from local brick-and-mortar shops. "In offering our products at these shops, we feel we are supporting small businesses which are primarily women-owned, who are the lifeblood of local making communities and who in turn foster local economic growth. Our community is our source of inspiration, and we are proud to feature our products in unique shops all over the world." ❋

PRODUCT DEVELOPMENT

My typical product design process begins with an idea of something I want for myself, usually to solve a problem. I let the idea percolate; I talk about it with my knitting group and the Cocoknits team. I gather images of other objects with elements I like or that inspire a new direction for the design. If I can, I make a prototype. If it is something like the Accessory Roll or Kraft Caddy, I make a paper pattern and then sew a functional prototype. This is what I send to the manufacturer for their reference.

For something like our Needle Gauge, I cannot prototype but I can consider similar designs, like a jeweller's diamond sizer, as I brainstorm. This product was in part inspired by the material itself. The mouldable plastic alternative, PLA, was something I came across when looking for an eco-friendly material that could be used instead of plastic. As I explored possible materials myself, and with my engineering partner, I let ideas come to me of what I would make with a mouldable material.

Once I have an idea and the materials figured out, an engineer helps me work with a manufacturer to bring it to life. While in production, we design simple packaging, consider how to describe and market this product to our customers, plan for photography and look forward to having something new ourselves! Finally, when the product is complete, packaged and packed up, we ship everything to our warehouse in California, as well as our international partners where small business owners in local communities help sell and distribute our products in their respective regions.

cocoknits.com
@cocoknits

RACHEL VALETTE

Crafting the Harvest

Growing up on an orchard in the remote foothills of Australia's Snowy Mountains, Rachel Valette had to make her own resources and create her own entertainment. "If I complained of being bored, my mum's first response was, 'go outside' or 'make something!'" she says. "The feelings of curiosity and delight that came with creating something with my own two hands, whether that was crafting or baking, are still with me today." Now in Calgary with her own family, she still follows her mother's advice. When she is not making cotton and jute rope bowls for her business, Crafting the Harvest, Rachel and her family head to the mountains for hiking and camping in the summer, and snowboarding and cross-country skiing in the winter.

"My mum has been my most influential teacher, my mentor and is now my biggest supporter," Rachel says. "She introduced me to knitting, cross-stitch and sewing at a young age. On the farm, repairing clothes and wearing hand-me-downs from my sisters was a necessity and came naturally. I was always dressed very colourfully and most days you could find me wearing a patterned skirt, hand-knitted wool jumper and cozy sheepskin boots!"

Though Rachel's style is simple, her bowls, bags and vessels show this make-do-and-mend aesthetic and appreciation for the impact of colour. White cotton rope is minimal and modern, with colourful accents from the thread. "I choose seasonal colours and sew the rope together using a sewing machine," she says. "Using zig-zag stitches and by starting in different shapes, a vessel is formed. Using my hands as a guide, the sides are shaped at various angles depending on how the rope is held while I am sewing."

"My designs reflect the simplicity of my life, one that is filled with quality and substance."

"Sourcing products and living a sustainable lifestyle are very similar and involve a process of constantly researching, questioning, learning, using, evolving and adapting."

As Rachel coils and sews, the rope gains strength, resulting in a sturdy but flexible unique piece. "A comparison can be made to the way in which a community is formed and gains strength as it grows," Rachel says.

The jute bowls are textural and earthy, but still minimal in their construction. "My designs reflect the simplicity of my life, one that is filled with quality and substance," she says. "My everyday life choices are entwined with my craft and create my personality—from the food I eat, the pieces that enter my home and the clothes I wear. My design reflects my lifestyle and vice versa."

Rachel's intention is to make minimal yet functional objects. "Beauty is in the eye of the beholder," she says. "Their function does not have to be specific. Perhaps they could be used for organization or storage, to house an indoor plant, be shared as a gift basket or simply exist as a piece of art! They are for anyone who wants to be intentional in their purchase and to move away from mass production and towards quality craftsmanship, sustainability and durability." ✷

"When looking for materials I draw a parallel and ask the same questions about the other things in my life: Where does my food come from? What is in my body and cleaning products, and who made my clothes? What better serves the message and lifestyle I want to cultivate?"

THE WHY

My business is an extension of who I am. In making these items, I follow the ethos of "less is more."

I make to create functional pieces that resonate joy for the owner.

I make to generate an additional income for my family.

I make things to serve a purpose and to be passed down to family and friends.

I love to see people enjoy a quality product that has been handmade with care and attention to detail.

I want to keep the art of crafting with one's hands relevant and approachable in modern times.

I want to pass on practical life skills to my children and community.

Success generates motivation; the more actions I take, the more it compounds.

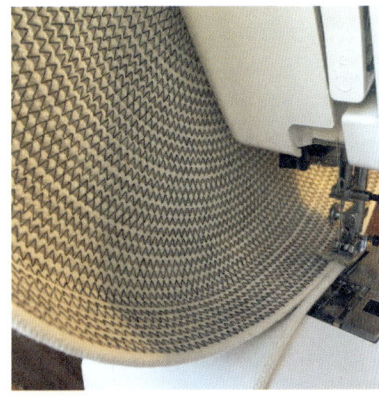

HOME TOGETHER

I am a one-woman business and I create my pieces from home so that I can be flexible to work around my lifestyle. This has most commonly been on my large kitchen table—the hub of the household. My workspace needs to be packed away quickly in storage shelves off to the side to make way for homework, activities and family meals. I have extra storage space in my basement for rope, shipping supplies and finished pieces. I don't have a lot of equipment: I use a sewing machine, cotton rope or jute on a spool, a tape measure, scissors, thread, a pincushion and a design book.

The pandemic changed the dynamic of the way I work drastically. I went from having the house to myself to sharing the workspace with my husband and two daughters. With everyone working from home, I need to be more conscious of the noise I make, the space I occupy and the time I spend on my craft.

craftingtheharvest.etsy.com
@craftingtheharvest

CRAFTING THE HARVEST

MADE IN WESTERN CANADA

Custom Woolen Mills

Maddy Purves-Smith grew up in a woolen mill, literally just footsteps from the family's home—her parents Fen Roessingh and Bill Purves-Smith started the business in the 1970s. "They were weavers interested in having their own wool made into yarn," explains Maddy. "They soon learned that the only places left in Western Canada for wool processing were shutting down—the owners had grown old and there was nobody to take the mills over from them. Game for a challenge, my parents brought those two historic mills together to form a new business."

Custom Woolen Mills is in rural Carstairs, a community about an hour's drive from Calgary, Alberta. They process wool and other animal fibres into woolen carded rovings, batts, yarns, quilted bedding and machine-knit socks, all using historical processing equipment. "Like a working museum, the oldest piece running each day is our batt carding machine from 1895, while the newest machines are our sock-knitting machines from the 1960s." There is also a retail shop and some dye-plant demonstration gardens.

"We are a vertical mill, where we do all levels of processing," describes Maddy. They receive the raw wool directly from farmers in Saskatchewan, British Columbia and closer to home, in Alberta. "We hand-sort it, then wash it and dry it. If we want to dye the wool a different colour, we usually do it just after washing. Next, we run it through our carding machines—they brush the wool to organize the fibres. From there, we can either send the carded wool for quilting into 100% wool-filled bedding, or we can spin it into yarn. The finished yarn is either ready for knitting into socks here at the mill, or for sale as hand-working yarn in our retail store."

"Our mission is to preserve the heritage of the local woolen mill. Sourcing all of our wool from Western Canadian farms and doing all the processing here at our mill in Alberta, we pride ourselves in providing a uniquely local service in a small-is-beautiful kind of way."

Maddy is passionate about the mill and is determined to preserve the heritage of the local woolen mill and her family's legacy. She recognizes that Custom Woolen Mills does a lot more than just make wool products: "We provide local farmers with value-added options for direct marketing their wool and improving their farm income. We offer local artisans access to products that haven't been shipped across the world several times, reducing environmental impact. We provide local jobs to our friends and neighbours—when you buy our textiles, you know that the people making them had the same labour rights that you do. We live where we work, so we care for our environment like the home that it is." ❊

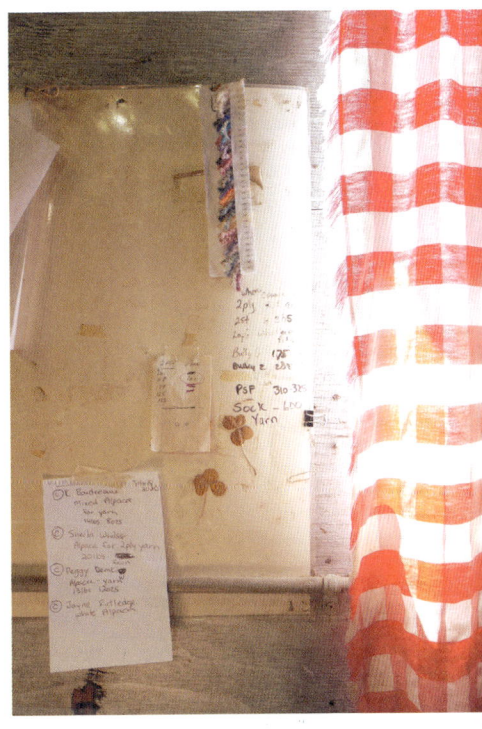

"Our mill is a strange mix of old and new. All of the machines are very old, but we keep them running with whatever new technology is necessary. The yarns are like historical yarns, but modern knitters use them."

WOOL FACTS

People have been hanging around with flocks of sheep for about as long as anyone has been keeping track. As far as fibre goes, it doesn't get much better than wool. Here are just a few things that make wool so great:

- Wool is fire retardant, water resistant, static resistant and wear resistant.
- Wool has excellent insulating properties that will keep you warm in the winter and cool in the summer.
- Wool can absorb up to 30% of its weight in water without feeling damp, making it comfortable even in the most uncomfortable situations.
- Wool is resilient and lightweight.
- Wool is biodegradable.
- Wool is reusable.
- Wool is a renewable resource.

CUSTOM-MADE

Our customers are just as varied and versatile as our products. In addition to our retail line, we also provide custom processing of people's own wool. We are able to provide fine washed locks and carded wools to fibre artists, luxury bedding to sleep connoisseurs, custom hand-woven blankets to farms for their market stalls, and insulation to log home builders. We can supply a single skein of yarn for a craft project, or if a customer has 100 ewes and wants to market their own farm label, Custom Woolen Mills has those products and services as well.

customwoolenmills.com
@customwoolenmills

MODEL: SOUMYA MOHANTY

MACHINE KNITS AND TATTING

Drew McKevitt

With a bachelor's degree in English literature and creative writing from Concordia University in Montreal, and many years working as managing editor of a poetry magazine, Drew McKevitt sees a correlation between her literary past and her current creative exploration: "Machine knitting can involve extremely meticulous manoeuvres and planning. I really enjoy this about it, because I think it speaks to the copyeditor in me."

Drew recently received a master's degree in textile design from Philadelphia University (now Jefferson) and is now based in Petawawa, Ontario, Canada. "I have been a hand knitter for many years, and I grew up around women who sewed, knit and made things for themselves and their homes, so it has always been part of my life," she says. "I sewed when I was a child, but my first attempts at knitting were disastrous—I didn't have the patience, and I got frustrated too easily. I didn't start really hand knitting until I was in my first year of university. At first I worked from patterns but quickly moved on to making my own hand-knitting patterns and designs. It wasn't until I went to grad school for textile design that I learned machine knitting and fell in love with it."

She learned technical skills in grad school: programming and creating machine-knit fabrics. "I also began to focus more on the fabric itself and not just the end use," she says. Drew balances an interest in technical knitting with an interest in organic, repeatable patterning. "For example, I collaborate with Suzanne Oude Hengel to make performance fabrics, which are extremely technical. My work with her is about researching yarns and structures, with a view to how they will perform and innovate athletic fabrics.

"Knitting can be very logical and planned, or it can be freeform. I like the idea of finding a balance between those two extremes. Sometimes I like to think about the knitting machine as a canvas, allowing myself to just make it up as I go along."

MODEL: SOUMYA MOHANTY

PHOTOGRAPHER: GABRIEL ORTIZ
MODEL: REGAN MARINER

Although they are technical, nothing is prescribed—the idea is still to innovate and hit on something exciting and new."

In contrast, Drew also makes hand-knotted and tatted jewellery and art pieces that are unconventional in their lack of patterning. "I guess I haven't found one idea to really immerse myself in completely," she says. "Some of my designs are more suited to fashion, others are performance fabrics and some are art pieces."

As a freelance designer, Drew can step into different aesthetics and project requirements—restrictions or parameters that can lead to new ideas. "It's freeing in a way—it allows me to focus on structure and use my craft to interpret another person's ideas."

"As a designer, it is important to me to work with people who care about the environment and are looking to contribute something meaningful to the already saturated marketplace. My designs are considered an attempt to innovate on what is currently out there. I think consumers are becoming more aware of how their clothes are produced, and this is a great thing." ✼

SAMPLING

With knitting, I often start by sampling an idea and then resampling it. I then make technical notes about the structure, yarn, tension, etc. Getting the fabric right can take quite a bit of time. It's nice when the sample makes an unexpected shape that can inform the final piece. I like to try to let the fabric decide what it will be, but that can be challenging.

I am motivated by the need to discover. I love sampling with different yarns and knit structures. I like to iterate ideas as much as possible. What's exciting for me is finding an unexpected outcome.

"Sometimes a mistake leads to something quite amazing. I'm always chasing a 'perfect mistake.'"

FAVOURITE FIBRES

Right now I really like using thin cotton thread for tatting (size 60 to 80). I'm also getting a lot of joy out of working with technical yarns, like elastics and nylons, for performance knits.

I tend to experiment with materials. I've tatted with PVC-coated filaments—which is an interesting combination. It makes lace, which is often fragile and soft, into something durable. I also like experimenting with adding resin to textiles. There's something nice about the conflict of using hard plastic with textiles, which are conventionally soft.

I also like the conflict of opacities and thicknesses when knitting. I often play with using a very thin yarn with a much thicker yarn.

"I am primarily a machine knitter these days, but I also work with my hands a lot as well. I am particularly obsessed with hand tatting at the moment. My approach is really intuitive. I don't follow a pattern—I just allow connections to happen organically."

SPECIMEN

Specimen is an ongoing project in which I take found natural objects (dried twigs, seed pods, etc.) and create a freeform tatted lace around them. Because the natural pieces I work with are fragile, the process is slow and meditative—I allow the object itself and my own intuition to determine the final appearance. When pieces are brittle, a delicate hand is necessary to interact with them without breaking them.

drewmckevitt.com
@drewmckevitt

120 YARN • THREAD • STRING

BASEMENT STUDIO

My studio is in the basement of my home, and it houses several domestic knitting machines and quite a bit of yarn. It was a struggle at first getting the space to work for what I needed. I've spent a lot of time arranging equipment and storage, and sourcing good lighting. Some days I spend a lot of hours knitting, so I didn't want the space to feel like a crowded basement with tons of boxes. At the same time, I didn't want it to feel like a living room either. It needed to be functional, but a little inviting.

PASSEMENTERIE

Elizabeth Ashdown

Working with a rare skill set, artist Elizabeth Ashdown specializes in the craft of hand-woven passementerie. "Traditionally, the term passementerie describes the art of making small-scale yet elaborate and ornamental trimmings and ribbons that are used to decorate grand interior schemes and furniture," she explains. Old-fashioned styles used braided gold or silver cord, coloured silks and beads—think tassels, fringes, rosettes and trims.

One of only three passementerie artisans in the UK, Elizabeth is the only one using the techniques to create art. "My work is an exploration of a traditional heritage craft technique," she says. "In the UK, passementerie is classed as an 'endangered' craft, which means that there are very few makers producing this craft."

"Passementerie is normally small in scale, as its intended purpose is to edge an object. I work with this small-scale nature, treating each piece as a component that I join together on the loom to create larger, almost lace-like artworks. I am very interested in exploring how woven technique, scale, material and repetition can be combined within my work."

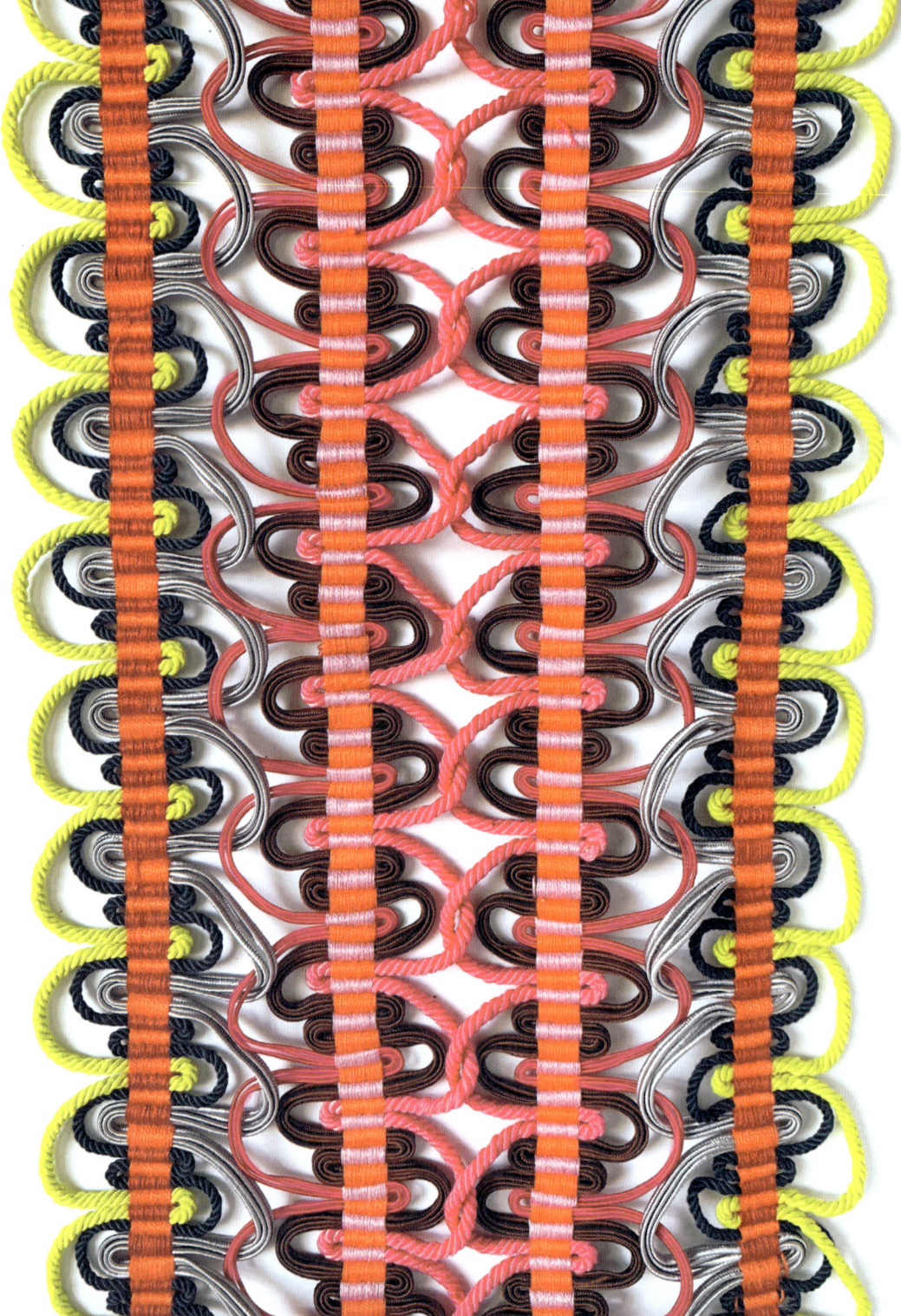

While earning a bachelor of art, Elizabeth quickly found her niche. "The weaving department was a revelation," she recalls. "I loved everything about weaving and I was immediately hooked. I love the process—from selecting yarns and dyeing, to warp winding, weaving and finishing. Taking individual threads and transforming them into woven pieces is magical."

"I've experimented with different textile disciplines and none of them have resonated with me in the same way as handweaving. With weaving, I am creating the design and the object simultaneously as part of the entire process and this is where my passion for the discipline lies." In 2012, she began playing with passementerie techniques, learning new techniques through books and by watching French videos on YouTube (as she did not speak French, hers was definitely a learn-as-you-go self-education).

Upon graduation in 2013, Elizabeth was awarded a prize that sponsored a trip to Paris to showcase her work in a trade show. "I exhibited passementerie samples that companies purchased for inspiration or to turn into large manufacturing lengths." She worked freelance in this realm, producing samples for clients for a number of years before turning towards a more artistic direction.

"I came to realize that my heart lay in creating artworks and bespoke pieces. I decided to undertake an MA in textiles at the Royal College of Art, in order to change and invigorate my practice. I knew that I wanted to continue to work with passementerie techniques, but this time in a totally different context. I spent two years playing around with scale, materials, colour and woven techniques."

Now, Elizabeth makes one-off and bespoke artworks through intricate weaving techniques combined with energetic colours and patterns. "I seek to give this art form a contemporary and fresh relevance by combining traditional making skills with a modern aesthetic, to create one-off art pieces, both large

"It is vitally important to me to carry on the skills and traditions of passementerie, ensuring that it remains relevant by altering its context to suit contemporary tastes and sensibilities.

I am sharing my viewpoint with the world and I am responding to what is happening around me. I may not obviously create work that makes a statement, but when I look at my pieces I can remember how I was feeling, or what I was responding to."

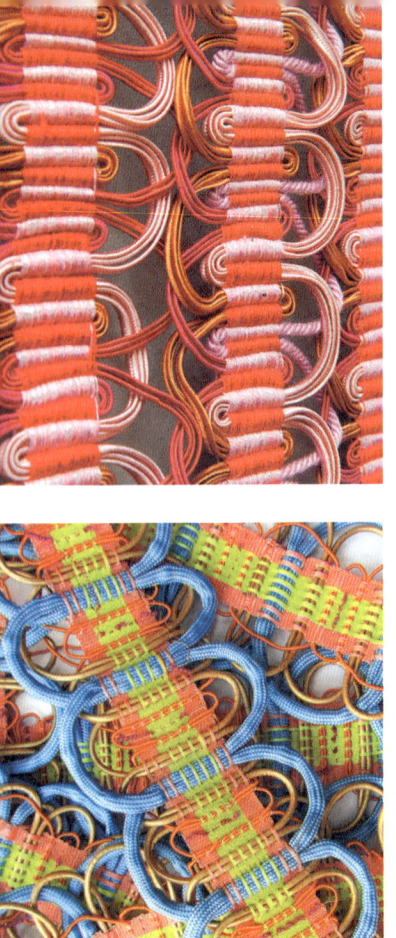

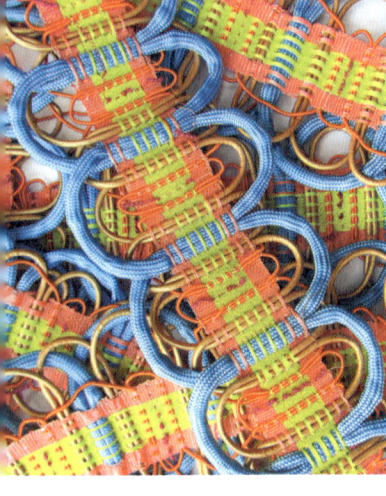

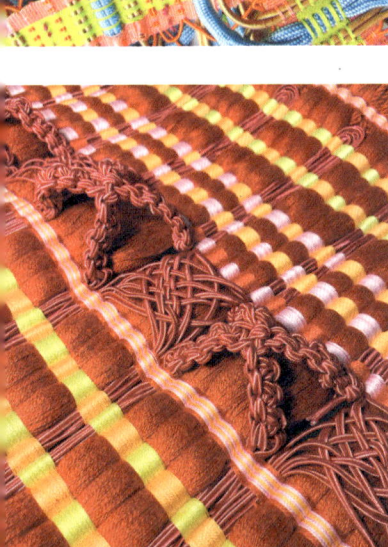

and small," she says. "I create bespoke art pieces for clients that are designed to be framed or used as wall hangings."

Her work is generated through exploration on the loom, and she describes her maximalist aesthetic as "energetic, rich, textural, lively and fun." Elizabeth sees this as a polarization between her work and her perceived personality. "I can come across as reserved, but when I look at my work it is obvious that the 'real' me is manifesting itself through the work I create."

With Elizabeth's intuitive and responsive manner to art making, embracing irregularity and imperfection is key. "When I remove a piece from the loom the warps will 'wiggle' a bit to create gentle curves, or a fringe will hang in a different way than I anticipated. I embrace all of these unexpected outcomes, as they further heighten each artwork's personality. The materials I use have their own inherent qualities that become even more apparent once removed from the tension on the loom. It's all about embracing the unexpected." ✣

STRONG AND RESILIENT SILK

Silk is such a wonderful material to work with for so many reasons—it is available in so many varieties, from super soft and thin, to chunky, textured and flat, and literally everything in between. It is an incredibly strong yet malleable material that lends itself perfectly to my style of work. Silk makes the most beautiful, full fringes and it also creates exquisite spun cords. I twist my own cords frequently using silk, and once spun, it creates a material that holds its shape perfectly to create the loops, crete and scallops that I use within my work.

Colour plays a very prominent role in my work and silk is the perfect material to hand dye and showcase colour. I use a lot of bright, contrasting colours within my artworks, and silk soaks up these colours beautifully, providing a gorgeous sheen once dry.

Silk dyes beautifully and it is also an incredibly strong and resilient material with very special qualities. The lustrous nature of the fibre adds a gorgeous sheen to my work. A central feature within my work is the use of cords to create patterns, loops and curves. I hand spin silk to create custom cords that I then weave with—once spun together the silk creates the most wonderful cords that hold their shape perfectly when woven.

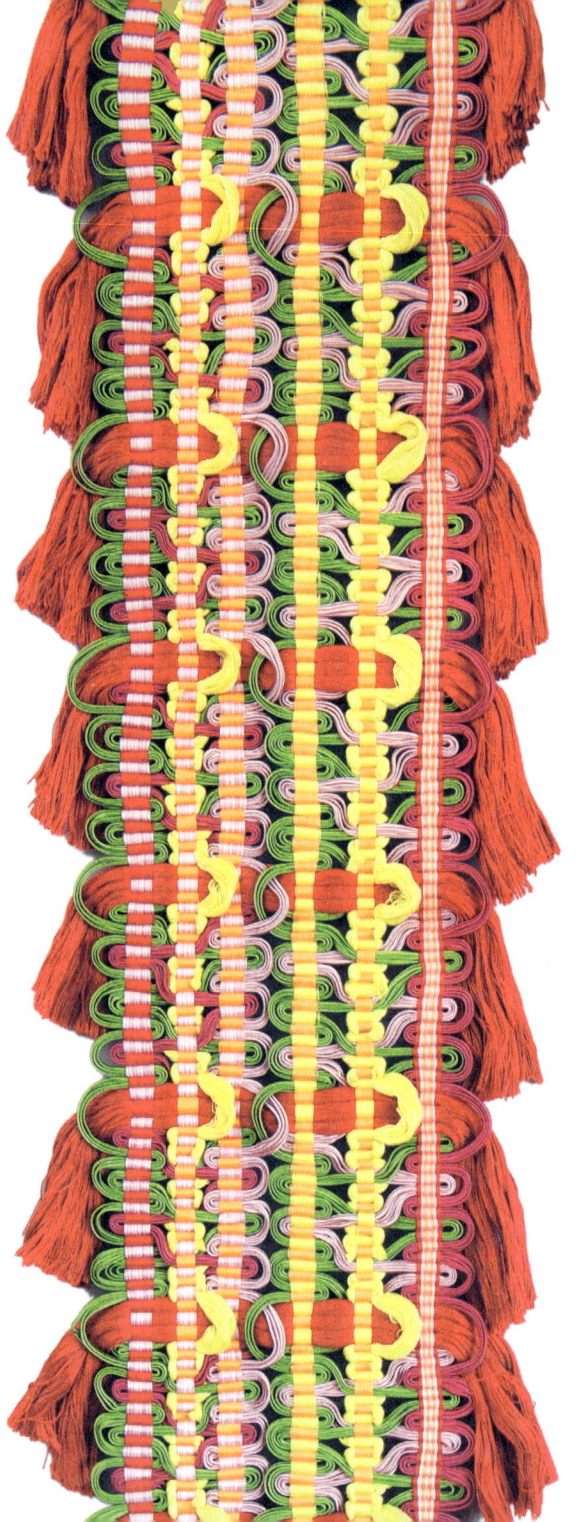

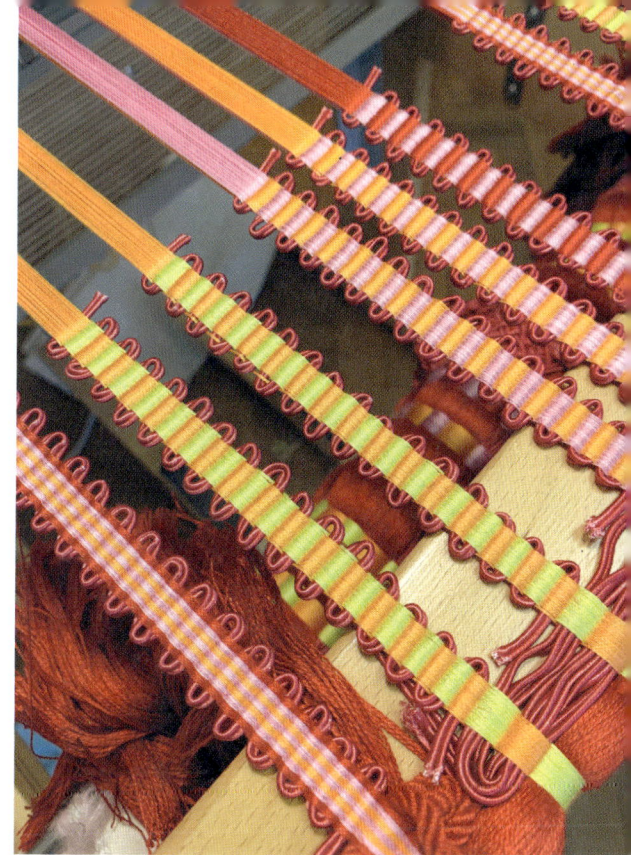

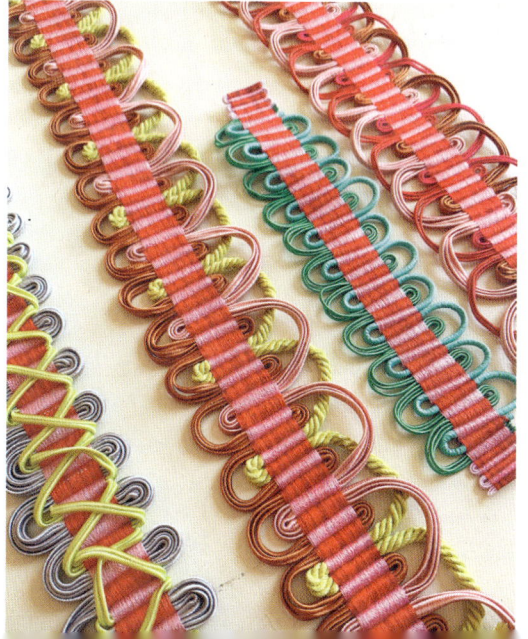

"My hands create my work at every stage of the process, and this is an incredibly important component for me."

elizabethashdown.co.uk
@ashdowntextiles

AN INTUITIVE PROCESS

I adore colour in all of its permutations, especially dynamic and energetic colour combinations. My use of colour is deeply intuitive, surprising, emotional and dramatic. I am always developing and playing with new colour combinations within my sketchbook. A lot of the time I dye yarn and cords in colours I like without having a defined purpose for them. I have a very well stocked yarn selection that I constantly pull from spontaneously when I am weaving.

I work in a very intuitive and free manner and all of my work is developed through play and exploration, whether in my sketchbook or on the loom. I follow my instincts when I am working and I have come to realize that this is the best way for me to work. Very rarely do I produce detailed drawings of what I am going to weave (unless I am working on a commission). I use drawing purely as a method of gaining inspiration and playing with ideas.

I begin with my sketchbooks as a starting point for inspiration. I play with colour in a spontaneous manner in my sketchbook or through combining coloured yarns.

I have to work within a certain set of technical parameters that govern how the loom can be set up and used. My next stage is planning the maths side of things. I then hand dye my warps, set up the loom and begin weaving. I produce samples to begin with to see what works and what doesn't work and then I refine my ideas from this point.

SHANNON WELSH & ANGELA WARTES-KAHL

Fibrevolution

Using flax to create fibre has been part of human history for millenia. "Linen is from the fibre flax plant," explains Shannon Welsh. "It is classified as a bast fibre (meaning a soft core) and shares this status with hemp, nettle, kenaf and a dozen other natural fibres around the world. Linen and hemp have historical significance in many cultures, from Egypt to the Netherlands and Russia to Ireland. Flax for fibre has been a part of our human existence for 36,000 years, give or take."

"Fibrevolution will facilitate the establishment of a linen and hemp industry in the US, from local fibre farmers through manufacturing to textile design, with a firm root in organic practices."

Shannon Welsh and Angela Wartes-Kahl are cofounders of Fibrevolution. Their vision with Fibrevolution is to "facilitate the establishment of a linen and hemp fibre industry in the US, from local fibre farmers through manufacturing to textile design, with a firm root in organic practices." They envision regional fibre manufacturing hubs, starting in Oregon, a region with a history of growing—and the capacity to grow—high-quality fibre flax that is processed into linen.

"Fourteen linen mills were in the Willamette Valley from South Portland to Eugene, Oregon, in the early 20th century," says Shannon. "Oregon is a specialty-crop state with 220-plus recognized commodities, is ranked fourth nationally for its transport infrastructure and has ideal transportation via airport, road, rail and sea." Fibrevolution's values and practices are deeply rooted in the Fibershed movement. "Their soil-to-soil circular textile model gives

you a sense of the connections between supply chain steps and how each part impacts the next. Our work focuses on the left side of this model—organic farming, integrating bast fibre and animal production, and regionally based fibre manufacturing." The first step is regenerative organic certification. "Then we build on that base with animal integration in grazing systems that move them over the land in quick subsections: taking into account time, forage quality, time of year and the number of animals, and deciding the next crop to follow the animals." Through this process, farmers are able to harness the carbon sink potential of grasslands.

Flax is a fairly quick-growing crop, averaging 100 days. Fibre flax seed should be sowed as soon as the soil can be worked in the spring—this takes advantage of the spring rains and eliminates the need for irrigation. It takes up to 60 days for the plants to flower, which lasts 15 to 25 days, followed by a month-long

FIBERSHED

The Fibershed movement aims to develop regional fibre systems that build soil and protect the health of the biosphere. The organization promotes "an international system of regional textile communities that enliven connection and ownership of soil-to-soil textile processes. These diverse textile cultures are designed to build soil carbon stocks on the working landscapes on which they depend, while directly enhancing the strength of regional economies. Both fiber and food systems now face a drastically changing climate, and must utilize the best of time-honoured knowledge and available science for their long-term ability to thrive." *fibershed.org*

maturation period. They have also experimented with overwintering crops begun in the fall.

For the past several years, Fibrevolution's field trials have taken place in strategic growing areas in Oregon's Willamette Valley. "Everything has been done by hand," says Shannon. Without specialized flax harvesting equipment in the USA, equipment needed to scale operations will have to be imported. Everything about how the flax is planted to how it is harvested affects the yield. "Every step in the processing of the fibre is either maintaining or diminishing the original fibre quality of colour, fineness, strength and length, and of course affects its organic certified status."

"If we have learned anything from our linen mentors," says the duo, "it's that fibre quality begins in the field. How the crop is grown, fertilized, and watered or not, along with plant density, weather, seed selection, harvest time and, most importantly, how long the crop is left to rett in the field, all determine

quality. The weather is our guide. Fibre flax is a crop that requires attention, and the timing of when it is pulled for linen production is crucial. Quality fibre is pulled when the crop is still partially green, and it needs to be timed appropriately for the retting process. You want the crop to be exposed to a little moisture during this process, but not constant downpours. So timing and following weather patterns is needed to ensure for a quality crop."

Integral to their ambitious multi-year plan is establishing regional fibre manufacturing hubs, starting in Oregon and elsewhere in the Midwest region. "Ultimately, Fibrevolution sees three mills in the next 10 years under our company umbrella. We want to create the prototype mill that will be replicated in other regions to meet natural fibres supply needs for the long term." ✻

PROCESSING TERMINOLOGY

RETTING

Fibre flax is pulled by the roots to preserve the long fibre in the stem. Once the fibre flax is pulled, it is laid out in windrows in the field for the retting process. Retting is the decomposition of pectins that bind fibres to the other parts of the stems or leaves, usually by the action of enzymes produced by bacteria or fungi. This process has the least environmental impact of the retting processes. The crop is turned halfway through. After it is fully retted, the fibre is round baled and ready to be transported for further processing.

RIPPLING

The process of removing seed pods from harvested flax stalks.

BREAKING

Part of the scutching process, which breaks up the woody matter in the flax stems.

SCUTCHING

The process of removing line fibres and extraneous matter such as shiv, earth, pebbles and weeds. When referring to this process in connection with other fibres, the word "decorticating" is usually used.

HACKLING

The operation of combing the line flax in order to remove short fibres, parallelize the remaining long (line) fibres and also remove any extraneous matter that might be mixed up with the line flax presented to the hackling frame.

Once hackling is complete, the fibre is ready to be sent to spinners or biocomposites markets.

"People often ask us the correct way to pronounce Fibrevolution— depending on the day we say our company name as Fibre Evolution or Fibre Revolution!"

fibre-evolution.com
@fibrevolution_pnw

BETH JORDAN

Freckle & Knot

Freckle & Knot began with a dream. "In the autumn of 2018, I had a dream," explains Beth Jordan. "I don't usually remember my dreams so this was significant. I dreamt about sewing into wood and woke up with a number of ideas to try it out on. It was that simple."

Perhaps not quite that simple, in that Beth's background, education and experience came together in that dream. She holds a multidisciplinary design degree with a specialty in ceramics and has been a secondary school art teacher. "Becoming a mother to two small boys changed that career path and left me feeling a bit creatively lost," she says. "I continued to be stimulated by creating, decorating a house or trying out new crafts but these things didn't seem to spark my imagination. But then I had a dream and all my training suddenly seemed to make sense. The skills of woodworking and textiles that I had accumulated through my degree and teaching career now met in the most harmonious and satisfying manner. Freckle & Knot was born."

Beth began experimenting with offcuts leftover from other projects. "Here my degree came into play," she says. "Using woodworking tools and a thread and needle were not new, I had the knowledge and away I went." In between her children's naps and after they had gone to bed for the night, Beth developed her skills and style, purposefully veering away from any traditional expectations of embroidery. This new technique reinvigorated the creativity that had been dormant while she focused on her two small children. "My dream woke me up from the mundane cycle of my life and gave me a renewed purpose. I was excited and filled with possibilities."

"I choose not to sand away the marks that tell the story of the wood: the stains, knots and holes of its previous life. To have these unique marks visible is to proclaim that they matter and they are worthy of notice, that they are beautiful. For the philosophical among us, this is a mirror to ourselves: our imperfections are unique, they matter; our story is precious. There is beauty in imperfection."

"I am drawn to the layers, textures and colours created in nature, which heavily influence my use of thread and yarn. I find that by creating work influenced by the flowers, plants and trees native to where I live, I can create authentic and original pieces."

Through her business moniker Freckle & Knot, Beth makes and sells floral embroidery set on reclaimed wood. "The embroidered homeware that I create range from one-off pieces to embroidery kits, to bespoke commissions. I use a range of woods that can be sustainably sourced or reclaimed: salvaged from demolition sites or saved from the side of the road or beach. I am passionate about reclaiming wood, saving pieces that have been deemed unusable or unneeded. I believe that knots, holes, stains and marks are beautiful, like freckles. They are not blemishes to be hidden away but beauty marks that display a unique and fascinating history. The wood is finished to a high quality and then adorned with threads and yarns to enhance its natural beauty, creating a new life for the wood as artwork." ✽

STITCHING ON WOOD

Embroidering on wood is similar to embroidering on fabric—however, quite often the stitch technique varies in order to achieve the same look in wood as in fabric. This technique has taken a lot of time and effort to perfect, so planning each embroidery design first is important.

The wood is selected based on its size and depth. It is then cut, drilled and sanded to a high standard, then buffed to a shine with oil. Finally, the real fun begins: embroidery.

I really enjoy using the thread to create a texture that contrasts with the smooth wood. Various knots such as bullion knots and French knots are great for this. The simple technique of varying the yarn and thread thickness is also quite an effective technique to achieve texture.

WORKING AT HOME

I work across many different mediums to create my pieces, and fortunately for me, my family doesn't mind that I have spread out across our house to make them. For woodworking, I use the garage, where I have kitted out my own wood workshop and store the majority of my wood finds. The hub of Freckle & Knot is run from my workroom, which is nestled at the top of the house. Here I design, create and pack the artwork and kits. It is where my ideas come into the real world. I like to use my computer to create designs but nothing beats paper and pencil, and the workroom is covered with sheets of ideas as I try to catch up with my whirring brain.

Freckle & Knot is run solely by me, but I have an important team of family and friends who support me. So even though my business is just one person at the moment, it is the endeavour of a whole family.

MILK HOUSE STUDIO

Hannah Burnworth

The maternal side of Hannah Burnworth's family all lived in the same small town where she grew up, in rural Indiana. "I spent a lot of time with my grandmother, cutting up her seed catalogues and collaging the flowers into new (and of course better) bouquets," she says. After completing each piece, her grandmother would assign the artwork a grade. "You would think a grandma would give their grandchild all A's, but mine didn't. Sometimes I got a B or C. So, I made my bouquets bigger and better. I can't ever remember it making me upset. I liked to remake the bouquets so I could spend more time with her."

This early influence inspired Hannah to pursue a master's degree in art education. She is now in her 15th year of teaching high school art—and now she gets to give the grades.

Following the birth of her first child seven years ago, Hannah turned to her own artwork to cope with postpartum. "I needed art to process my new role in the world," she explains. "I needed to prove to myself that I could have something that was my own." Through workshops, stitched collages and handmade books, Milk House Studio became her creative outlet, as well as a source of supplemental income.

"I make papergoods, or more accurately, paper art designed to enhance spaces and lives. Not printed or mass-produced papergoods, but one-of-a-kind, stitched, mixed-media pieces, collages and handmade books. The creations are made from found and handmade papers, occasionally fabric, and usually lots of thread."

Hannah starts with a variety of papers, such as envelopes, napkins and old bingo and library catalogue cards. "If I am doing a commission, I might start with

"My work is a compilation of muted yet colourful hues. It is carefully designed, yet free flowing. It is deliberate, yet intuitive. Much like my own personality, and my story of motherhood, order is often thrown to the wind by a more powerful energy. Loose threads have become a symbol of both the binding order and the freeing chaos."

a certain colour palette. I begin to intuitively cut and arrange and paint and cut and arrange and paint, and finally, I reach a point when a piece is working. I tack pieces down with small dots of glue. At that point, I let everything dry. If I still like the composition the next day, I begin to stitch (with my sewing machine), adding lines as new elements to enhance and add texture to the piece."

This last step, of sewing over her work, developed from a simple problem: the messy stickiness of adhesives. "I originally started stitching on my work as an alternative to gluing. Over time, the thread became a prime ingredient, an element binding a piece not only physically, but visually, and eventually conceptually. Strings tether us together, just as women and mothers do."

Hannah creates for her own personal enjoyment, to explore the conceptual meaning and to spread joy and community in the process. "The pieces are a way of helping me understand my world, and I love it when they help someone else understand theirs." ✤

"I believe the creative process is enlightening, healing and unifying. Visual language bridges gaps in a way no other language can. Social, racial, political and religious bias falls away in the language of art. At the same time, art can be used as a tool to share powerfully unique perspectives. Art teaches me and my students that there are multiple solutions to every problem, that there is not just one right way and that differences are beautiful."

FAVOURITE FIBRE

I use cotton and linen spools with my machine. Quite literally, they are threads of my life: thread binds garments, blankets and my own artwork together. The individual thread combined with others makes a stronger collective. Thread is symbolic of the power of community. Using thread is a nod to women's work; it reminds us of the strength of a woman in binding her home and family.

manchestermilkhouse.com
@milkhousestudio

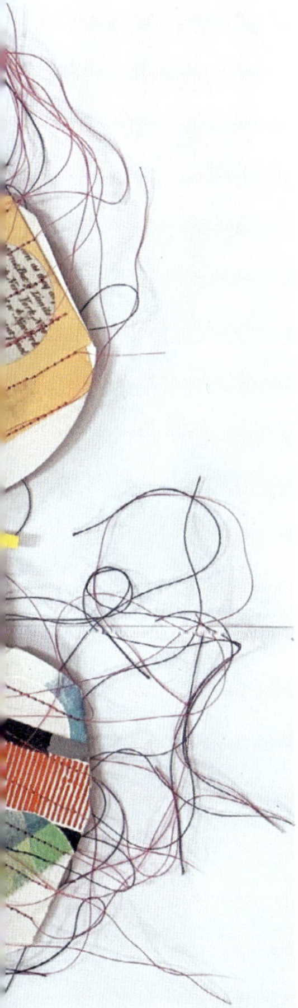

HOME AND SCHOOL

I work alongside my students in my classroom, stealing moments here and there to snip and sew. I also stay after school a few days each week to finish projects. Students are surprisingly good critics and I have learned so much from them over the years.

At home, I used to work in a studio behind my home that was used to milk cows many years ago. Thus my business name: Milk House Studio. But, like nearly everything else in my life, the milk house has been commandeered by my two children and filled with bikes and bug collections, and I now work at the dining room table in our country house that was built in 1864.

PRODUCT OF THE EARTH

Hemptique

Hemp has always been a part of Peter Nyari's culture and upbringing. He was raised in Hungary, where his family has used hemp for generations. "This plant can provide you with shelter, clothing and a multitude of other uses," he says. Noticing that industrial hemp-based products were missing from the marketplace, he realized there was an opportunity to grow a business while making a positive difference. Through his company, Hemptique, Peter and his team bring hemp cordage, craft threads, ropes and fabrics to consumers.

"Act local, think global" is Hemptique's purpose in action. Peter explains: "It keeps us aligned with our primary goal of continually providing the best in eco-friendly and sustainable products while enabling us to maintaining our learning and adapting mindset. The Hemptique team closely collaborates with an ever-increasing group of like-minded people. We strive to educate people about the awesome uses of hemp, and how it can provide them and their environment with healthy solutions. We show people that there are healthy and sustainable alternatives that can help them to reduce and eliminate their dependence on synthetic items. When you introduce hemp into your daily life, you are enriching and nourishing your body and your surroundings. You are creating a healthier world for future generations as well."

Hemp is a quick-growing crop, generally taking 110 days to mature. "After harvesting, retting and drying of the hemp stalks, the process of turning hemp into a finished product continues with decorticating, scutching, hackling, roving, combing and spinning the goldish/blond fine fibre into fine hemp yarn to be made into a multitude of high-quality, human- and planet-friendly finished products."

"Our philosophy is that well-made and long-lasting natural products contribute to optimal environmental and personal health, as well as quality and sustainability."

Their materials originate from Europe and Asia. "From our office in Southern California, we coordinate our global network of product development and product fulfillment activities," says Peter. "With our international flair and expertise, Hemptique is an innovative, zero or minimal carbon footprint–focused leader; one that focuses on craft and lifestyle products that are made from hemp, organic and recycled natural fibres."

The creative team in California designs products and innovative uses for the Hemptique offerings. "Our lifestyle and craft products have been expanded to include fun and trend-setting products which include macramé and themed magical colour combinations and much more. Hemptique prides itself on designing, developing and supplying trendy, fashionable and functional products that are environmentally sustainable and socially responsible." ✼

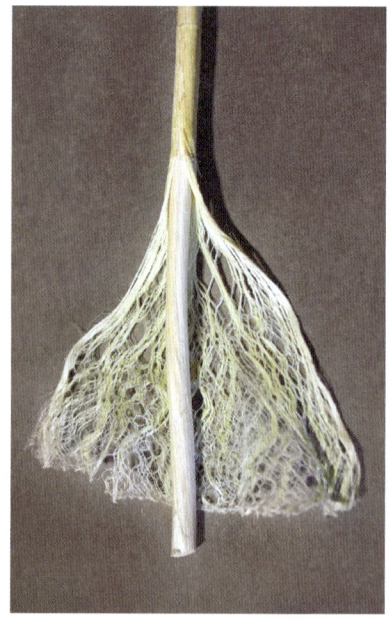

FIBRE TYPES

The image above shows a hemp stem. The outer material contains the prized bast fibres and the inner is the hurd, which is made up of short fibres. The short fibres produced during the separation process are known as "tow" and the long fibres are called "line fibre." Line fibre can be incredibly long—depending on the height of the plant, a single strand may be up to five metres in length. Once separated, the line fibre is cleaned and carded to size, cut and baled, ready to be further processed and spun. The tow fibre is just compressed and baled.

GROWING HEMP

Our hemp fibre supply model follows a traditional method of hemp textile production.

CULTIVATION

Seeds are sown densely to produce tall, slender stems that contain a greater amount of fine fibres.

HARVESTING

Takes place after flowering but before the seeds set, as fibres tend to become coarser around the time of seed formation.

RETTING

The process whereby naturally occurring bacteria and fungi, or chemicals, break down the pectins that bind the hemp fibres to be released. Common techniques include:

WATER RETTING

Involves soaking the stems in water tanks, ponds or streams for around seven to ten days. Warmed water laden with bacteria is most effective.

DEW RETTING

Entails laying the crop on the ground for three to six weeks, turning the plants occasionally to allow for even retting.

FIBRE SEPARATION

BREAKING

Stalks are passed between fluted rollers to crush and break the hurd into small pieces, separating some of the fibre in the process. Though once a very involved and labour-intensive process, separation of the bast from the hurd has been somewhat simplified through use of a machine called a decorticator, which enables the leaves to be left on the stalks during the breaking, although this makes for a messier process requiring more sorting after completion.

SCUTCHING

The broken stems are then beaten and scraped, separating more short fibre and the remaining hurd material from the long fibre.

REFINEMENT

HACKLING

The fibres are then hackled (combed) to remove any remaining woody particles and to further align the fibres into a continuous sliver.

hemptique.com
@hemptique

ROVING

This sliver is twisted and drawn out further to improve strength, then wound on spinning bobbins.

SPINNING

Generally, to produce a better, finer yarn, the fibres are then thoroughly wetted in a small trough of water as part of the spinning process, known as wet spinning. Fibres can also be dry spun, which often results in a coarser yarn.

HOME-GROWN CLOTH

Huston Textile Co.

Following his service in the United States Army, Douglas Huston and his wife, Kat, decided to build a business, one that "truly reflects what the American Dream means to us," says Douglas. "After the birth of our first child, we founded Huston Textile Co. inside our home garage in the fall of 2012. A few years later we opened shop in a converted military hangar in Mather, California, just outside of Sacramento. Huston Textile Co. began with a fascination for vintage, American-made machinery that soon evolved into a passion for recreating heirloom fabrics. All of our textiles are American-made,

"We make high-quality, small-batch and bespoke cloth reminiscent of the golden age of textiles, woven in California from the finest sustainably grown fibres."

"At Huston Textile Co., we hope to reignite the domestic textile industry while sharing our knowledge about textiles and their environmental impact to ensure a healthy future for all."

right here in California, from natural, American-grown raw materials. As one of the only selvage fabric makers left in the United States, we are proud to take part in the resurgence of vintage-quality fabrics and the revival of American textile production."

Working with natural, domestically sourced fibres, Huston Textile Co. specializes in working with organic, sustainable raw materials. "We go to great lengths to help farmers and ranchers regional to us get their fibres through the textile supply stream," explains Douglas. "We know for smaller ranchers and farmers this is a complicated process, and having a little help along the way can bring their fibre to full cloth."

Huston Textile Co. believes in community-supported cloth. "The company's mission is to provide the highest quality small-batch and bespoke cloth while sourcing natural fibres from the US to make a truly high-quality, American-made product reminiscent of the golden age of textiles."

"We work on equipment that has patents as far back as the early 1890s. Most of the equipment we use is considered antique to the textile industry, as technology has changed the way most mills create fabric."

Taking a farm-to-fabric approach, they work closely with their suppliers, obtaining organic cotton from West Texas and wool from Northern California. The fibres are mainly from farmers and ranchers who practice carbon-sequestration. They also work with ranchers in supporting the restoration of wetlands, and programs that bring healthy soil into the process of garment creation.

"These responsibly farmed materials are transported to our spinner to be made into the highest standard of yarn and thread," explains Douglas. "From there, some yarns are kept in their beautiful natural shades, while others are dyed responsibly with natural botanical colours or low-impact dyes." The yarns are put on cones and shipped to Huston Textile Co., where they warp, beam and weave these yarns into sturdy selvage fabrics, including denim, chambray (woven with blue yarn in the warp and white in the weft), canvas, car curtain (shade cloth), union cloth (fabric woven with two or more fibres, such as wool and cotton) and pincheck (cotton cloth with white dots on blue).

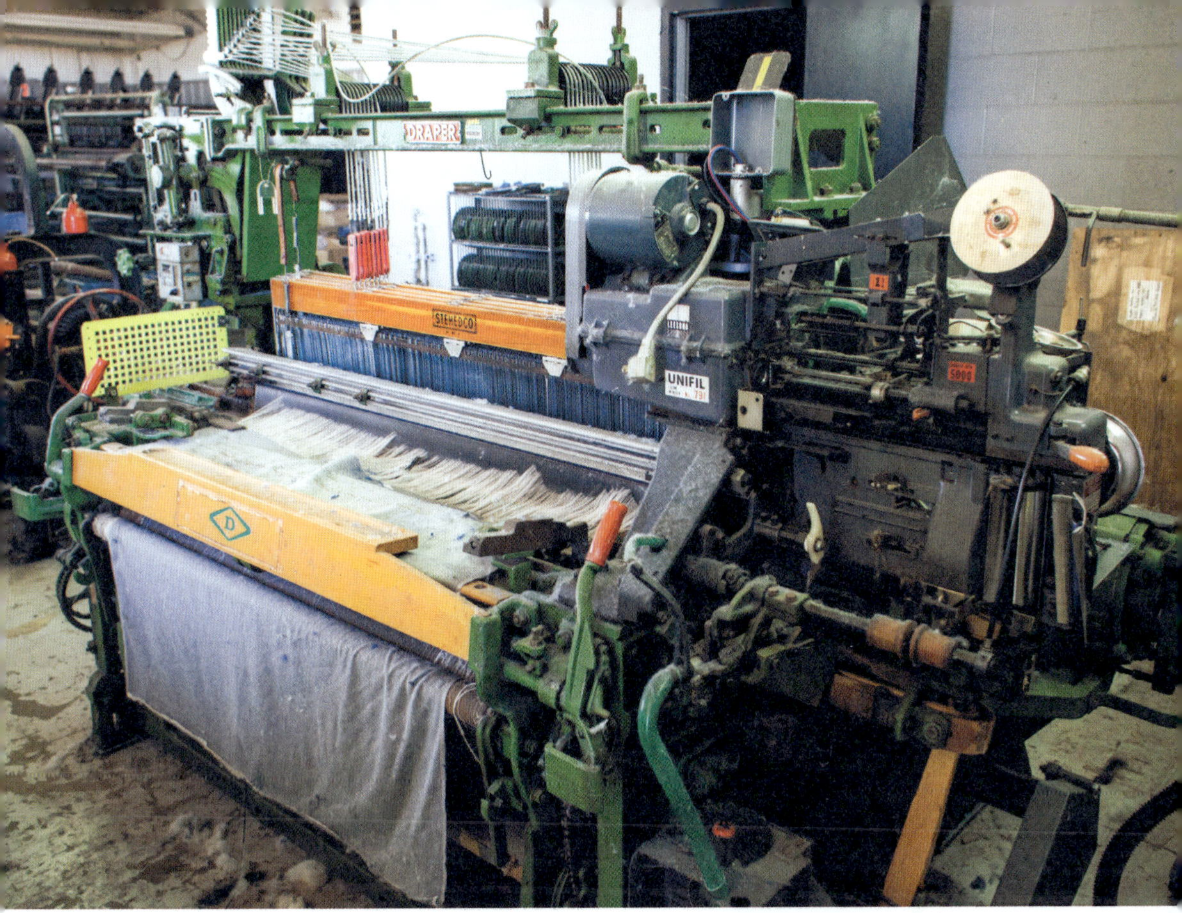

These basics demonstrate Huston Textile Co.'s respect of tradition and hard work. The appreciation of making do and of hard work is woven into the company culture. "Growing up in a single-parent household, I was privileged to watch my mom find ways to support us; in this process, she taught me how to sew," says Douglas. "When I combined the skills she taught me with my natural curiosity for understanding and fixing machines, weaving just seemed to fit seamlessly. The art of fabric design, construction and vintage, American-made machinery brought a spark of life to my dreams." ✤

HUSTON TEXTILE CO.

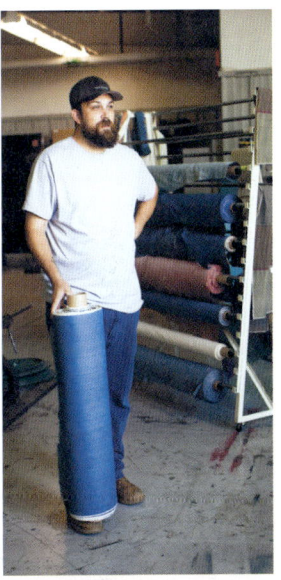

FACTORY IN A HANGAR

Our factory is located just outside of Sacramento, California, in a converted military hangar, on the runway of the former Mather Air Force Base. Once a warehouse for airplane parts, the space is now home to a dozen vintage textile looms, including old Draper shuttle looms, and other textile-producing machinery that date as far back as the 1920s.

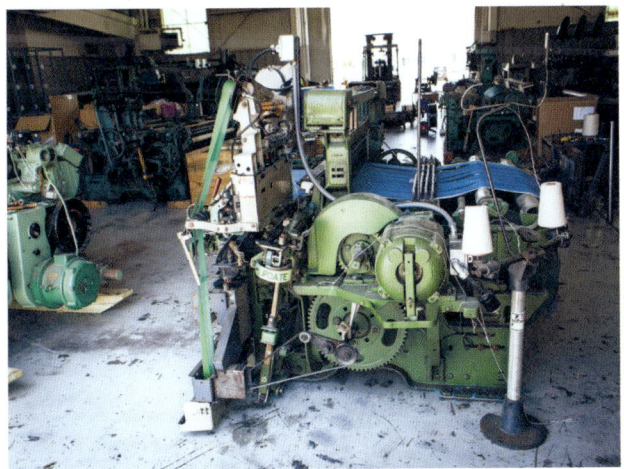

HUSTON TEXTILE CO.

JAPANESE FOR YARN

ITO Yarn & Design

Art historian and designer Tanja Lay has always held a fascination with Japanese art and design. "As a textile and fibre enthusiast, Japanese fashion designers like Yohji Yamamoto, Issey Miyake and Comme des Garçons were a revelation to me in the '80s in the use of materials and fabrics, as well as shapes and the reflection of the body," describes Tanja. "Later on, I discovered the textiles by Reiko Sudo of Nuno and the knit works of Setsuko Torii. I experimented with fibres and dyes, with body shapes and multi-stranded knitting."

In the mid-2000s, Tanja decided to make her fibre hobby into a profession by opening a yarn store in Berlin, Germany. "My intention was to bring unusual fibres and exceptional yarns to other fibre enthusiasts and to show new concepts of working with yarns. Multi-stranded knitting that combined yarns and materials I had discovered in Japan were not common in Europe at that time. Also, thin yarns and yarns with special materials like paper were not available easily."

A Japanese friend helped Tanja contact yarn producers in Japan, and in the process she discovered a mill that was very interested in selling overseas. The mill had a minimum production of around 100 kilograms per colour, a quantity that Tanja's little shop concept would never be able to sell. "Our Japanese partners were interested in bringing their wonderful yarns to a wider audience. Thus a brand and joint venture were the only conclusion for cooperating, buying and selling Japanese yarns at a larger level."

Tanja and her founding partner mill began the yarn brand, ITO—Fine yarns from Japan, in 2009 as a wholesale business. "ITO started with a handful of yarn qualities from our partner mill. Since these yarns

"ITO's mission is to bring unique Japanese yarns to a wide audience of crafters and fibre lovers outside of Japan. Through the years, ITO has expanded this mission into a broader range of fibre-related products, by adding needles, hooks and notions, as well as fabrics and dyes, to serve the crafting community with distinctive Japanese crafting supplies."

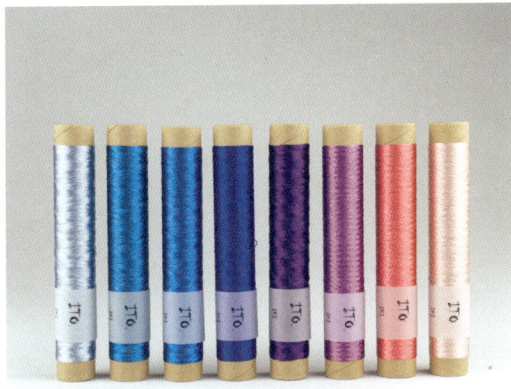

TIME-INTENSIVE DEVELOPMENT

Since ITO is a joint venture, the development of yarns, colour concepts or other products is a time-intensive process, but it is also the part that, as the creative director for Europe, I probably enjoy most. Usually, our partner sends us samples of new product developments. If it is a new yarn development, for example, we will knit samples to see the drape and feel, test it for pilling, wash it and also knit it in combination with yarns from the existing assortment. We will also do some benchmarking to see if a similar yarn exists and, in communication with the supplier, to work out the unique idea behind the development. Sometimes this leads to reworking the yarn idea in terms of composition, thickness, twist or other properties. Once the final yarn idea is settled, we will show the new development to designers, fibre artists and retail partners and ask them to test it as well and give us their opinion. Next, the colour palette will be developed by the Japanese artisans and dye house. For a single colour we sometimes get one suggestion, other times we get anything from three to up to twenty different lap dips and will discuss these with our partner. Developing a new yarn can take anywhere from one to three years; developing colour palettes is usually a ten- to twelve-month project.

were received well, our partner started to involve other mills, dye houses and specialized companies for twisting or other finishing techniques that are special to Japan. In this way we built a network of suppliers for ITO. This was necessary because each small company is specialized, for example in ring spinning or mule spinning, speckle dyeing, yarn dyeing or top dyeing, or fancy yarn production like chenille. Together in this joint venture we also contacted different producers for needles, ready to wear, dyes and fabrics."

Today, ITO offers over 30 yarns, including sewing and embroidery threads. Tanja carefully selects yarns that are uniquely Japanese in their characteristics. "For example, ITO Sensai is a silk mohair yarn with 60% mohair and 40% silk, with a yardage of 240 metres per 20 grams. In 2009, ITO was the first company to offer a silk mohair yarn of that fineness, which was very innovative and difficult to spin, and had such a high percentage of silk. Moreover, the mohair is sourced from a farm that is certified for sustainable farming and recognized for its excellent quality clips, making ITO Sensai exceptionally soft." Other products include ITO Washi, a paper mix with linen-like qualities, and ITO Kino, a recycled top-dyed silk noil produced from the leftovers of spun filament silk that has a distinct tweedy look. "These yarns are quite different from other hand-knitting yarns that are readily

available," says Tanja. "All ITO yarns can be wonderfully mixed with two or more strands to create fabrics with different drapes and properties."

The variety of offerings requires a network of over 40 different suppliers, from mills to dye houses to needle makers and fabric producers. Although some family-run businesses have been around for generations—sometimes an astounding eight generations—many companies face problems with labour costs and succession. "Marketing and selling ITO yarns is much more than just selling unique yarns," Tanja explains. "It also means preserving textile traditions and hopefully helping them continue in the future."

Very old manufacturers need not be set in old ways: "Innovation and tradition do not have to be opposites," Tanja claims. "The Japanese craftsmanship of multi-generational family companies is definitely rooted in tradition, but on the other hand, the drive to innovate and reinvent themselves keeps them alive." For this joint venture to work, technology and good communication are vital for keeping the partners in touch. "Even if crafting itself is a non-digital activity and the joy of crafting can be a relief from the very technological life we're living in, technology is equally important for connecting and organizing." ✻

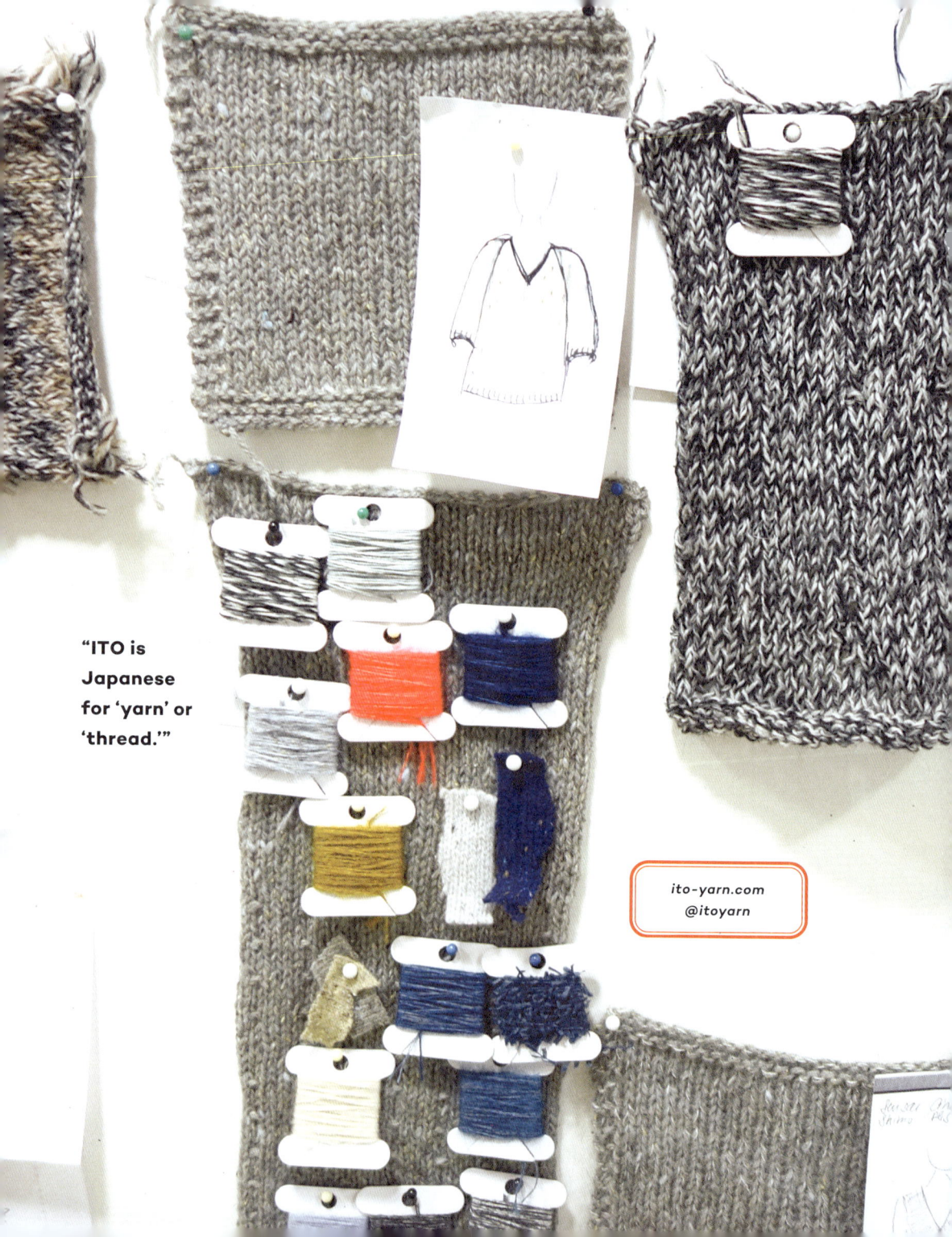

"ITO is Japanese for 'yarn' or 'thread.'"

ito-yarn.com
@itoyarn

PRODUCT DESIGN

Design is very important to us. From choosing the brand name ITO to designing the logo, the Japanese origin and Japanese craftmanship had to be communicated in a clear and simple yet strong and straightforward way. Also, selling the yarns on cones and in small balls, as is more usual in Japan, was a way of being different, and we have seen other yarn companies copying it lately. Another crucial area is colour. Japan has a different tradition using colours and a remarkable colour sense. A big difference compared to Western European or North American yarns is that the same colour in different yarns has slightly different tones. This is not just because different materials take colour differently—we also learned from our Japanese partners that when combining different yarns of the same colour, it is more interesting and pleasant for the eye if the same colours are a bit different. When combining yarns, this will give depth to the final fabric.

ELASTIC CLAY

Jeremy R. Brooks

Artist Jeremy R. Brooks has a BFA in art and design and an MFA in ceramic art. "I have balanced my career between working as an artist and teaching at the university level," he says. He is an assistant professor of ceramics at Coastal Carolina University in Conway, South Carolina. "I create a variety of work through a rather eclectic studio practice and describe myself as an artist who works through the specificity of the ceramic medium," Jeremy explains. His fine art practice is varied in its aesthetic approaches and themes. In Rockwellian Homobilia, for example, he has reinterpreted Norman Rockwell illustrations and ceramic collectibles on plates and sculptures that subvert their sentimentality and illustrate the historical marginalization of those in the LGBTQ+ community. Other work takes a three-dimensional pop art approach to play with the perception of taste as a sense and taste as an aesthetic sensibility. These works explore identity, sensuality, eroticism and cultural comprehensions.

Apart from that body of work, Jeremy has an ongoing interest in hybrid clay materials. "I have always felt that ceramics is so much more than what it is pigeonholed to be, and work like this has helped me challenge many preconceived notions concerning clay construction and ceramics," he says. He has developed a recipe to lend elasticity to clay, using, among other common ingredients, a filler component that he does not reveal publicly. "A portion of my research has fixated around a unique blend of clay materials that possess qualities of elasticity rather than qualities of plasticity traditionally found in common clay recipes. To put it plainly, it behaves more like rubber than clay, and sets up very quickly once the components are measured and mixed."

"I continually strive to challenge my understanding of what it means for me to make things. This has lead me to make a variety of work that can vary in style, appearance, construction method and/or subject matter from one piece to the next. The work featured here, for example, is but one facet of my creative practice, which is very different from anything else I make. I have found that maintaining a diverse studio practice has allowed me to share my ideas to a rather wide audience."

The elastic clay is extruded into long strands. Typically, long linear strips of clay would be used in coiled constructions but Jeremy works with these strands using techniques borrowed from the fibre arts. "Once the material has set, it is not brittle like greenware, but instead very stretchy and elastic," he explains. "A coil made of this clay can easily be tied into a tight knot. This method may be used to join different pieces together, or the clay can be crocheted, knitted or woven into more dynamic forms." Jeremy starts with a basic slip knot of the elastic clay and then crafts small vessels through knitting or crochet. "I identify this body of work as Knot Pots, which is a homophonous play on words." From a ceramic perspective, they are not pots in a utilitarian sense and the term "vessel" might be more apt. "Vessels conceptually focus around how a pottery form contains an idea rather than how it holds or facilitates a specific function," he says.

"While this elastic clay is not an easy material to work with, it does present a number of technical challenges that captivate my inquisitive mind. Opening a kiln with new material tests is always a surprise, and sometimes I find the potential in new material tests to be more gratifying than the resolution of a finished art object. I have been researching this clay for over eight years now, and feel that I am only starting to realize its full potential. Creatively speaking, it is an exciting place to be." ❋

MAKING ELASTIC CLAY

I make small batches of elastic clay in a lab using a combination of traditional and nontraditional ceramic materials. To make a porcelain-based elastic clay, for example, I use a blend of kaolin (clay), feldspar (flux), frit (glass) and commercial stains (metal oxide colourants), along with an undisclosed filler that creates elasticity in the clay body. Precision and care must be observed when handling these materials. It can take several hours to measure, mix and extrude this clay into the long fibres necessary to create a single piece.

This clay is extremely sticky, just like taffy when it is prepared. It will begin to set within 10 to 15 minutes of mixing but can take up to 24 hours for it to fully cure. Once cured, the clay is no longer sticky or pliable like traditional clay. It is instead quite firm and incredibly stretchy, similar to a rubber band. This elasticity allows me to work with it in ways that would not be possible with traditional, plastic-based clays. This clay can be tied into a variety of knots or tightly woven into more complex structures. It can also be formed into flat, rubbery sheets rather than long, linear fibres when it is prepared. Sheets of elastic clay can be cut into precise shapes using a sharp blade or pierced with a hole puncher to create spaces to cast on additional fibrous material. From the perspective of a ceramic artist, this material offers a number of innovative approaches to nontraditional, clay-based construction.

klai-body.com
@decalcomaniac

WORKING WITH ELASTIC CLAY

The elastic clay does not dry up like traditional clay when it is handled, so I can take as much time as necessary to make a single piece. I use a small, 12-prong circle loom to knit the foot ring and base of each vessel. Once complete, I remove this section from the loom and cast on additional material to crochet the walls using a size I-9 (5.50 mm) hook. Rows are predominantly made through a combination of single crochet and freeform stitches. I also incorporate a variety of contrasting oddments within the walls of each piece to further introduce variation within the form. Upon completion, each piece is stamped with my potter's mark on a small slab of clay that is framed within the vessel's foot ring. The work is fired in a kiln to a mid-range temperature of over 2,000°F. Firing removes all elasticity from the material, transforming the elastic clay into rigid porcelain. The clay shrinks approximately 30% and is subject to pyroplastic deformation during the firing process. This causes the vessel to warp in all sorts of unexpected ways—sometimes good, sometimes bad. As a result, not every piece survives the firing.

JEREMY R. BROOKS

CASHMERE FROM KYRGYZSTAN

June Cashmere

"June Cashmere seeks to improve economic conditions for Kyrgyzstan's nomadic shepherds and to encourage economic development in Kyrgyzstan through the ethical and sustainable production of cashmere yarn."

Sy Belohlavek, a native of Columbus, Ohio, is the founder of June Cashmere, a fibre company that sources cashmere from small family farms in Kyrgyzstan, in Central Asia. "I grew up living overseas a lot, since my parents are in development work," says Sy. "As a college student, I was required to spend time abroad, and I wanted to go to the most unknown and intriguing place, and for me that was Kyrgyzstan. I first went in 2001 on a cross-cultural trip as a student, and I fell in love." In 2010, he and his family moved to Kyrgyzstan, where Sy established his company—"June" being the Kyrgyz word for animal fibre.

Six years later, while back in Columbus, he met with textile writer Amy P. Swanson, who wrote an article about June Cashmere for *Selvedge* magazine. When Sy had to return to Kyrgyzstan in 2017, he invited Amy to lead the yarn company's wholesale sales back in the USA.

Sy and his team purchase cashmere directly from shepherds, who gently hand comb the soft cashmere fibre from their goats. "Our work addresses sustainability and ethical issues surrounding cashmere production, lifts Kyrgyzstan as a world-class cashmere producer and preserves the traditional nomadic lifestyle as well as the local Kyrgyz goat species, the 'jaidiri,'" says Amy.

Currently, the fibre has to be shipped to Belgium for scouring and then to England for dehairing, the process that removes the guard hairs so that only pure cashmere remains. "Using the longest, most uniform fibres, our mill in England spins the fibre into yarn, then sends it to Scotland to be dyed. Once dyed, it is wound into skeins and shipped to our headquarters in Columbus, Ohio, to be labelled and packaged for

SY BELOHLAVEK

AMY P. SWANSON

distribution. Our mills are small family processors who have long-standing experience working with cashmere."

Sy is working on getting vital cashmere dehairer equipment from England into Kyrgyzstan in order to set up a local dehairing facility. "This would broaden our work with shepherds throughout Kyrgyzstan, provide jobs at the facility and allow us to expand international access to sustainably and ethically produced cashmere," explains Amy. "It would also lessen our shipping carbon footprint by completing more of the manufacturing process in Kyrgyzstan."

With Sy's attention on the development of the mill, Amy and her husband are invested in the yarn production portion of the company. Amy runs the day-to-day operations as June Cashmere's director. By operating June Cashmere out of her home in Columbus, Ohio, Amy tries to keep operating expenses as low as possible so that company income can go toward repurchasing fibre from shepherds to manufacture yarn. "It is incredibly hard work, building the June Cashmere brand and running the yarn company, as anyone in any small business knows," says Amy, "but being able to engage my love of textiles with a company doing such good work is a gift I am thankful for daily." ✺

"We use the longest and finest, most uniform fibres, resulting in a yarn with a cotton-like hand that blooms and softens with wear with little to no pilling. Cashmere is a limited annual commodity, requiring specified processing. It should last a lifetime—but this is a departure from the over-processed, overly soft, cheaply manufactured yarn that the North American market is accustomed to."

"We educate shepherds in best husbandry and fibre-collection practices, paying fair value directly to shepherds for their cashmere fibre."

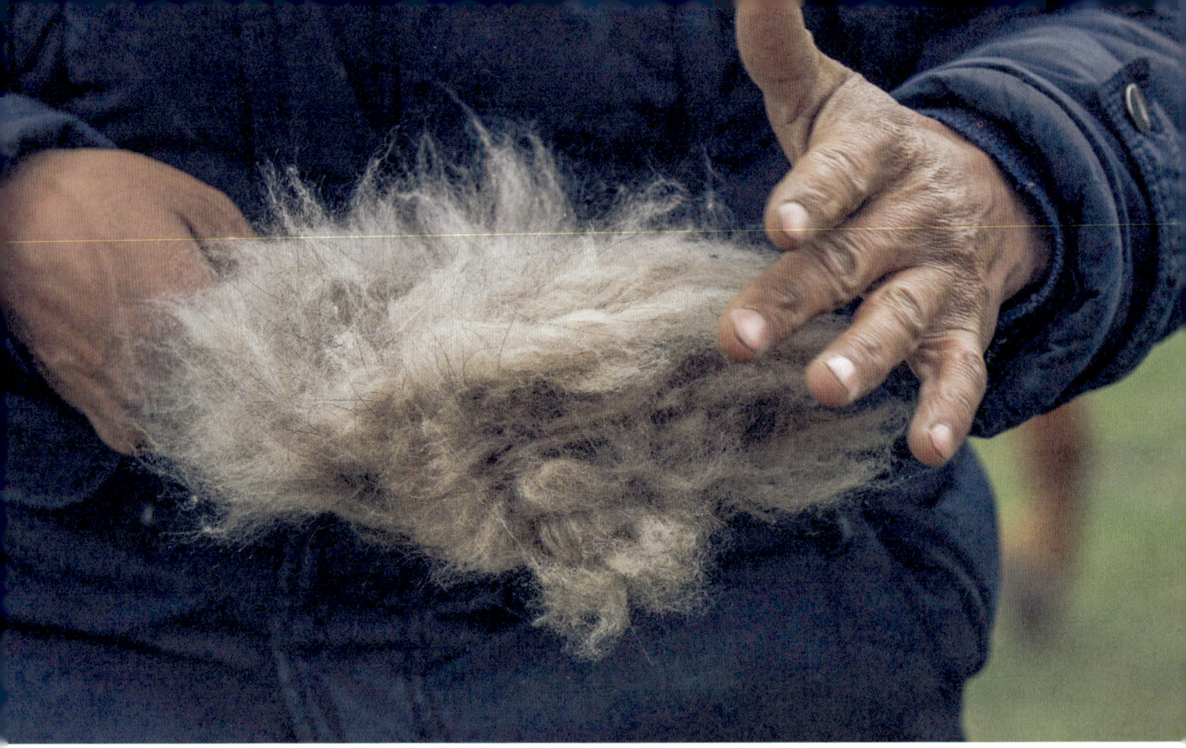

LOCAL GOATS

We source our cashmere from roughly 1,200 semi-nomadic shepherd families in 35 villages along one of the ancient Silk Road passes, the Chong-Alai mountain region, a 20,000-foot mountain range in Southern Kyrgyzstan with a wide valley running east to west. The villages are located in the valley (elevation 14,000 feet) and shepherds spend the summers living in yurts, allowing their animals to graze in the mountains. Families own on average 10 goats native to the region—called "jaidiri" in Kyrgyz, meaning "local goat." A goat is the cheapest animal for a family to own, allowing the poorest families to benefit from selling their cashmere fibre.

Cashmere is the downy undercoat that grows on a goat to provide it with necessary extra warmth for the harsh, cold winters of mountainous Kyrgyzstan. The cashmere naturally molts in spring, providing about four ounces of fibre per goat. From fibre collection to a finished skein of yarn, about 30 to 40% of the commodity is lost. Six goats are necessary to yield enough cashmere for a knitted sweater.

In the spring, shepherd families, often women, comb their goats as the cashmere undercoat naturally molts off. Often, teenage sons bicycle the fibre to meet the June Cashmere vehicle on the day it is in the region to purchase fibre. A three-tiered purchasing system encourages best husbandry and fibre collection practices, as the longest, finest fibres yield the most income. Fair market value for cashmere is paid directly to the shepherds. Previously, middlemen arrived to shear the goats, paid very little for the fibre and sold the fibre to larger processors to earn a profit. By selling to June Cashmere, shepherds earn about 35% more than from selling to previous purchasers and benefit from new income long after other crops have yielded income, providing an economic boost as some families prepare to migrate up the mountains for the summer and other families begin planting crops—potatoes being a main crop.

junecashmere.com
@junecashmere

D.K. WRIGHT CONSTRUCTION

Kelly Wright

Kelly Wright has a special place in her heart for wool in all its forms: fabric, rug yarn, tapestry yarn and crewel yarn. "My grandparents had upwards of 200 sheep on their farm," she says. "I herded them down to the pond to graze in the morning and back into the aluminum-sided barn in the evening, brought them feed and water, replaced their salt blocks, helped with lambing and watched shearing. I love the whole process of caring for animals and using their wool—the feel of it, the smell of it, the way it holds colour and catches the light, the way it felts up and becomes voluminous, the way it holds stitches and makes beautiful defined little loops, and finally the feeling of it in a rug underfoot." Her grandparent's farm in Missouri held other influences, too. "My grandmother had a storehouse of vintage haberdashery and crafting supplies (dreams of a wool shop she never opened)," Kelly recalls. "On the farm, I learned to care for and respect the environment and animals, self-sufficiency and how to make things."

Describing herself as a "chronic needleworker," Kelly's affinity for these crafts includes many activities: "Embroidery, knitting, quilting, sewing, needlepoint, rug hooking, twining are all special to me because these crafts appeal to my innate sense of balance and regularity while affording incredible artistic freedom through the use of colour."

In the 1990s, Kelly left the United States for Berlin. Her friends there were craftspeople and painters who shared her love for old things and beautiful studio spaces. "The creative energy was at once exciting and soothing," she says. "In a leap of faith, I just started making rugs professionally." Kelly dyes fibres and makes braided, hooked and embroidered rugs, and sells kits and supplies online through her shop,

"Handmade textiles and textile art are made loop by loop, stitch by stitch. It entails a meaningful and productive process that requires dedication and care, and cannot be rushed. Engaging in that process with the intent of making people somehow more connected, satisfied and comforted is its own reward and motivation. I like to think that every handmade rug is a thing of beauty, simply because it reminds people of the value of the process and dedication itself."

D. K. Wright Construction. "Using quality tools and materials is important. Since most of the techniques I employ are North American and not yet really established in Europe, I import some things like needles and no-slip hoops, but I also build my own line of frames and have worked really hard building a network in Germany and the rest of Europe to source amazing, locally produced needlepoint yarn, rug hooks, wool fabric, gripper strips and foundation cloth, and I have my own line of European-made rug yarn."

Some years ago, Kelly returned to America as a student at Amy Oxford's Rug Hooking School, for training in the Amy Oxford method of punch needle rugmaking. "The experience was transformative, I found my tribe," she says. "Now, I certify Oxford Rug Hooking instructors myself in my school just south of Munich."

"Making rugs with recycled or naturally sustainable materials is a way to slow yourself down. When you commit to making a rug by hand or commissioning a handmade rug, you are engaging with and shaping your environment into a thoughtful, warm and personal expression of your intentions, needs and hopes. You are choosing a way to maintain the relevance of traditional crafts, a gentle form of production over consumption and to interact with those materials and that process on a daily basis." ❊

INSPIRATION

I draw on the incredibly beautiful Bavarian landscape and woods, my kids and my dogs for inspiration. I am always finding inspiration in the works of old masters, antique rugs and quilts, old magazines and wallpaper. There is no end to inspiration or good ideas—there are times when ideas come in an onslaught, one right after the other, so strong they will keep you up at night. The challenge is to bring inspiration full circle and have the discipline and will to drive an idea through all the stages of becoming a rug— becoming part, if you will, of our daily fabric.

"I am thankful to be a part of this community—I have found fibre artists to be among the most generous, original, inventive and giving people I have ever met. The connections and friendships made through a common love of fibre are remarkable."

dkw-construction.de
@d.k.wright

WINTERGARDEN

My studio is a converted wintergarden back of the historical house I live in with my family and dogs. It is an open space built into a hill with an incredible view of the Alps to the east, saturated with the history of the house and fit with windows that let daylight and weather and the sounds of the goings on in town surround me (the commuter train, voices of people walking or skateboarding home, the "thwock" of the tennis courts, cows lowing in the pasture and the neighbourhood rooster). I love the space in early morning when the sun rises or late at night with rain pounding from all directions. One April there was a late snow that had started to melt at the tree line toward the bottom of the hill, and a sudden shower brought a fully arced rainbow and it was like seeing the entrance to Narnia.

GATHER TEXTILES

Kim McCollum

Before she became a weaver, Edmonton, Alberta-based artist Kim McCollum was a competitive runner. "You would think weaving would be the furthest thing from running," says Kim, "but I find it has a lot in common. The calming cadence of right-left-right-left-right-left of running is similar to the passing of the shuttle. It requires a similar focus, endurance and balance of meditative calm and challenge."

And much like running, craft teaches us life lessons: "I had a weaving teacher who told me, 'Never tie a knot where a bow will do.' Weaving is full of these little bits of tangible and metaphorical wisdom that make it meaningful for me."

Our world is ever-shifting towards a digital society, and Kim is aware of the material knowledge that we might be losing. "I use a weaving loom that hasn't changed much in thousands of years," she says. "I also use Photoshop and weaving software to plan out my compositions. The dialogue between these two ways of working is an important part of what I am interested in as an artist—thinking about how the very old and very new relate. The process of working with threads is a way for me to feel a connection with the physical world while exploring bigger concepts and ideas."

Weaving has become both the process and the subject of her work. "Sometimes I make weavings, sometimes I make weavings that become things, other times I make paintings about weavings."

Weaving drafts, or patterns, have become the subject matter of many paintings. Kim is inspired to closely study these resources, found in old sample books and weaving publications, and to preserve the knowledge, ideas and stories held within. "I see my artwork as an attempt to reframe how these patterns

"As soon as I sat down at a floor loom I knew it was going to be my thing. I had this weird feeling that I was remembering how to weave, instead of learning for the first time."

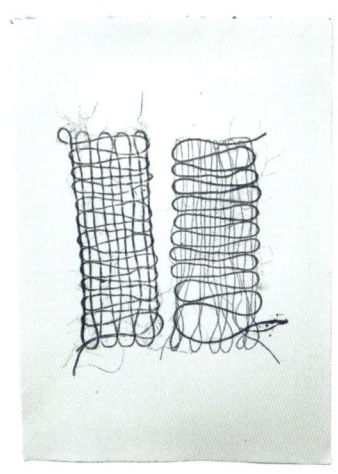

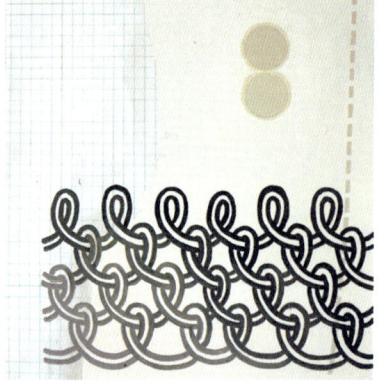

are typically viewed and to have their value and purpose reconsidered." The resulting work could be a wearable item, a textile for the wall or a painted piece or drawing.

Kim has completed the Master Weaver program at Olds College and an MFA at the University of Alberta. Her zest for weaving has taken her farther afield, too: "Learning everything I can about weaving has taken me to Morocco, India, Mexico and all over Canada and the United States. It has also taken me into many weaver's basements and storage lockers full of dismantled looms."

With sewist Angela Kelly, Kim is also co-owner of Gather Textiles in Edmonton. The pair met at a weaving workshop Kim was teaching. "We collaborated on a couple of projects together where I would weave a textile and she would sew it into a garment. There was a lot of interest around what we were doing in the local community, and it ended up growing into a fully stocked weaving supply shop, a teaching resource for weavers and a studio where we host about 30 workshops every year."

Having a business partner and customers to take into consideration does influence one's work, and it is good to have a sewist with whom to collaborate. "We often do a good bit of technical sampling before coming to a textile that will work in the way we want," Kim says. "We primarily use eight-shaft floor looms at Gather, and always use our own designs. Anne brings a whole world of knowledge and experience to the table that pushes me to explore new ideas and new ways of doing things." With Kim's minimalist aesthetic, she is sometimes teased by the team at Gather for "being the one that wants the colour sucked out of everything," but it's a gentle ribbing. "I love colour, just not too many all at once. The truth is that texture and structure is more interesting to me, and too many colours can be so loud that those subtle things can't speak." ✻

"A visible grid structure is a signature of my work. I often avoid structure in my day-to-day life, so starting off with a predictable grid structure in my work is a kind of ritual that prepares me for art making."

"I find inspiration in the quiet moments of making. It can take days to set up a loom for a project, or draw the tiny grid that hides under most of my paintings. These moments allow me to think deeply about what I am doing and often lead to the next piece."

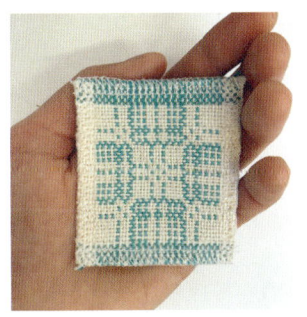

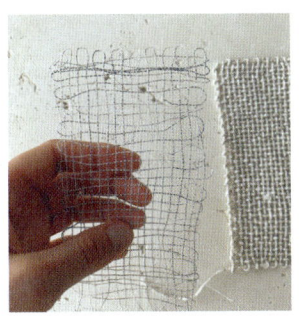
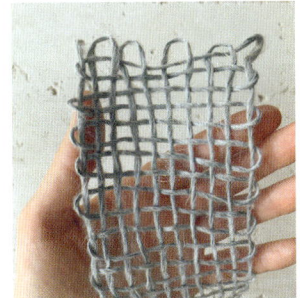

FAVOURITE FIBRE

Considering that I co-own a studio that sells a large variety of weaving yarns, it might be surprising that I love natural undyed cotton the best of all of them. It weaves up like a canvas and becomes a surface for anything. When we first started the studio, we were always running out of it, so now we constantly stock around 100 cones because we never want that to happen again!

TWO SPACES

Currently I work out of two major spaces. My primary studio space is in my home, where I have a huge old loom that is allowed to get paint on it. This is where I do my painting, drawing and research. I have piles of books on my favourite artists: Anni Albers, Agnes Martin, Hilma af Klint. I also collect old weaving books with any information on drafts, or weaving related mythology or folklore.

I also have a shared studio space at Gather Textiles, where I have access to all sorts of looms. I really like moving between my solitary space at home, where I can move at a slower pace and think through my projects, and then the hustle and bustle of the studio at Gather, where the energy of the space and the weavers is really exciting.

"In my paintings, I often leave the raw canvas exposed, allowing the intersections of thread to be visible. The visual structure of the grid is important in my work and I like the idea of it existing within the actual canvas itself as well as painted on top."

kimmccollumart.com
@gather_textiles

KIM McCOLLUM

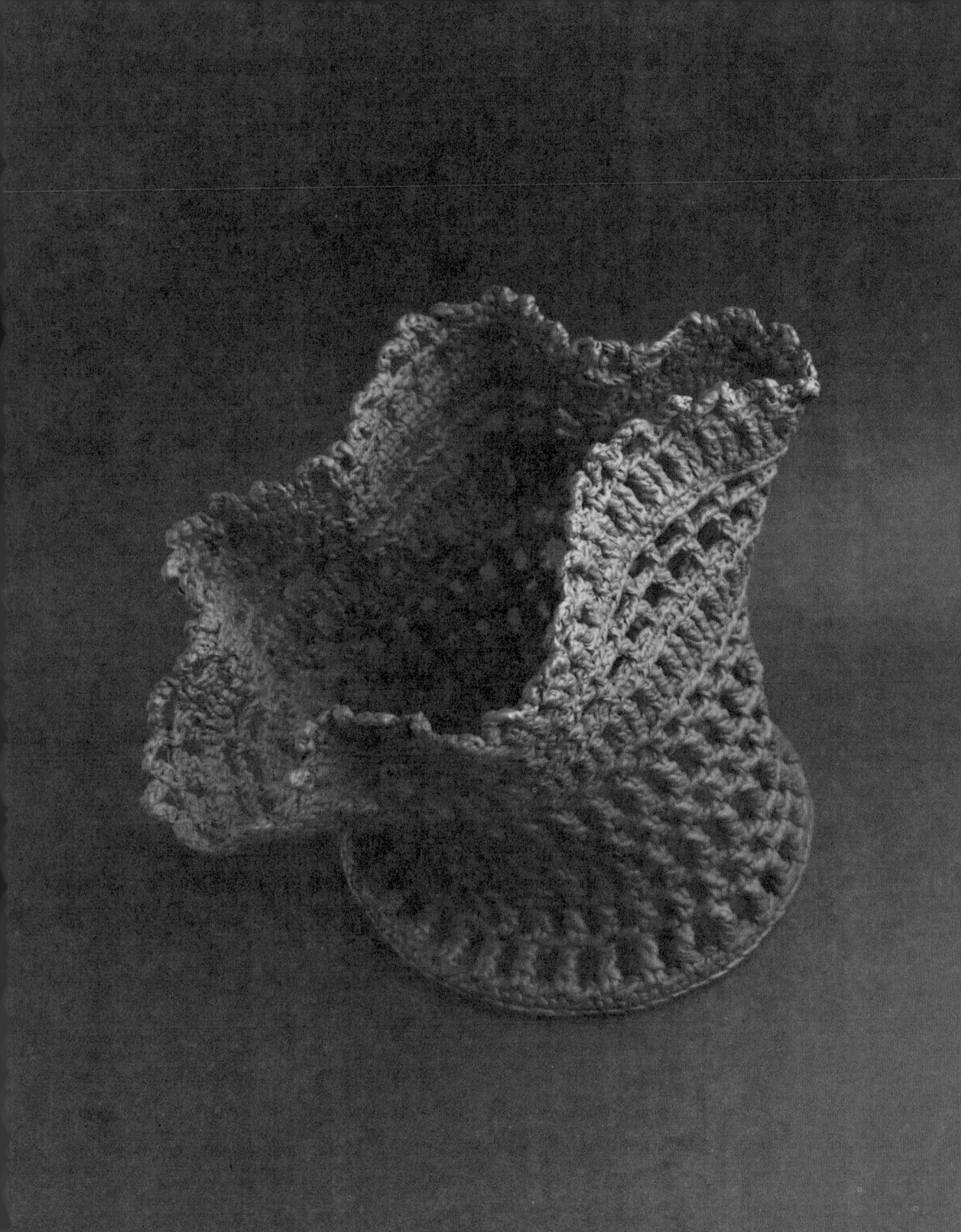

TEXTILES, CERAMICS & PAPER

Liz Sofield

Liz Sofield counts herself lucky to have been immersed in a creative environment from day one. Liz grew up in New Zealand, where her nanna was a tailoress who passed her skills on to Liz's mother, who in turn taught her daughters how to sew, knit and crochet. "A natural transition was to study textile design in Wellington," she says, "and later interior design in Auckland, and work as a designer, designing hand-printed furnishing fabric, woven homewares, bed linen and bespoke rugs."

Several location changes later (she is now based in Brisbane, Australia)—and becoming a mother of twins—helped Liz transition from designer to artist. "This is how my two art practices, textile paper art and crochet porcelain, have evolved. When my son, Liam, was seven (he is now a pre-teen), he became obsessed with making paper planes. So I would sit for hours with him and his twin sister, Rosabella, making planes and paper flowers. This playing and curiosity sparked a fascination with origami, and I began combining it with my hand stitching."

Liz folds watercolour paper using traditional origami techniques, creating forms that play with light and shadow, wrapped and accentuated with a precise web of hand stitching. "Rhythms, textures and symmetry are what inspire me," she says. "It starts with playing with paper and sketching patterns, evolving into an artwork."

A friendship led to Liz's discovery of clay as a material: "My friend invited me to classes at our local pottery club a few years ago and there I fell in love with clay. I wanted to combine this new passion with my existing textile-based work, so I started researching ways to combine fibre and clay, and discovered the technique of dipping fibre into liquid clay."

"My style is delicate and intricate in the way I use patterns and rhythms. The precision required to create the work is a way for me to feel some sense of control, and the repetition helps with my mind's constant chatter and creates a visual calmness I wish to reflect."

LIMITED ON PURPOSE

My colour palette and yarn selection are very limited. This is intentional, as it is very calming to work with and emphasizes the interesting shadows and textures, but doesn't distract from the form or pattern. I predominantly use cotton, as it has a very beautiful tactile feel.

To create these works, Liz crochets using soft cotton yarn, which she then submerges and paints with liquid porcelain. Fired in a kiln, it is transformed into a delicate, light porcelain sculpture. "This technique intrigues me, the way it plays with your senses," she says.

Liz uses her art as a way to make sense of the world and her emotions. "As a maker, I work in quiet corners of contemplation, the rhythmical nature of creation, meditative in its process, and a joyful act of living."

Sadly, her mother now suffers from dementia. "Why is it so important that we remember things? But aren't we all meant to be living in the moment?" she ponders. Her work includes small details that might be unimportant to a casual viewer. "It's the memories that make us unique, that capture our heart and make us who we are. As I sit creating, thoughts, feelings and memories arise, a subconscious act of remembering. I do not want my work to be thought of in sadness—no, not at all. My work is a celebration; a way of linking the past, present and future."

"If along the way other people engage in what I create, that is fabulous to think that I have translated that joy." ✲

"My workspace is as basic as a desk in a corner of our lounge/entrance/kitchen area. I work alone in the hub of the house surrounded by the chaos of family life."

lizsofield.com
@liz.sofield.artist

THREADING A NICHE

Maine Thread Company

The Maine Thread Company is a family-owned company in Lewiston, Maine, USA. "In the mid-1950s, my grandfather and our founder, Alfred 'Honey' Baril, were living in Lowell, Massachusetts, working at C. V. Watson Company," recounts Rusty Vallee, Maine Thread Company president and CEO. "When the company relocated to Auburn, Maine, he and others in the workforce moved with it. Gradually, he rose up the ranks and became the general manager of the shoe factory. Soon after, Honey saw an opportunity to both further his career and to better support his family. He started his own business as a supplier to the booming shoe industry in the Lewiston-Auburn area, and Maine Thread Company was born in 1965."

Their threads used to be made from linen, then nylon. Now polyester has become the fibre of choice for hand sewing. Their speciality is thread with tapered ends. "One can easily needle each end of the thread when sewing together the plug and vamp of the shoe, which is called an 'upper.' The upper is the leather that covers the front and sides of the foot." For decades, manufacturing this niche item was the backbone of their business, selling almost exclusively to large factories.

Today, they still supply tapered ends to large factories, but Maine Thread Company is also reaching a new audience. "We've also become known in the cottage industry for our smaller offerings of waxed cord," says Rusty. "We've branched out to accommodate the smaller companies, Etsy sellers and individual crafters who do leather working, jewellery making and pine needle basketry." Rusty believes that his customers' experiences and feedback define their brand, and they pride themselves on quality, dependability and

"We are part of a growing group of individuals and businesses who value making quality products here in America. The products we manufacture are used by truly fantastic crafters who make up the ever-growing maker culture. We supply to inventors, designers, artisans— people who create and make things by hand."

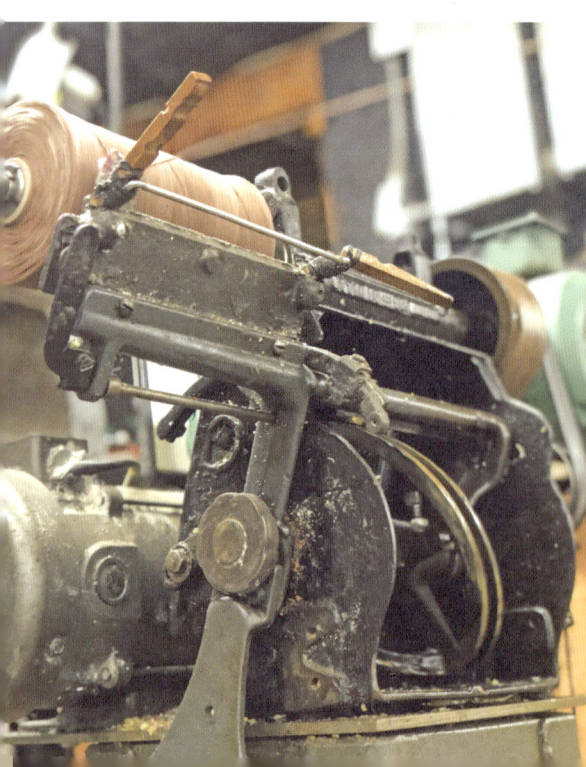

PROCESS

Our process starts with single strands of yarn. Before we get the yarn in-house, we work with two companies to prepare the yarn. One company textures the yarn to our specifications and the other company dyes our choice of colours. When the textured and dyed single-ply yarn arrives at the factory, we start the process of spinning yarn into thread.

First, we wind single strands of yarn together to create the desired thickness (anywhere from one to eight strands). Next, the strands of yarn are twisted together on our Ring Twister. After twisting, the thread is back wound from the wooden bobbin onto a large cone to be "conditioned" (like a steam bath) to prepare for the application of wax. The thread is then run through our wax tanks and wound onto reels. From there, the thread either is wound onto tubes for our smaller offerings, or begins the process of being cut and tapered.

integrity. "A few years ago we decided to build a more consistent image and brand based on those values. We developed a logo (it's hard to believe we went without a logo for over 50 years), which is present on our spool wraps and packaging, and we tried to create more of a cohesive image across our products, website and social media. Building a brand has given us the opportunity to articulate what we value as a family and as a company, and to find ways to communicate that to our community and customers."

With three generations of the family working together at the company, tradition is built in to their culture. Manufacturing is also part of the history of Lewiston. "It's important to us to continue the tradition because of what it means to be committed to making products here in the USA," says Rusty. "In addition to the family, we have four dedicated, long-term team members who make what we do each day possible. Each member of our seven-person staff has a specialty or an area of the business they're really familiar with—but at the end of the day, we all do whatever needs to get done."

Getting things done involves working on old, but appreciated, machinery. "Our process and materials are a mix of new and old. We use modern-day fibres and machines of the past. We have embraced specialty waxes and polyester, as it has become the top choice for hand sewers, while continuing to use machinery that, in some cases, has been around for more than a hundred years. We adapt and change with growing technologies, but some cases call for sticking with what's been working for us. There are newer machines that do the jobs that ours do but with more bells and whistles, but our best and most long-lasting machines are made of metal, gears, belts and pulleys that can be tweaked and manipulated by hand. Newer machines are made with electronics, digital screens and plastic. Fixing them can be the difference between turning a wrench or replacing a motherboard. In our business, we'd often rather turn a wrench." ❋

PEPPERELL MILL

We occupy two floors of a building in the Pepperell Mill in Lewiston, Maine. The mill dates back to 1860 when it was the Lewiston Bleachery and Dyeworks. We're surrounded by brick, wooden beams and remnants of equipment that were used to power the mill when all the factories were hydro-powered by the nearby canal systems in the Androscoggin River during Maine's industrial heyday. The upper level has an office, warehouse and manufacturing space where we do some of the waxing, winding and specialty projects. The lower level consists of our textile factory, where we twist, wind, wax, cut, taper and pack our thread products for footwear companies. The factory is filled with the loud and distinctive humming of the ring twister, the chugging of the air compressor and the rhythmic ticking of the backwinder, with conversations and classic rock filling the gaps. Our factory space has met its share of challenges: we've accrued some damage over the years and even experienced a flood—but it still serves our business well and we're proud to help in keeping the mill alive.

mainethread.com
@mainethread

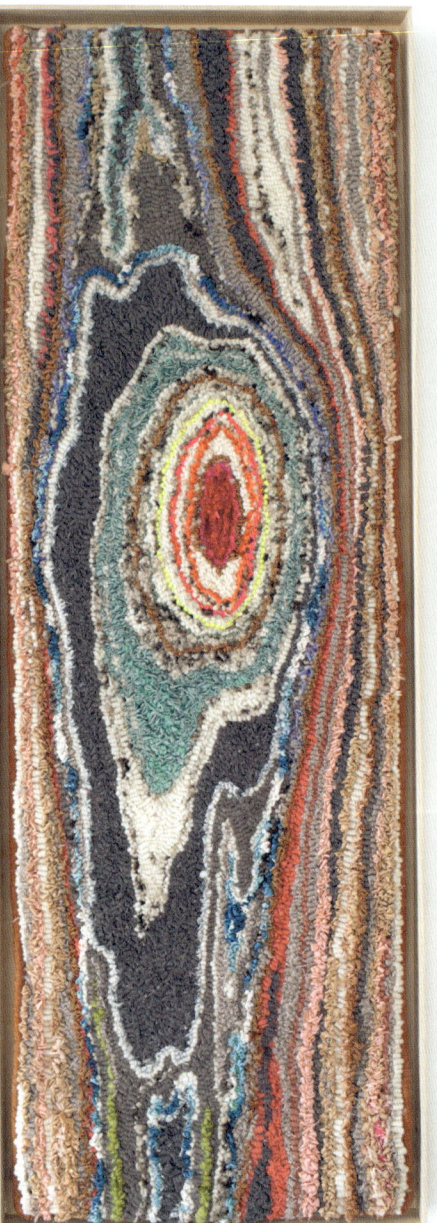

TINY ACTS OF MAKING

Marina Dempster

Marina Dempster embraces traditional craft techniques such as hooking, punching, knitting, sewing, tufting and Huichol yarn painting and beading, combining them in an effort to paint with threads and yarn. "I have been playing with threads ever since ritually organizing my granny's sewing drawer as a wee one, and learning to sew a button, mend a sock or hand turn her old Singer." Marina remembers giving a tutorial on that classic string game, cat's cradle, to her elementary school classmates. "French knitting, knotting, rug hooking, even braiding fern plants or making daisy chains were all 'happy places.'"

Her textile art intertwines form with function, weaving in various recycled and mixed materials—even discarded yoga mats, her own clothes and her husband's jeans are incorporated into her art. "The foraging of the materials themselves then propels me farther forward," Marina says. "In this process, I am experimenting with how the materials behave and what they can contribute metaphorically."

For Marina, the process, and indeed the resulting art, embodies "a deep and universal reckoning" that explores the transition from shame to grace, fear to love and woe to wisdom.

Any transition is basically story: "I love yarn's ability to tell a story in increments. A narrative formed by tiny acts of pure intention, stitch by stitch or loop by loop, feels much like a line of cursive writing, or the ever-evolving lines on our hands and faces. I prefer using worn and upcycled materials to create my own yarns because they carry their own soulful energy and weight. I am enchanted by the alchemy and reinvention that is possible through the materials, which also mirrors my own mutability." ✽

"Most fibre artists spend a certain amount of time mending, reeling or untangling, and these are true metaphors for life. I love the generous nature of the fibre community, who through sharing skills and working together, honour and expand borderless tactile languages and traditions."

DUALITIES

A cushion can provide comfort for deep rest and joyful intimacy, or it can be a throwaway object with a purely decorative function. My Dear Friends// Near Enemies series uses words to expose the often well-worn dualities inherent in our thinking which can make us our own worst enemies. Words within words expose unconscious blindspots that may be the source of our suffering and projections, or they might offer an antidote to our enmeshment. The choice is always there. I use a combination of punch needle and tufting with pure wool in the series.

INFLUENCED BY HUICHOL ART

My fibre practice was ignited in my early twenties when I was invited to help facilitate a workshop hosted by the Textile Museum of Canada and the Gardiner Museum. A Huichol artist had travelled from his remote Indigenous community in the Sierra Madre Occidental mountain region in Northern Mexico to generously share the pre-Columbian technique of transformational "yarn painting." I was captivated by its aroma of beeswax and pine resin (cera de Campeche)—the base into which yarns are delicately embedded with fingertips—and by its powerful symbolic resonances of yarn, pattern and colour.

As I was born in Mexico, practicing this technique felt like both an expression of my Mexican connection and a means to advocate for the resilient yet vulnerable culture of the Huichol.

Then a strange thing began to happen. Physical forms began to find me—in hallways, and in the street—that begged for my waxing and elaborate embellishment. I adopted these abandoned forms, mostly mannequin forms or moulds relating to parts of the body. When I began to play outside the traditional boundaries of the technique by using these forms, my contemporary sculptural practice began to gain momentum.

THE POWER OF LANGUAGE

It's a "knotty" business talking about "waxing," "hooking," "punching" or working with (tufting) "guns." What is this "tuft love" about? I believe that inherent to working with yarn, string or thread is the power to reclaim, repair and reinvent with grace, persistence, courage, resilience and hope.

In boxing, "the hook" has knockout power. I feel that working with fibre, traditionally dismissed as a "domestic" art, packs a powerful punch to expressing social protest, and to confronting cultural issues in a wide variety of contexts and settings. The craftivism of "Victory quilts," the Pussyhat Project initiated by Krista Suh and Jayna Zweiman, the defiant installations of Sheila Hicks, the ecological masterpieces of Vanessa Barragão and the staggeringly beautiful honorific quilts of Bisa Butler, for example, have the power to speak to truth, transcend hierarchies, make language evolve and change restrictive narratives. I love that my work can also be empowering as a reminder of both personal and collective experiences, values and visions.

I see fully embracing a creative career as a kind of activism. In the words of Henri Matisse, "Creativity takes courage." Having a creative career is my way of taking joyful responsibility for myself: a daily ritual of creative practice enables me to develop a more intimate relationship with my natural rhythms and inner voice.

"Making feels like my best friend—supportive, calming and emboldening at the same time."

marinadempster.com
@marinadempsterstudio

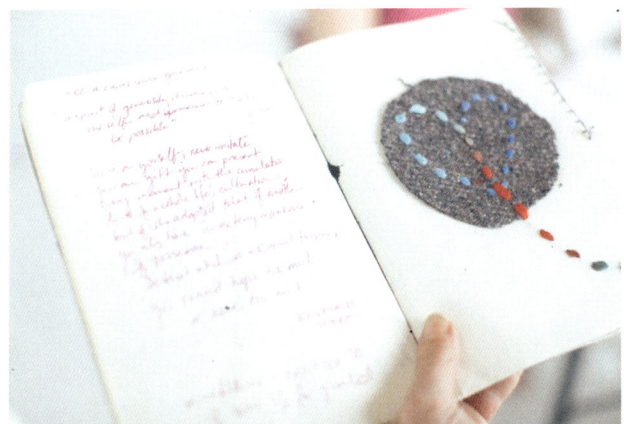

ARTIST IN RESIDENCE

I am currently the inaugural artist in residence at the Orchard Lyceum, an innovative creative space in Toronto (a commercial gallery, community studio and small, private arts-based middle school). In situating students in the context of a working studio and gallery environment, the intention is to invoke their natural tendencies toward industry and practical enquiry and to expand their capacity to express themselves artistically.

I mentor the students to earn my light-filled studio space and a coveted spot on the exhibition calendar. It is a magical place. Last year, to fill the holes in the concrete floors, we embedded symbolic charms and filled them with clear resin. The studio tables on wheels were lovingly crafted from the salvaged floors of a defunct bowling alley.

By virtue of being in this environment, every day is both a prize and a surprise; there is always an opportunity to create, innovate, curate and collaborate. My 12-year-old daughter, Paloma, is one of the students, so she and I have the very special opportunity of witnessing and supporting each other in our element at an exciting time in each of our lives.

MĀORI WOMEN ART COLLECTIVE

Mata Aho Collective

The Mata Aho Collective is an art collective in Aotearoa (the Māori name for New Zealand). It was established in 2012 by four women—Erena Baker (Te Atiawa ki Whakarongotai, Ngāti Toa Rangaātira), Sarah Hudson (Ngāti Awa, Ngāi Tūhoe), Bridget Reweti (Ngāti Ranginui, Ngāi Te Rangi) and Terri Te Tau (Rangitāne rāua ko Ngāti Kahungunu ki Wairarapa)—all of whom are graduates of Toioho ki Āpiti and CoCA Massey University and share Māori cultural heritage.

The women relish their "four-brain, eight hands" approach to making art, since it enables a "sense of supportive freedom" as the quartet creates works that are bigger in scope and physicality than any one of them can attempt individually. "Our strength as a group is our collective authorship," the four say. "Our aim is to construct projects in such a way that it isn't possible to tell who has contributed which part, and

"We want to increase the visibility of Indigenous artists at national art institutions. It is inspiring to bring people along with us and bring issues affecting Māori to a world stage."

ABOVE Making *Te Whare Pora* (2012). Faux mink blankets. Exhibited at Enjoy Public Art Gallery. Victoria University of Wellington collection.

LEFT *Tauira* (2018). Synthetic marine rope. Exhibited in *Embodied Knowledge*, Dowse Art Museum, Wellington.

often we can't tell either." Creating as part of a group with shared responsibilities in which the whole is more important than the self can be found throughout Indigenous art histories, especially women's practices, they explain.

"We are interested in the hidden histories of Māori sewing. In many collection stores, both in Aotearoa, New Zealand, and overseas, are a plethora of bone needles, but few examples of what was sewn." Fortunately, the four have been able to visit historical examples of weaving created by their ancestors, housed in museum collections around the world. "Visiting these collection stores is a tangible connection to the skill and technical ability of our ancestors." And it influences their own techniques, too: "Recently our practice has used the visual language and techniques of customary Maori weaving and finger twining, translated to large-scale industrial materials."

Their installations are site specific and respond to the setting and culture in which they will reside through the use of typically domestic sewing or weaving techniques, but scaled well beyond personal dimensions. Using industrial materials makes the work accessible while also enabling construction on these very large scales. "Although some of our materials are constructed for industrial purposes, they're all linked through fibre—whether it's industrial marine rope or hi-vis fabric for road workers. We have recently used marine rope and tarpaulin in large-scale projects. These materials are usually easily accessible in bulk and the colours are typically high visibility, for safety and strength, in anticipation of a long, hardy life outdoors. We use what we call 'modern Māori materials'—industrial, utilitarian materials that are easily accessible within our communities. The material or fibre we use for each project is usually one of the first things we lock in when starting a new project. We then experiment and push the boundaries of that material

ABOVE Mata Aho in front of *AKA* (2019). Copolymer fibre marine rope, steel. Exhibited in *Àbadakone | Continuous Fire | Feu Continuel*, National Gallery of Canada, Ottawa. Photo courtesy of National Gallery of Canada.

to try to present this modern Indigenous material in a new and exciting way."

"As installation artists, we joke that we are engineers who went to art school. There's a lot of maths that goes into our practice, from figuring out how much material we will need, to calculating a repetitive pattern, to ensuring the safety and longevity of a work in a public space."

Creating installations that take up a large amount of volume in galleries and institutions is done by design and with purpose: "It is our goal to exhibit in large national institutions and take up large amounts of space as Indigenous women. Representation matters—for an audience to come into a gallery and have to take notice is a really powerful thing. We hope that by doing this, other female Indigenous artists gain confidence to do the same." ❋

THIS PAGE *Mahuika* (2019). Barrier mesh, wool and cable ties. Exhibited in the 2019 Honolulu Biennial, Hawai'i State Art Museum.

mataahocollective.com
@mataahocollective

MAKESHIFT

We don't have a permanent studio. We long for a warehouse space, perhaps with a giant sail-makers table to create and test our large-scale works, but we each live in different parts of the country and such an opportunity has yet to materialize. Collectively, we own an industrial sewing machine and a hoist. For a recent project, *AKA* (2019), we had to store, sort and weave almost a tonne of marine rope. This was an intensely physical project, for which we shared a 12-metre-high studio with a group of volcanologists and a furnace that simulated eruptions. We had to use plastic sheeting that is usually used in commercial greenhouses to cover our work to protect it from ash, which was ever present in the studio. With the four of us, we get to attempt big works that we might not necessarily consider in our individual practices. We prioritize working together and get assistance from family, who look after kids and sometimes feed us.

FAMILY FARM

Millpost Merino

The Millpost farm is on Ngunawal/Ngambri country, on the southern tablelands of New South Wales, Australia. It is nestled in a valley, where the undulating landscape is beautifully treed, with regrowth forest, windbreaks, woodlots and shade trees. After heavy rains, Millpost Creek flows through the farm, and several springs feed the creek. Various birds, frogs, kangaroos, wallabies and wombats live in this land.

The Watson family has owned this land for nearly a century, mostly raising sheep. Currently, David Watson and Judith Turley, along with their three sons, Harry, Roy and Murray, and their families tend the land and livestock. "It can be a tough way to make money but it's a great life," says matriarch Judith, "so in order to make farming a viable livelihood for the two generations we are diversifying into as many income streams as possible. Turning some of our sheep's wool into knitting yarn is one of them."

"We produce superfine wool from 2,000 to 3,000 Merino sheep," she describes. "Right now we have only about 750 sheep because we were forced to destock during the summer of 2019 to 2020, due to extreme drought. Although conditions have now improved, and we are hoping to increase numbers when our ewes lamb next month, it may be some years before we have such a large flock again. Therefore it is a good thing that since 2017 we have been value-adding a small percentage of our wool clip by having it processed into knitting yarn."

The family follows the principles of permaculture and takes a regenerative approach to agriculture. "From the start, reafforestation of the farm has been one of our highest priorities, and our sons, particularly Roy, are carrying on that tradition with gusto both on

"We would like to see the yarn from our wool clip transformed into a range of useful, sustainable and enduring products because merino wool is a brilliant fibre that the world needs, whereas man-made fibres are part of the industrial system which has brought the planet into an era of danger and despair."

and off Millpost," says Judith. Tree planting is one integral part of keeping the land healthy. "Over 40 years we have set aside hundreds of acres for biodiversity enhancement and protection, including wildlife corridors and riparian zones. Our goal has always been to farm ethically and humanely while protecting and enriching the natural environment. We hoped to show other farmers that it's possible to make enough money from the land without destroying the resource." They are also working to restore the creek, protecting it from erosion by allowing the banks to revegetate, rather than letting sheep graze there.

Clustered into a small hamlet are stone, timber and mud-brick cottages that house the various families. There is also a shearing shed, machinery shed, workshop, meat house and bicycle workshop. "Many water tanks store water from every roof. The tanks supply most of our domestic water," says Judith. "Next to the shearing shed are timber sheep yards and a shelter shed, which are very old. Each of our houses

"We have used permaculture principles in the management of Millpost farm from the very beginning and will continue to do so into the future, having seen that this approach has served us well, particularly for climate change adaptation."

has a substantial vegetable garden. There are hundreds of fruit and nut trees, pines and shade trees such as oaks, elms, ash and other deciduous species around the dwellings and sheep yards."

It is a lot of work. "There is no off-season!" exclaims Judith. "When not doing sheep work we are busy with growing food. That involves compost making and soil improvement, seed sowing, weeding, a lot of watering, harvesting and processing such as bottling, freezing, etc." They also have a small herd of dairy cows and raise poultry for eggs and meat.

Being self-sufficient and sustainable is integral to life at Millpost. "Globalization has contributed to the destruction of Australia's once-thriving manufacturing sector, with dire consequences for agriculture. We are dedicated to supporting the revival of wool processing and manufacturing here in Australia, given that our country produces the best wool in the world. It has given us great satisfaction to see our wool turned into a valuable, unique product that we hope will eventually provide us with a better income than selling wool through the auction system for export ever did. Better still, in this subalpine climate, our highly wearable, warm wool is making our winters more comfortable than before, as the several knitters in our family turn it into scarves, shawls, socks, jumpers and more!" ✱

KEEPING SHEEP

We have a self-replacing flock (we don't buy in sheep except for rams, and we breed our own rams as well), so much of the work revolves around breeding. Until a few years back, we joined the ewes and rams in autumn, lambed in spring, the lambs were marked two months later and the whole flock was shorn in mid-summer. Crutching, which is when sheep get a haircut to prevent wool-blindness and a bum-shave to remove dags and stained wool, happened about six months after shearing (and still does).

Summer shearing meant the sheep were carrying a full fleece through some of the hottest months of the year, and our summers are getting hotter and hotter. Also, we are now experimenting with shearing our more mature ewes in winter. The theory is that, at lambing, a shorn ewe will be more likely to seek shelter from cold conditions than one with a full fleece.

Also, a ewe can have trouble getting back on her feet after lambing, particularly if her wool is wet. For a couple of years, we have been shearing the older ewes in August. So far we've had improved lambing results. The younger sheep now are shorn in mid-spring, after lambing.

All year round there is constant vigilance for pest problems such as flystrike. The daily routine involves moving sheep onto fresh pasture (more like every two or three days, in fact) by opening gates into new paddocks or moving electric fencing, checking or moving their water supply and noting whether they are all in good health and have sufficient food, shelter and shade.

Other sheep-related work includes pasture regeneration, tree planting for shade and shelter, and checking for intestinal worm infestations (doing a "worm count" with the microscope), and management of kangaroos that compete with sheep for feed.

"Millpost Merino is an exciting new direction for our family farm. After more than 30 years of selling all our wool at auction, we took the plunge and sent the best of our clip off to New Zealand to be processed into these balls and hanks. We hope there are knitters and crocheters out there who are pleased by the prospect of creating garments from Aussie wool from Aussie sheep."

FROM BALE TO SKEIN

After shearing, several bales of greasy wool are transported to the port of Sydney, then shipped to a wool-scour at Timaru, on the South Island of New Zealand. The clean wool then travels to Design Spun in Napier, on the North Island, where it is made into tops, spun, dyed and labelled. The finished product, consisting of balls, cones and skeins of wool, is shipped back to Australia.

millpostmerino.com
@millpostmerino

EMILY KATZ

Modern Macramé

At 19, Emily Katz dropped out of art school to travel through Europe. Upon returning to Portland, Oregon, in 2003, she began a line of freehand embroidered art clothing. "I have always found myself on the cusp of a creative renaissance, from art clothing to sustainable women's wear, to macramé," she states. Her current business, Modern Macramé, was founded in 2014 and offers macramé and craft supplies, curated artisan goods from around the world, experiential craft education and custom fibre-inspired installations. "We prioritize sustainable practices and materials, with a focus on modern beauty and design. We are a tight-knit team of women working to make the world more beautiful and creative."

With its loops and knots, the art of macramé has created a lot of connections for Emily. It even helped mend an important relationship. "In 2012, I reconnected with my mom, who I was estranged from for over 20 years, via the request to have her teach me to make a macramé plant hanger." Emily hung the plant hangers in her guest bathroom, and the following year when editors from a Japanese magazine were visiting to create a DIY home feature, they were impressed. "I told them I had made them with my mom and then the next day they came over and I taught my first ever macramé workshop to Japanese magazine editors in my living room. From there I began travelling the world and teaching workshops in macramé." With growing demand for high-quality materials and an ever-growing social media following, Modern Macramé was born. "We began with workshops, then writing a book, then selling rope. Our biggest seller is our five-millimetre cotton three-ply twisted rope in 32 colours. We were the first in the USA to offer this product."

"At Modern Macramé, I take all the photos, work with the team on branding, marketing, design and other creative, and help run the business. It is a team effort."

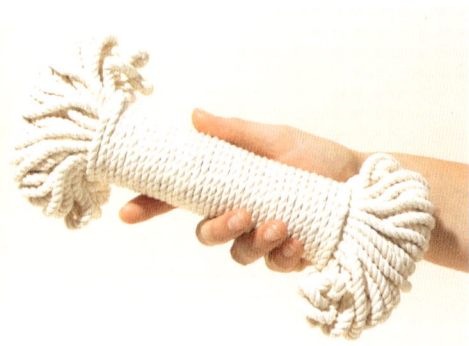

SUPPLY

Much of our materials come from Turkey. I visited there in 2017 and had planned to in 2020 before Covid.

The cotton yarn is purchased, custom dyed, then spun into string. It is then either wrapped onto a cone or bundle, or turned into rope through a process of machine twisting.

It is then sent to us via boat, unloaded to our warehouse/studio in Portland and lovingly sent to our customers.

We are also working with a new manufacturer in Sweden who works with only 100% GOTS-certified organic cotton. We have goals to create vertical USA-based manufacturing for high-quality farm-to-design products as well.

With over 280 thousand Instagram followers, Emily and her team have created a business that goes much deeper than a crafty trend. "We believe strongly that we are more than just a company selling rope and string," Emily says. "We just went through a devoted rebrand and website launch with the customer in mind so they feel supported, trust in us and feel empowered to create from their heart." They collaborate with other artists to make exclusive beads, notions and tools. "We work with interior designers to execute large high-end design installations. At our core, we are about connection, and love collaborating with others."

Supporting their community through education and inspiration is key. They have launched a Craft Club, monthly video tutorials and a community for their eager audience. "We believe in raising people up to be the best versions of their creative selves, and we want everyone to know what macramé is and to love it," says Emily. "My dream continues to grow so I can support and inspire as many creative women as possible to realize their creative potential through craft. Modern Macramé is not just about rope and making crafts, it is about deeply connecting to who you are." ✻

modernmacrame.com
@modernmacrame

"For me, the tradition of macramé relates to connecting over craft through my matriarchal line. Like many crafts, they are passed down through generations. My work in sharing my love of craft is also rooted in connection and the sharing of knowledge."

STUDIO

In Portland, we work out of a 2,000-square-foot warehouse studio. I just upgraded to my own 400-square-foot studio within our space with my own door! It is very exciting. We have our shipping and warehousing on one side, and the rest is creative offices for my team and my own design and video space.

PAINT AND STITCH

Nadia Nizamudin

Nadia Nizamudin grew up wanting to be a fashion designer. "I used to love running my hands through my mom's clothes in the wardrobe, feeling the textures of the wool, the silk, the chiffon," she remembers. An appreciation of textiles runs in the family. Her maternal grandmother and mother both do various handcrafts like crochet, cross-stitch and knitting. "But we all started out with sewing and have sewn things for our homes, ourselves and our families."

While pregnant with her first child, Nadia took painting classes. "I needed a means to escape, and

"I use my embroidery as a means to relax and escape. Also, starting a piece and finishing it does wonders for my sense of purpose and accomplishment. It is tiny, but tiny victories count."

DMC THREADS

I love the plain old DMC embroidery threads, mostly because they are accessible, easy to get, come in a lot of colours and are durable. I have experimented with organic and plant-dyed floss and totally love them, but I reserve them for special or personal work because they are pricier, although I love the feel of them between my fingers.

since I couldn't cycle or run at that time, the art classes felt right. After the baby was born I became more and more obsessed about making art, this time insistently finding ways to fuse my paint with my textiles."

When the baby was born, Nadia started a kidswear business, but success forced her to make a decision. "It snowballed bigger than just a side business and I had to make the decision to end it while the going was good," she says. She began to use the bolts of unused fabric as practice canvas for painting. "I love the tactile quality of embroidery—also the chaos of textures and colours." For the first time in her life, she felt there was no pressure on her art making. "I can decide what concepts I would like to do, what colours, and then work on them. The fact that people love them and collect my work is a bonus."

Based in Selangor, Malaysia, these days Nadia is drawn in many directions and describes herself as "a visual artist working with fibre and mixed-media collage, a self-conscious poet, an awkward mother, a tired triathlete and an overworked engineer."

Embroidery is an antidote to these demands, especially with the simple stitches that she favours. "I love that the embroidery is at the same time a mental challenge and a meditative practice. I love nothing more than to unwind listening to a podcast and just stitching away, one line at a time." She carries her embroidery work with her, especially when travelling for work. "People know me for bringing my embroidery to oil rigs to work on at night."

Nadia's bright, seemingly cheerful colour palette belies some darker content. Her work speaks about grief, postpartum depression, domestic abuse and child sexual abuse. Some are taken aback by these themes, but this contrast between medium and message also helps to call attention to important issues. "My main goal is to make artwork that resonates with the things and issues that I am passionate about," Nadia says. "This is the reason why I have been pushing

more and more to be in exhibitions, because I love having people discuss my work and understand the depth and context of the story behind it rather than just find it visually pleasing."

Her work has been included in campaigns for gender injustices in the workplace and providing postpartum anxiety awareness. Nadia donates a portion of her profits to social organizations like PS the Children (Protect and Save the Children), an NGO that works in prevention, intervention and treatment of child sexual abuse in Malaysia.

Nadia could not have anticipated the impact art making would have on her life, nor the significance of those early attempts at needlework. "My best moment was when my mom unearthed an old embroidery hoop that once belonged to my grandmother and she gave it to me after she'd seen how far I had come along with my embroidery. I keep it in my studio and only use it when I am stitching on a personal project." ✱

"The chevron stitch is probably my signature stitch. I incorporate it in almost every single piece. I also use bright, loud colours because the concept of my work is already dark."

nadianizamudin.com
@nadianizamudin

HOME COMFORTS

Because embroidery is portable, and because I travel so much, I have a portable studio in a bag. In it are all my favourite acrylic tubes (must have: white and magenta), one to two brushes, all colours of yarn, needles, a scissor, a sketchbook (for when the inspiration hits), a magazine and glue (for collage inspirations), several different sizes of embroidery hoops and then my painted fabric, all neatly folded and ready to be stitched.

My main studio is at my parents', whose house I go to every weekend (or every other weekend). It is also a sewing room for my mom and me, and it is just so full of fabric. It has a small shelf that sits all my embroidery and sewing books, and a large sturdy table where I do all my painting and block printing.

But the real studio is usually my living room sofa, where I lay out all my yarn, floss and tools and get to work. I stitch on two to three different projects at once, because I love to keep things fresh, so I like having the pieces around me.

PRETEXT STUDIO

Nadine Flagel

Nadine Flagel's mission is to "make art out of making do." The Vancouver, Canada-based artist and academic creates hooked rugs out of upcycled textiles from hand-me-downs and thrift shops. "Although reusing fabric is technically challenging," she admits, "it makes this an ethical, sustainable endeavour. The resulting works pose strategic interventions in a mainstream culture preoccupied with consumption and fast fashion."

Early in Nadine's pursuit of a PhD in English literature, a friend in Halifax, Nova Scotia, took her to visit Doris Eaton, the famed East Coast rug hooker, and founder of the Rug Hooking Guild of Nova Scotia. "The dense soft colours of the hooked rugs and the sustainability of the art form were a revelation and an inspiration," she says.

Rug hooking provided Nadine with a much-needed tangible break from "the relentless critical thinking that goes along with completing a PhD dissertation and teaching literature." In 2007, during parental leave with her second child, Nadine invested time in documenting her past textile work and in developing an original art practice. "This quickly led to teaching rug hooking and selling supplies. I have since developed a socially engaged art practice in which I collaborate to make community art pieces, create hooked rugs on commission, exhibit work internationally, study with other rug makers, and publish articles and conduct ongoing research on craft, design and art."

Nadine has become more comfortable in bridging her two worlds: text and textiles. "Oddly, my area of academic specialization is intertextuality, or the way books refer to (or upcycle) other books," she says. She recognizes the structural and thematic similarities

"Rug hooking is not only a sensual fine craft but also an art form worthy of intellectual critical and political labour. At its core level of technique and materials, rug hooking is the labour-intensive act of pulling together elements that were not originally designed to be side by side. Rug hooking requires a significant act of reloving the forgotten, of finding the potential of the discarded."

> "There is a revelation in the act of looping and folding fabric; as in origami, folding creates meaning and shape."

between her artistic and academic interests. "Interested in the repurposing of both texts and textiles, I find that both practices rely on cutting up existing text(ile)s, on aesthetic and sensual appeal, on thrift and on putting old things into new combinations, thereby intensifying and multiplying meanings."

Whether making a patchwork quilt or hooking a rug, the use of reclaimed fabrics is the act of storytelling. "These stories aren't just in the pictures or patterns; they are in the textiles and fibres themselves. The juxtapositions of texture, colour and form that are so fascinating to me are only possible with reclaimed fibres."

"All the fibres I use are rich with labour and resources and creativity and stories well before I find them. Working with these is not like working with raw materials; it's finding a way to put existing stories side by side." ✱

FAVOURITE FIBRES

The linen foundation cloth I use has the most beautiful hand. It's unbleached flax with a primitive weave which is strong yet elastic and lets you see where you're going. This linen is my hero, although you don't often see it in a finished piece.

I've experimented with hooking various fibres. Strips of medium-weight, tight-weave wool fabric are the best for keeping loop shape and direction, and providing defined detail. My favourite width is one quarter inch, but you can cut it down to a tiny fraction of an inch wide (three threads wide!) and it will still hold together while you hook it.

Hooking a beautiful light silk charmeuse is glorious, but it's very different; it's all about pulling up the silk fabric to let it bloom and shimmer, and letting go of control.

THE RUG-MAKING PROCESS

GATHERING

I often gather material and generate ideas at the same time. Working with reused fabric is constraining, and I build around what I can find. Certainly, sometimes I benefit from 20 years of collecting wool and find everything I need at home. But sometimes I'm in a small town with 15 minutes to spare and one thrift store, or I'm looking for T-shirts during a pandemic and the thrift shops are closed.

I vigorously launder garments then deconstruct them. Buttons, zippers, shoulder pads and scarf fringes go to the school craft room or local upcyclers. I turn chosen fabrics into fibre by ripping or cutting them into strips. Wool is cut about a quarter inch wide and up to 25 inches long. Cottons and silks get ripped into strips varying from a half inch to two inches wide, depending on thickness.

MAKING

A frame similar to an embroidery hoop sits on my lap and holds a piece of linen foundation cloth taut, so I can reach the top and bottom. From the top, I insert a rug hook, which is like a crochet hook with a bulbous wooden handle, through the loosely woven cloth. Underneath, I hold a strip of fabric, ribbon, yarn, roving or other fibre. Then I pull the fibre strips into loops above the surface of the linen. It requires 10 to 12 loops per square inch to cover the linen and create a rug pile.

One of the most interesting differences between rug hooking and other forms of rug making (such as latch hooking or rug braiding) is that a hooked rug has no knots, glue or stitching. The pressure of the loops, excellent workmanship and the felting of fibres are the factors holding a hooked rug together. There is something terribly precarious about that but also reassuring. Things hold together more easily and are stronger than we give them credit for.

FINISHING

Finishing is my farewell to a piece, so I try not to rush it. When the hooking is finally done, the rug is blocked (steamed and stretched). Then it needs finishing: framing, mounting or hanging. A classic finish for a floor rug is a whipstitch edge, so the whole rug is protected with a raised edge.

"Making a rug is slow art. People often ask me how long it takes to complete a rug. I tell them rug hooking warps the time-space continuum, and this is only partly a joke. Rug hooking is a ritualistic and in some ways senseless looping of time—senseless because it is so slow that progress is hard to measure. Yet persistence pays off in terms of the pieces produced, and in more ineffable results. We all have to make things we can't measure so we understand that use, efficiency and productivity are not the point of existence."

A FAMILIAL FEELING

My family lives in a small Vancouver bungalow, where every space does triple duty. My primary workspace is the living/dining room. I hook, mend and quilt from the corner of our couch. Current projects live in brightly coloured woven baskets in the living room. Occasionally I spread out fibres, fabrics, patterns, an ironing board, a sewing machine and more all over this room.

I usually work alone at night. My children help cut fabric strips; they like hand-cranking the fabric-slitting machine, which is similar to a pasta cutter. A table my grandfather made holds tools (he was a carpenter), and my grandmother's cedar-lined chest contains much of my wool (she knitted).

I have a deep closet and a dozen other nooks stacked with clear plastic containers for fabric scraps, old silk ties and cashmere sweaters, yarns, a dye pot and so on. The disadvantage is I can't see what I have; the advantage is that I am frequently sorting through this collection. New projects require me to pull out everything so I can touch and see, choose the fibres and textiles I need, then pack it all up again.

pretextstudio.com
@pretextstudio

Natalie Ciccoricco

Natalie Ciccoricco grew up in the Netherlands and describes herself as having been "creative in one way or another" for most of her life. She earned a master of arts at Utrecht University, learning about art history, film, cultural heritage and education. And yet, she never thought she would be a professional artist. "It was a lot of learning and very little doing," she says.

Once out of college, she worked as a translator, language consultant and localization tester in the computer gaming industry. "While I was working as a translator, I started to feel the need to work with my hands more and more. It felt so good to do something different than sitting behind a computer all day. It's really important for me to have a creative outlet."

She and her husband became home owners on another continent—in the San Francisco Bay Area—and she began making more art. "Embroidery on paper has been my main medium of choice since I started making art," Natalie says. The interest stemmed from some thrifted embroidery thread that her mother gave to her and her sister. "She gave it to us to do something creative with. I always kept it and wanted to do something with it, and when I first learned about artists using embroidery thread on paper, I got really inspired to start using it." Natalie enjoys playing with geometric shapes and straight lines, giving simple materials a new life and a new story. "I'm always thinking of new ways to explore this medium."

Keeping things simple in her art-making process has proven to be a useful trait. Being at home extensively during the Covid-19 pandemic, Natalie and her toddler have gathered sticks and stones, river rocks and broken tiles around their house and on nature hikes. "I recently started creating embroidery

"I create because I just have to do it. It is the natural flow of things that demands it. One of my main motivations is to bring some beauty into the world. It motivates me to know that my artworks bring others joy."

artworks incorporating natural materials. Exploring the juxtaposition between geometric shapes and organic elements, these new works have been an ongoing exercise to find beauty and hope in challenging times." Aside from organic materials, Natalie uses old books, postcards, magazines and found ephemera in her work, bringing textural colour motifs to life on old imagery. "Repurposing materials and letting nothing go to waste is a very important segment of my work. From old books and magazines to sticks and stones, I like to give materials a new life. I hope it makes people think about the ugly side of consumerism and how much waste it produces, as well as the importance of slowing down and seeing beauty in the little things." ✽

"Nature is such a great source of inspiration. There is no substitute for being in nature. It heals my soul and brings me to a place of calm. Being still and observing the world around me is a strong catalyst for creative ideas."

PERFECT THREADS

I absolutely love DMC six-strand embroidery thread. The quality is amazing and it comes in any colour imaginable. Furthermore, you can split the strand to the desired thickness. I love the satin sheen it has and how the colours look different at different times in the day. Using the thread to pick out a colour scheme for a project is one of my favourite things to do.

mrsciccoricco.com
@mrsciccoricco

STAY-AT-HOME

My studio is just a small desk on a landing outside of my son's bedroom. It is tiny. I dream of a bigger studio, as I usually have boxes of materials and finished artworks floating through the house, especially while I'm getting ready for a new art show.

I have a lot of embroidery thread, neatly organized and colour sorted in clear plastic boxes. Other than that, most of my materials consist of all kinds of paper and old books and magazines.

I work by myself, but I would love to one day have assistance with packing and shipping artwork, answering emails and admin stuff. It can be challenging to do it all while being a stay-at-home mom as well.

THERESA FURRER

Nine Lives Twine

Yarn is made from animal fibres. Wool, angora, alpaca, cashmere—we don't even think twice about these fibres from sheep, rabbits, alpacas and goats. But have you ever knitted with chiengora or catgora? Is your furry little companion also a potential fibre source? The answer is yes, and Theresa Furrer specializes in hand-spinning yarn made from the collected brushings from pets. "I started Nine Lives Twine for the sole purpose of creating lasting mementos for people who cherish their pets," Theresa explains. "Weaving together my love for animals and my creativity, along with losing a pet of my own and some serious reflection about my life's purpose, is what sparked the idea."

Theresa has a decades-long interest in yarn, but she never had the time to spin her own, despite having a spinning wheel. However, after donating part of her liver to her father and requiring three months off to recover from this major surgery, Theresa had time to try something new—and also the purpose and determination to truly follow her heart and live more fully. "Fate definitely played a part in aligning the stars from me."

Theresa lives in western Pennsylvania with her 21-year-old Devon Rex cat, two eight-year-old Sphynx cats, "and my husband," she adds. "You can usually find me covered in dog and cat hair, and I wouldn't have it any other way. It's definitely ironic that I work with pet hair and have hairless cats. And my last name really is Furrer!"

Through spun yarn, and knitted and crocheted keepsakes, Theresa makes fibre that is sentimental and extremely personal. It is a service that goes beyond being just a product; it is an emotional release for the recipient. "I take what I consider to be love and intention behind the intimate act of someone

"I'm so grateful that my work has been recognized around the world for both the love and intention behind it. While it is a unique niche yarn, the appeal to pet lovers is universal. People from all walks of life have touched me with their stories of love and devotion for their pets. It is these people, with hearts of gold for animals, who truly inspire my work."

brushing their pet and intertwine that into a yarn that continues the life cycle of that energy. Pet hair is beautiful, soft, unique to one animal and becomes a source of healing as yarn once the pet has passed on. Helping pet owners honour and celebrate their pets, whether they are still living or passed on, with a unique yarn or keepsake is truly a service I'm so grateful to be able to provide. My work helps hearts to heal and provides not only comfort but a lasting treasure."

Theresa believes that every animal has a story to tell and wisdom to share, and she is honoured to be part of it. ✸

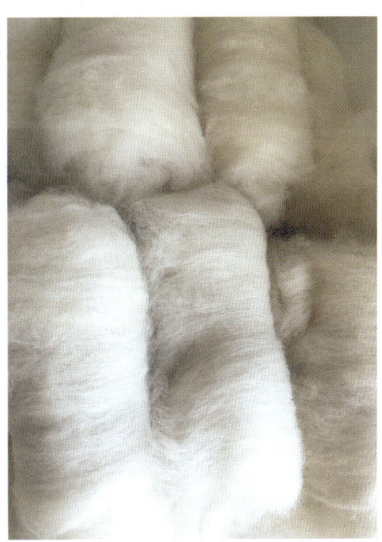

CHIENGORA

Yarn made from dog hair existed even before written history. Once made and used out of necessity, it is now a novel yarn, or what is known as slow yarn. While it has fallen out of mainstream use it still serves a purpose. I love knowing that I am keeping that tradition alive for dog lovers and yarn enthusiasts. The origins of hand spinning have been lost in time, though there is evidence dating back 20,000 years. It is certainly an ancient art that is timeless. My process is simple, straightforward and doesn't employ industrial, mechanical methods. I'm taking raw materials, and my hands play a part in making yarn with it every step of the way. Once people realize the amount of effort and time that goes toward hand spinning a skein of yarn from pet hair, they often ask if it's worth it. Absolutely! There are no shortcuts to be had and the end result is magnificent; it truly is a labour of love for me.

THE NINE LIVES FIBRE PROCESS

BRUSHING

Clients brush their pets and collect those brushings over time. Some breeds of dog blow their coats at certain times of year and this can create a large volume of brushings. Cat hair is usually collected over a longer period of time; they send the brushings to me once they are ready to have yarn made. I work with any amount, large or small.

RECEIVING

I inspect, weigh and book the service once the fibre has arrived.

INSPECTION

I hand pick any debris or matted hair from the fibre. This takes a large amount of time, but is an important part of ensuring a high-quality yarn. In some cases the fibre must be washed and dried before carding it.

OPENING THE FIBRES

Some hair can be put through my manual bench picker to open up the fibres before carding. When that's not the case, it is opened up by hand.

CARDING

The fibre is hand carded into rolags or drum carded into batts. Again, it's a long and laborious process but the time spent preparing the fibre for spinning is so important! Opening up each handful of pet hair into a lofty cloud of fluff is the goal.

SPINNING

The carded fibre is hand spun, usually on a double treadle wheel, and plied into a sport-weight yarn on my production spinner. It's then washed to set the twist, air dried and finished as centre pull balls.

ninelivestwine.com

NINE LIVES TWINE

PAPER YARN, TWINE AND RAFFIA

PaperPhine

While working on a master's program in textile art and design at the University of Art and Design in Linz, Austria, Linda Thalmann became interested in the history of European-made paper yarns. "European paper yarns (and paper in general) was a more widespread and popular material in Europe after the First and especially the Second World War," she explains. "Other resources (cotton, wool, etc.) were scarce, but wood and therefore paper was still available and turned into paper yarn and everyday textiles. When other supplies were available again, paper and paper yarns disappeared again. So our yarns have a largely forgotten legacy and are now rediscovered by creatives around the world."

During her studies, it wasn't possible to buy the thin paper yarns that she desired, and so slowly, an idea for the business began to grow as she sourced paper yarns from various suppliers. PaperPhine was founded in 2009.

"Paper yarns and paper twines—ranging from thin like a thread to thick like a rope—are made in the European tradition from sustainably grown European wood, and dyed with environmentally friendly dyes and processes." Manila hemp is used for the few Japanese paper yarns that PaperPhine offers: "They have some unique technical properties not found in European-style paper yarns and a beautiful, soft feel and papery sheen." Linda is able to source specific paper yarns for her offerings, selecting the thicknesses and technical qualities of the yarn and directing the dyehouse on the palette.

Using beautiful reused wooden bobbins and simple labelling, Linda creates the sort of product she would want to buy personally. "Luckily a lot of

"We love how we can make people admire and wonder in awe how a humble material made out of wood-like paper can be turned into beautiful threads and ropes, making their own lives a bit more beautiful while not damaging the environment. Especially in the West, paper, paper textiles and paper yarns have never been as highly valued as in the East, and we think it's about time to change that."

"We're always looking for new paper yarns and twines worldwide to incorporate into our product range, as long as they're made out of paper and meet our quality and environmental criteria."

customers seem to share our sense of design and presentation," she says. "We're providing access to an environmentally friendly, sustainable yarn/twine that is hard or impossible to come by otherwise and that is a great alternative to many other less environmentally friendly yarns and twines."

For crochet, knitting, weaving, jewellery making, bookbinding, gift wrapping and more, the use of paper yarn and raffia is really up to the imagination of the user. "Think of a yarn that is strong enough for carpets and furniture making, supple and elegant enough to hold together the finest and most elaborate invitation suites on handmade paper, and rigid enough and vibrantly dyed for paper jewellery and art projects—all while being vegan and fully recyclable though your household's paper bin." ✻

PAPERPHINE

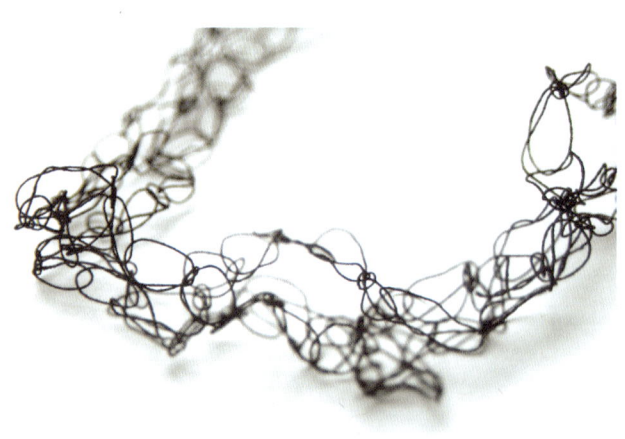

"We love to use our own paper yarns and try out new and old techniques, incorporating the specific properties of our paper-based products if there is any time left besides running the business. Due to the uniqueness of our paper yarns, we're also often helping our customers with questions regarding their own creative projects (and yes, our paper yarns can get wet!)."

STUDIO

Our studio is in the middle of Vienna, Austria, and packed with paper yarns, paper twines, paper raffia... boxes filled with old bobbins, heaps of new bobbins, and drawers filled with very secret samples of special paper yarns and samples of yarns that we never offered for sale to customers. Worktables for working on our own paper yarn projects (which do not happen nearly often enough—there is just never enough time) can be found next to packing tables filled with packages that need to get out. It's a very busy, small studio, juggling creative with business-related work.

paperphine.com
@paperphine

HAND-DYED IN PERU

Pichinku Fibers

"Pichinku's mission is to help preserve cultural traditions, and in doing so provide skilled and dignified work to women artisans by offering a safe environment where they can learn, converse and grow."

Dana Blair is the founder and managing director of Pichinku Fibers. "Pichinku (pee-cheen-koo, meaning 'little bird' in the native Quechua language) is a social enterprise that produces all-natural yarn, botanically dyed in small batches by the skilled hands of women artisans in Cusco, Peru," says Dana. "Pichinku yarn is sustainable, environmentally friendly and socially conscious. Each skein is part of the ancient heritage of the Andes mountains and supports the health of its people and breathtaking landscapes."

Born in Honolulu and raised in a small town in southwestern Pennsylvania, Dana has always been the wanderer in her family, fascinated by world travel, people and culture. "When it came time to leave quaint Belle Vernon for college, I was off to study anthropology at Pennsylvania State University," she says. "And when I started travelling internationally, I never stopped." She visited Europe a handful of times and travelled extensively in South America, but did not feel such a deep cultural connection until she went to Peru. "When I moved to Cusco in 2013, supposedly for a one-year contract working with textiles, I had no idea what awaited me. Just days after arriving, I was working hand-in-hand with a network of artisans who were the living, breathing practitioners of a 5,000-year-old tradition. And I was overjoyed, to say the least. Not only was it fascinating and dynamic, but there was also huge potential to make a positive impact in the lives of other people."

"One year quickly turned into more than seven here in the Andes, now with a business, home and family of my own." Her work is dedicated to empowering women and helping them gain independence: "I made Pichinku for the women who inspired me to stay in

288 YARN · THREAD · STRING

Peru. I was awestruck by their talent, knowledge and strength, but devastated by the difficulty of their daily lives. They face financial and medical hardship, lack of access to education and, consequently, have few options for making an income to support their families. Yet they're capable of making woven masterpieces using no mechanized equipment and dyeing a rainbow of vibrant colours with just the plants found around their homes. I thought, and still think, that it's extraordinary and wanted to do something to support it."

Since 2013, Dana has worked with three Peruvian sisters, Leonarda, Angela and Santusa. Together, the "Pichinku girls" have over 50 years of combined experience working with natural fibres and fibre arts.

Sourcing their base yarn from Peruvian suppliers who share their commitment to sustainable production, Pichinku dyes the yarn from a seemingly limitless palette of colours made from seasonally available leaves, bark and roots foraged by hand from the mountains and valleys surrounding the workshop. "This past year we moved to our new workshop home, La Casona Pichinku, a 19th-century Spanish colonial house in the Sacred Valley of Cusco," says Dana. "Nestled in a lush mountain valley, we work outside in a private orchard full of fruit trees, our vegetable garden and sunshine. Our equipment is simple, all hand operated. It's work that's best accomplished and most enjoyed when done slowly. There are a few large stovetops, metal pots, rinse basins and lots of buckets. There are shelves lined with needles, hooks, swifts and ball winders inside. Almost everything is speckled with colour from bubbling dye pots." ✻

NEW CONNECTIONS

Incorporating new technologies and products has been integral to preserving the very same traditions that inspired Pichinku and guide our daily work. We have learned these traditional techniques from our mothers and grandmothers, who learned from them being passed down through many generations of their families and communities. But with the arrival of synthetic materials, natural dyes and fibres were less commonly used.

We had to find a middle ground between traditional and modern. We follow pattern and yarn trends, to incorporate new, popular weights and blends to our collection and keep "on the pulse." Access to social media platforms like Instagram and Ravelry have also been integral to the evolution and promotion of our work.

These newer resources are still challenging for artisans who aren't familiar with the Internet. The collaborative structure of our team—combining skills from different technological and cultural backgrounds—is the basis for a successful business.

SLOW COLOUR

If looked at with a wide lens, all of our yarns take weeks to produce. We begin by sourcing the raw materials, which might be found nearby along the river or many hours away on a steep mountainside. Back at the workshop, we scour the undyed yarn with biodegradable detergent and, depending on the colour that we're making, will take that yarn through either a mordant or tannin process, sometimes both.

Then on to the dye, unquestionably the most exciting and dynamic part. Plants are ground, scraped, pounded, fermented, etc., before being boiled to release their vibrant colours. To avoid us having to pick out leftover material later on, plants are strained from the dye water before adding the yarn. The first dip is thrilling every single time, seeing the natural colour fill a blank canvas.

Dye water and yarn in the pots are heated to varying temperatures, maybe adding a fixative material or additional mordant to strengthen the chemical bind or modify the colour. For deeper tones, we'll often leave yarn to rest in its bath for anywhere from a few hours to a couple of days. When it's time to wash and lay out to dry, protein fibres are treated to full sunshine, whereas cellulose fibres (like cotton) cool off in the shade. Each skein is reviewed by hand, cleaned of any plant bits that have stuck around, and hung in storage to be packaged later on.

I have an incredibly deep appreciation for this process—for the people and materials involved in it. Although we've received complaints about lead times, I consider the wait to be part of the aggregated value of such a unique product. It's like our work tells stories of our present and past.

> pichinkufibers.com
> @pichinkuyarn

DESIGN AT ITS HEART

Purl Soho

"In our New York City store and online, the heart of our business is and always has been our community of customers and readers."

From day one, as a tiny shop in New York City's Soho neighbourhood, Purl Soho has been known for its carefully curated aesthetic—a modern take on traditional fibre arts. And that is entirely by design, since founder Joelle Hoverson along with co-owners Jennifer Hoverson Jahnke and Page Marchese Norman are the visionaries behind Purl Soho. Editors, artists, educators and stylists in past lifetimes, they share a passion for exceptional design: the timeless, the classic and the beautiful.

"We opened in 2002 as a place to share our love for natural fibres with people who might feel the same way," says Joelle. "At the time, there weren't that many shops that focused on these kinds of yarns, and we felt there should be more!" A few years later, they opened an even tinier shop, this time for fabric—Purl Patchwork. "We wanted to bring our love for textile arts to the world of not just knitting and crochet, but home sewing and quilt making as well. In 2010 we brought it all together under one roof at our current store at 459 Broome Street."

The beloved shop is a destination for locals and city visitors. "Our shop is suffused with colour and texture, bounty and beauty, and our staff offers a friendly welcome and a genuine desire to share information and lend a helping hand," says Joelle. Purl Soho has a loyal following on Instagram and customers worldwide who shop the Purl Soho website, as well as their own brand of yarns, fabrics, notions, patterns and kits. To meet this demand, the company has a dedicated fulfillment centre, located in southern California: "Big, beautiful and functional, this space provides a high-quality work environment for our staff there. Thankfully, during the coronavirus crisis,

JOELLE HOVERSON   JENNIFER HOVERSON JAHNKE   PAGE MARCHESE NORMAN

"Everything we do starts with a love for beautiful materials and a deep respect for needlecraft traditions. The techniques we employ and teach are as old as the hills, from hand knitting, loom weaving and embroidery up to the relative modernity of machine sewing. It is a daily challenge and reward to bring our own voice to the history of crafting, and we love nothing more than when we're an hour into a discussion on which cast on to use or which way to bind a quilt."

it has been spacious and ventilated enough to allow us to maintain safe working conditions."

Purl Soho works with mills all over the globe to develop their yarns, including in Peru, Australia, Mongolia, Japan, Italy, the United States, China, Uruguay, the United Kingdom and Romania. "We are always working to expand the provenance of our materials, with the goal of directly accessing their source—for instance, cashmere from Mongolia."

Each new line is considered thoroughly. "Our general process for approving new yarns is very organic and from the gut: Does it stir something deep inside us? Do we want to put a skein of it under our pillow at night? Do we have to cast on with it right now? Then we want it!" From the base yarn, the Purl Soho team takes great joy in developing the collection's colour story. "We love to identify an inspiration, to set a mood, to argue about the exact shade of yellow and to watch the garden grow!" ✤

"Part of our success comes from the integrity of our brand vision. From a custom measuring tape to a hand-dyed yarn collection, we aspire to create very special products that people care about forever. Every aspect, including packaging and labelling, styling and photography, meets our standard of warmth and elegance, familiarity and surprise. We think our customers understand this level of care in ways both conscious and unconscious."

THE GENTLE CARDIGAN
DESIGNED AND MODELLED
FOR PURL SOHO BY
BRANDI CHEYENNE HARPER

@brandicheyenneharper
brandicheyenneharper.com

"Our goal is to bring fibre crafts into the modern discourse while honouring their rich traditions and histories. Great design is an important component of this, but we believe beautiful materials and exquisite tools are just as important. Our commitment to this level of quality at all stages of the making process has always distinguished Purl Soho."

BUSINESS WITH HEART

We aim to be a trusted resource for high-quality fibres and supplies, as well as needlecraft design. And the goal that really gets our hearts pumping is that of bringing joy into people's lives, inspiring and educating our customers, sparking creative fires and building a community.

The manufacturing of yarn is so closely tied to the land and to the animals and people who live on it, and we are always looking for opportunities to improve all those relationships. Raw fibre can be difficult to trace, but most of the alpaca and some of the merino we use comes from certified sources, and all of our cotton is organically grown. We work with mills who are responsible employers, providing good, self-sustaining jobs to local communities.

In addition, we believe that, while hand-crafting changes hearts, action is also required. We take our voice seriously and often donate portions of our profits to causes that matter to us and to many people in our community, from natural disasters to racial equality and justice.

purlsoho.com
@purlsoho

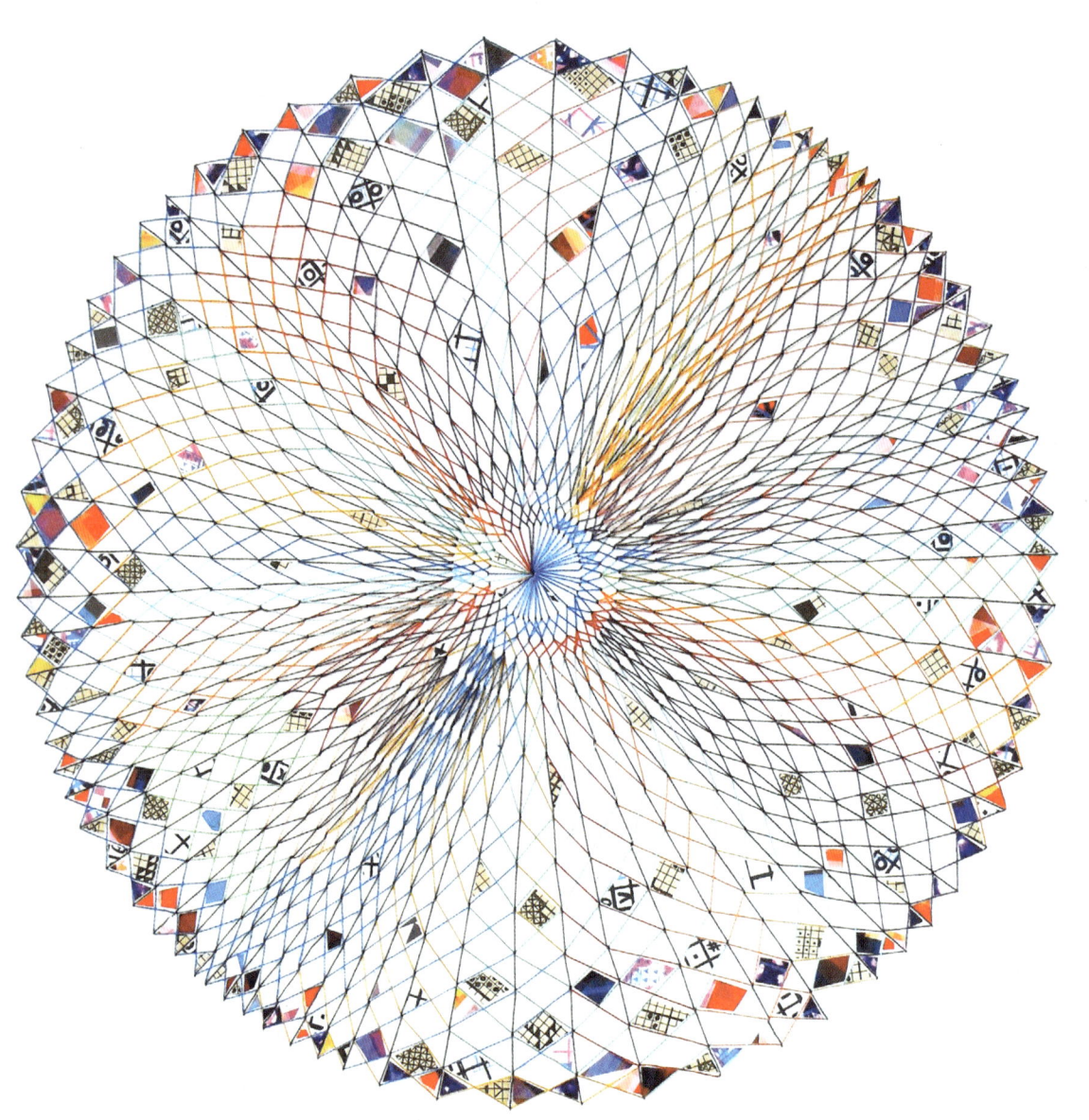

STITCHED & PRINTED

Rachel Parker

Rachel Parker is a surface pattern designer in Kettering, Northamptonshire, in the United Kingdom. "I studied textiles at Norwich University of the Arts, which is where I first realized that some lucky person has the job of designing patterns for almost every product you can imagine. I wanted that person to be me!" Rachel is grateful to have since seen her patterns on silk scarves, rugs, embroidery kits, blankets, chairs and even printed tables. Her abstract surface patterns extend into stitching, too. "I love to stitch and many of my abstract designs are inspired by embroidery, grids, chart symbols and the abstract geometric shapes found within them. I scan my stitched pieces to use as a starting point for my digital pattern designs and also sell the original embroidered artwork online."

Rachel likes to play with the perceived traditions of embroidery and needlework, and combine stitching with modern methods such as digital printing. "Cross-stitch is probably the furthest you could get from fine art—you're thinking about those twee craft kits of cats and country houses right? I decided to come at it from a graphic design angle, treating each square as a pixel and dissecting the printed patterns to use as collage materials. I also started to focus my attention on the back of the work; I love that when you flip a piece of embroidery over there's a whole other world of abstract shapes created without thought or intention. There's a lot of beauty in creative chaos."

Creating frameable art pieces for the home, Rachel creates stitched patterns and repeated motifs that sometimes includes bits of ephemera, paper fragments or collaged elements. She draws her patterns onto midweight paper, attaches watercolour paper and carefully punches holes through both

"You have to have a lot of patience to get on with embroidery—many people can think of nothing worse than battling with needle and thread! I find it quite a meditative process and I enjoy the fact that it's a craft that can't be rushed."

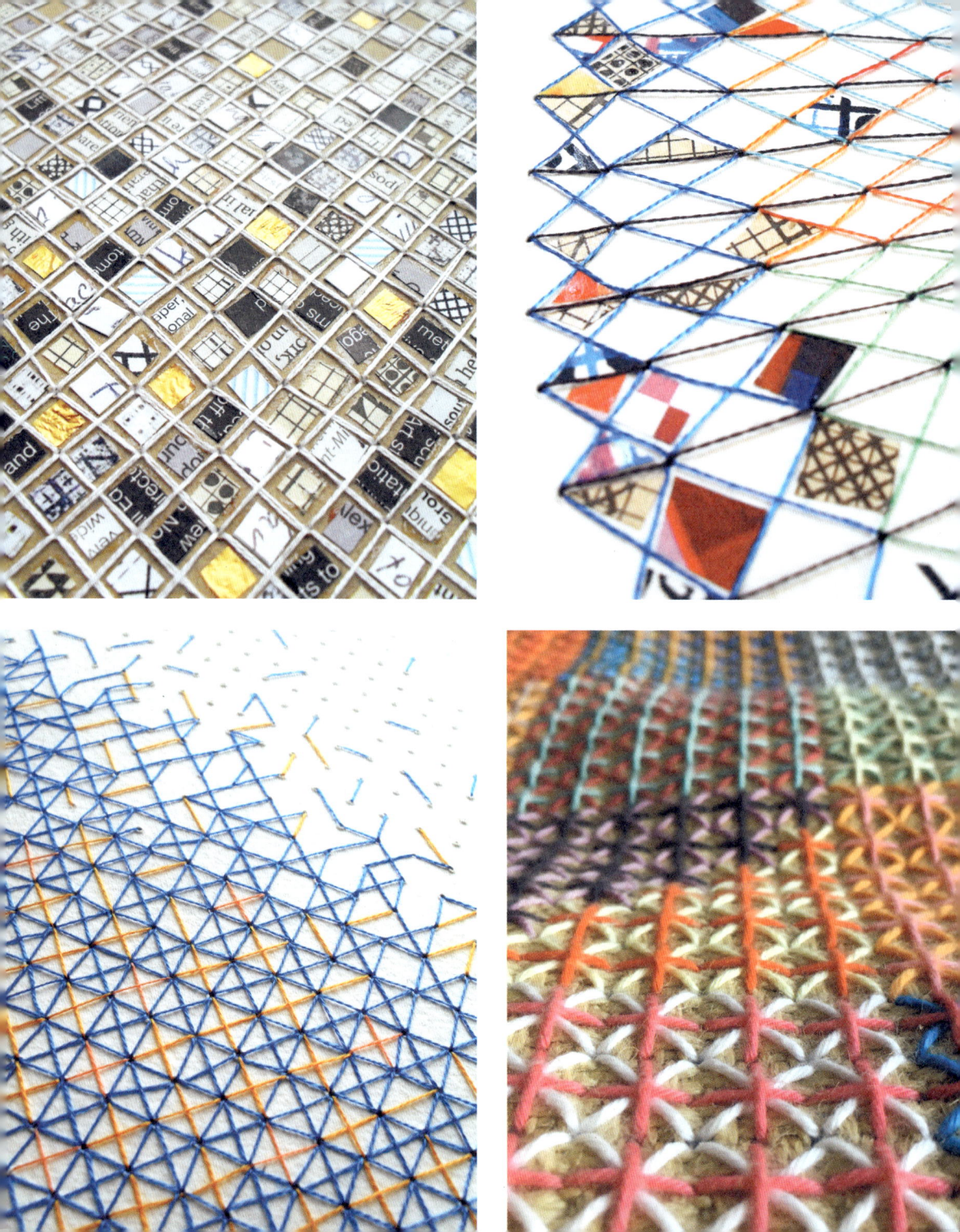

"There's obviously a wealth of inspiration to be found online but I try not to fall down that digital hole too often. It's so easy to compare yourself and your work to someone else and feel like you somehow fall short."

pieces. With this method, she can reuse the template. "In the end, I'm left with a network of holes which I then stitch into. If I'm careful I can reuse the paper template a few times if I'm creating multiples."

Embroidering onto crisp white paper helps highlight Rachel's colour selection. "My embroidered pieces usually have a graphic design look to them due to the geometric shapes and segments of colour," she says.

For her digital pattern designs, Rachel often scans the stitched artwork and uses it as a basis for a repeat pattern. "I like the juxtaposition between the craft and the digital, the slow and the speedy, old and new." ✳

"I think a lot of us have this compulsion to create something which we can't really put into words. If I haven't had the time or the opportunity to be creative for a few days I can feel myself getting irritable; it's not quite a dark cloud descending but it's not far off. I love to make things. Most of the time my creations will never make me any money, sometimes I'll never show them to anyone else, but I have the satisfaction of being able to say, 'I made this thing.'"

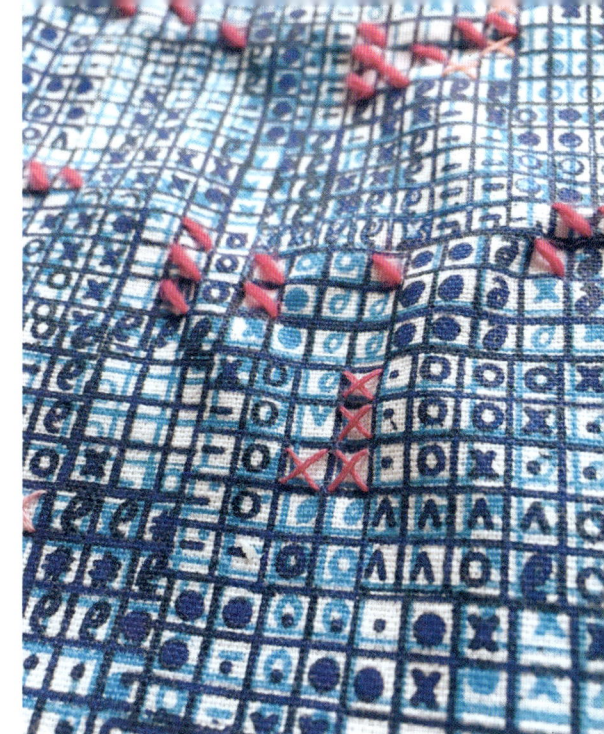

COTTON THREADS

I love working with embroidery cotton because you can split it into six strands to create different depth of lines. It's a bit like drawing with different thicknesses of pen. There are hundreds of colours to choose from and they just look so beautiful. (I did experiment with dyeing my own threads at one point but I couldn't get the intensity of colour that I wanted and it seemed like a whole extra step in an already lengthy process, so I abandoned that one.) Anything much thicker than fine embroidery cotton can be too bulky to pull through the paper without tearing, which is always a consideration.

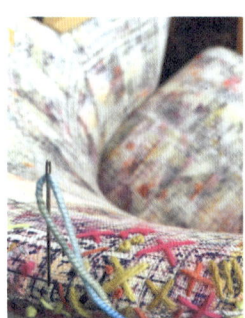

LAYERS OF PATTERN

Sometimes I embroider back into the digitally printed fabric—this was the case with a collaboration I did with Studio Elizabeth Rose. I designed a fabric inspired by collaged embroidery patterns that were upholstered onto a beautiful mid-century chair. I then embellished the back and arms of the chair, filling in areas of the grid with fluid freeform stitches. It was a painstaking task but I loved the outcome, and the process of treating a piece of furniture as a canvas was very freeing.

rachelparkerdesigns.co.uk
@rachelparkerdesigns

STUDIO SPACE

I'm currently working in a very small space which I try to fill with as much colour as possible! By the time you read this I should have upgraded to a slightly larger "studio" (a spare room), if our move goes to plan. Luckily my practice doesn't require a whole lot of space—I have my desk with my computer and scanner, my sketchbooks and many (too many) boxes of fabrics and threads. The threads are currently stored in yellow storage boxes with dividers for different colour groups, although they never stay that way for long. I work at home, accompanied by my Sproodle dog, Louie. He doesn't know a whole lot about design but is very enthusiastic nonetheless.

I'd love to share a studio space with other creative people so we can bounce ideas off each other, but I also enjoy the quiet solitude of my current setup and the space for reflection that it provides. Gustav Klimt said, "Art is a line around your thoughts," which has always resonated with me.

DAUGHTER & FATHER DUO

Roving Textiles

Michelle Chesson and her dad, Paul, design and build handcrafted wooden looms and tools. Michelle also creates one-of-a-kind wall hangings and teaches beginner weavers through her e-course. "Recently I've started gathering some of my favourite fibres and some pretty rare ones, too, and made them available to other fibre artists online," says Michelle.

Michelle studied graphic design, and then anthropology. "I was clearly confused!" she laughs. "In my mid-twenties I had the opportunity to travel to Australia, where I ended up falling in love and getting married, and then moving there for five years. I became a yoga teacher and worked in a surf shop, still cruising through life—until I saw an astrologer who told me I would move across the world and find my life's passion and that I would make a living from it." A decade later, she and her Australian husband settled in Canada, in Bradford, Ontario.

The cold Canadian winters indirectly inspired her newfound infatuation with weaving—Michelle and her family would travel to Mexico to escape the cold, and she was captivated with all the colourful weaving they admired in the markets. But at home in Bradford, she couldn't find any local suppliers for looms, or weaving instructors.

"Not one to be defeated, I splurged on a loom from the other side of the world and figured I'd teach myself," Michelle says. "I was soon blown away by the online fibre community (who knew that was a thing?!). Their enthusiasm and support only fuelled my new passion. Soon friends, family and even strangers began asking me to teach them to weave!"

At that point, she turned to her dad. "He grew up on a farm and was put to work and learned basic

"I believe in keeping it simple. From the design and functionality of our looms to the simplicity of our branding and packaging, we believe in being clean, uncomplicated and transparent. We strive to design looms that are easy to use and assemble, and with minimal packaging to minimize waste and our impact on the environment."

woodworking, electrical, plumbing—the works! After retiring from a computer programming career, he too discovered his life passion in building anything and everything from wood. So when I pitched my idea that we collaborate to design and build our own looms and tools, not only did he deliver, but his craftsmanship was better than I ever thought possible. I started business in 2015 and during this time we purchased our home, had two kids and have grown our little business with two employees and lots of help from my husband and parents."

Their company, Roving Textiles, is known for its 30-inch adjustable tapestry weaving loom, named the Ace. The Byron is 40 inches. "Both looms are designed with a weavers posture in mind, including legs for an upright weaving experience. What makes these looms unique is that both also adjust in height, allowing you to make a variety of wall hanging sizes, as well as having more than one piece on the loom at a time." Paul also makes a variety of combs, needles, shuttles and holders.

"Each of our weaving looms is a labour of love," Michelle explains. "From turning our crazy ideas into something beautiful and useful, to visiting the local wood mill to photographing our products for our online shop, our family works hard to bring you quality weaving companions. Every piece of wood used is hand selected. Every little notch, edge and groove is handcrafted. Every piece is sanded to feel super cozy in your hand. We hope you can feel the love." ✣

"This work has brought my dad and me together to share our common love of creating with our hands. Our mission is to inspire connection and mindfulness through creativity."

THE STORY OF A LOOM

I get a multitude of requests and ideas from weavers. Mix in my own weaving needs, and the seeds of a loom are sown. I collect these ideas and bring them to my dad and he starts sketching and planning and designing. (Sometimes he secretly comes up with new ideas and surprises me!) We go through a couple of prototypes and I try everything out to make sure it feels good. Dad then heads to the mill and picks out the wood. He likes to find pieces with neat-looking knots and of course a beautiful wood grain. Then he hunkers down in his happy place, working with his hands, creating outstanding products.

When the looms are ready, my parents come for a visit to drop them off (but really it's to see their grandchildren!). I photograph them and list them on our website and get them ready to be sent out into the world.

rovingtextiles.com
@rovingtextiles

MADE AT HOME

Everything is made in-house, literally! My dad makes all the looms in his workshop, in my childhood home. In 2016, my husband and I purchased our current home. It's a raised bungalow with a huge fireplace right in the centre of the house. When you enter, just to your left is a big room, the only room on this floor. This is my studio. It's big and open with lots of natural light. I love the grand feeling of the statement fireplace in my creative space and the airy feeling of the vaulted ceilings. I'm so grateful to work at home, with my family, but just far enough away from the chaos upstairs to feel like I have my own special space.

GIFTS FROM THE ART-GODS

Ruth Miller

The impetus for Ruth Miller's embroidered life-size (and larger) portraits goes beyond simply creating a resemblance. "Most pieces are a vehicle for the exploration of a narrative extending from my own inner life," explains Ruth. "The people whose bodies I use as subjects are a way to add variety to my work, to keep me from making self-portrait after self-portrait." The very process of making art, and especially with a method that requires such an investment of time and labour, like embroidery, becomes a portrait of the self nevertheless. "Occasionally, photographs of the models suggest or remind me of the threads of my inner conversation. But whatever the source, these narratives make me visible to myself and help me to resolve personal issues. My hope is that they do the same for others."

The process for making a piece, which can take a year or more, begins with an idea: "Most of my ideas arrive as gifts from the art-gods rather than as a decision to explore a certain subject," Ruth says. She will find a suitable model to be photographed as reference and then make a line drawing to refine ideas and composition. "Photocopies of that drawing are used to create shaded and coloured references. I use the graph method to transfer the image with pencil to a cloth stapled over a canvas stretcher. This technique is ancient and low-tech but effective."

"I cover the cloth with various straight stitches. Needle in and needle out; that's about it. The difficulty (or the magic) is in deciding what colour to use, how long to make the stitch and in which direction it should be placed. Whichever section proves to be incorrect or awkward is removed with tweezers and nail scissors and restitched. In order for stitching to take a backseat to storytelling, I aim for a less-textured

"I always want to understand life more deeply. I examine the physical surfaces of things as well as the psychological cores of experiences. As I work, I focus on both, and the mysteries of both drive me to keep going further."

surface. Therefore, stitches are seldom placed one atop another. Instead, I leave gaps for the stitches I think will be needed to complete the effect I'm after."

Ruth attended the High School of Music and Art and the Cooper Union School of Art in New York City. "It was at Cooper that I received the instruction in drawing and colour theory that is the basis of my current work. I studied sculpture, architectural drawing, art history, photography, calligraphy and printmaking, as well as painting, but I never warmed up to using paint. In fact, I liked almost all of it better than painting, even though at that time I thought 'artist' was synonymous with 'painter.'" At 16, Ruth saw figurative woven tapestries by Senegalese artist Papa Ibra Tall.

"I would describe my portraits as being very but not hyper-realistic. This style developed over time as I sought to understand how the brain sees and what reality is. I'm never satisfied and so am required to achieve a better or more interesting likeness in the next one."

WOOL ON LINEN

I use Paternayan brand 100% wool tapestry yarns, available online. Their high-quality yarns are tough, colourfast, soft but with a slight sheen and available in over 400 colours that allow for subtle contouring of the figures.

I prefer to use linen as a backing fabric because it hardly stretches at all. This means the yarns won't distort the shape of the fabric when stitched. If most of a piece's image will be light, I use white or cream-coloured fabric; if dark, I use taupe. This is because there are always tiny gaps between most of the stitches that let the backing peek through. The gaps are visible in the finished pieces, even if I don't notice them while working. If the contrast is too great, it acts like static on airwaves. My intended effects are compromised. So the differences in backing fabric colours help me minimize those contrasts.

"Something about colour is additive: one shade makes me want to put others next to it, to find companions for it. Colour is more inspiring than form, even though, in practice, I have to apply the colour to the drawn subject to create the appearance of form."

"I was inspired to switch from paint to yarn as a way to create painterly images. I had no idea it would eventually play such a prominent role in my life."

However, Ruth's art career didn't begin until much later. "I was still a teenager when I began my first forays into the adult world of work. While my technical skills might have led me to start an art career right then and there, I lacked the confidence to even attempt it." She spent decades at "stress-inducing jobs in corporate and government employment," which she credits to toughening her up. "They helped me realize those jobs were no more secure than the art world. I became determined to pursue a career in line with my personal inclinations and temperament. Art could allow me to work at home in peace."

Ruth reflects upon her journey in art. "The trajectory of my art career might seem impractical or counter-intuitive to some. Why bother to work on such a large scale in a medium that requires such an extravagant use of time? And why be so meticulous with it? Indeed, why start so late in life? Every day we hear of artists who are 20 times more prolific than I will ever be—50 years younger, too. But every day, I'm rewarded with the byproducts from the constant search for technical excellence and deeper understanding. I believe I'm a stronger, more fulfilled person for having approached my work and life in this way, and encourage others to do similarly. Not to use embroidery necessarily but to challenge themselves to go beyond the typical, to find a pursuit, make it truly their own and let the effort transform them. Start with a commitment and let life show you the next steps." ✳

"I love the softness and cleanliness of yarn. It has an emotional warmth that's not separate from its implied physical warmth. Everyone owns something made of fibres. This gives fibre-based art an automatic connection with audiences. Along with realistic drawing, the almost three-dimensional quality of stitches makes the subjects of my portraits seem somehow closer, like live inhabitants of the rooms in which they live."

EMBROIDERY STUDIO

My studio is 25 feet by 24 feet, with windows on three sides to let in daylight, which is absolutely necessary. Its ceiling has four large LED fixtures. No lamps are used. In case I have difficulty seeing, on occasion I use a held-held magnifying glass. The yarns are separated into colour families and stored in 38 translucent plastic boxes. Embroidery fabrics are kept in an old suitcase. Three long tables hold sewing, beading and woodworking paraphernalia. Three bookcases hold reference books and drawing materials. Stored art is kept safely wrapped in plastic inside cardboard boxes.

I prefer to work seated on the floor with the stretcher propped on furniture and held horizontally so I can look down while placing the stitches. Every so often, I place the work vertically and stand to judge the composition from across the room. This is because I know people will see the work while moving in from a distance as well as close up.

Each piece is planned in as much detail as possible but may also change in response to momentary inspirations.

CRAFT SCHOOL OZ

Ruth Woods

Ruth Woods remembers watching the 1975 film *Mahogany*, in which Diana Ross plays a Fashion Designer (capital F and capital D). It had such an impact on the young Ruth that she set aside her previous idea of becoming a nurse. "Literally overnight I changed my mind," she says. "I was 14 at the time and I was starting to make my own clothes but had never really thought about the people who designed them."

Her hometown of Leicester in the United Kingdom had many clothing and footwear factories. When Ruth left school at age 17, she worked as a sewing machinist. "This wasn't the plan and I really didn't enjoy it at all, but it gave me a solid groundwork in the construction of garments and how to make them quickly and easily—so definitely not in a dressmaking style but a mass-production technique. I could make tops in a matter of minutes. I was quick but I had to have my own industrial sewing machines—a straight stitch and an overlocker. They were the best things I ever bought and I still have my trusted industrial Singer sewing machine today—40 years later!"

A year later, she landed the position of assistant knitwear designer at another factory. "It was a busy, dusty and noisy factory far from the glamour portrayed in the Diana Ross movie!" The experience provided a foundation for her own business: "I could buy the end of cones from work and mix all types of fibres—many were from Milan in Italy and they were very special." Yarn, fabrics and design were part of both her work and play. It was the punk era of the 1970s, and people were free with their ideas. Ruth designed a range of clothes for a few boutiques in the city. "I loved big baggy jumpers made from many types of yarn."

"Sometimes I think my brain is going to explode, as I have too many ideas and not enough time to explore them."

"Later when I had a family I worked from home, and this was perfect because I chose when I wanted to work, fitting in with family life. I was constantly designing clothing and knitwear. Living in a city where clothing and knitwear was produced, there was access to great yarns and textiles, and this made it easy to be creative."

Ruth has had businesses manufacturing children's and women's clothes, followed by a time of working in government. "This became a very non-creative time, but it gave me an opportunity to visit and live with a community in Arnhem Land in the very north of Australia." There, she met Mavis Ganambarr, an Indigenous artisan who taught Ruth the basics of coiling baskets. "We would sit together and weave at the weekends on the beach. She inspired me and I continued basket making, and I later joined the Basketmakers of Victoria and pursued my basketry journey using many different plant fibres, materials and techniques."

SLOW STITCHING

I also work with fabrics to create textile stitched pieces I call "slow stitching." It's kind of a play on words with the slow movement, having a more meditative approach and again using upcycled fabrics. This is hugely satisfying work; the subtleness of threads and fabrics are so pleasurable to look at. This is taught as though it was a piece of art, looking at the composition, colour and texture.

Motivated by wanting to curtail the waste of discarded textiles, Ruth began to play with reclaimed fabrics within basketry. "I really started to develop this idea of sustainable materials and was soon teaching a course face to face to hundreds of people, and then I developed an online course. This has become my full-time business, and even though it's hard work it's the most enjoyable yet." Having a thousand students so far, Ruth is proud of the impact teaching can have. "I love to think that I have inspired, encouraged and taught skills to people, for them to go on a journey of confidently exploring and finding creativity to be as fun, rewarding and exciting as I do."

Her success as a teacher is partly due to her empathetic approach. "I'm dyslexic and struggled with learning at a young age, so creativity was my saving grace. I think this is reflected in my teaching, and I never want anyone to feel stupid, because they could get the hang of things straight away."

"My biggest enjoyment is when I have a student who comes to class and they're really apprehensive, but once we get started and I introduce the craft, they become excited to explore the materials in a completely different way. They have permission to explore and to investigate and to make mistakes. They go home inspired and excited," says Ruth. "This is a total privilege." ✻

FAVOURITE FIBRES

I make and I teach basket courses that use sustainable materials, which include recycled fabrics and plant fibre. So using up what we have or picking plants from the garden is either free or very low cost. I do buy threads and sustainably sourced natural raffia.

I love wool, linen and all-natural fibres. I have two spinning wheels which I haven't used for a few years, but when I open a bag of beautiful fleece—English Leicester is my favourite—and start to spin I find it such a delight. Turning it into yarn and being able to make something with it is particularly exciting. I also incorporate it into my textile baskets.

When I'm stitching my baskets I love to use wax linen thread—it feels good and because it's waxed it has a strength and stability about it. I'll sort out colours of fabric, creating bundles—I'll cut them into strips, ready to be turned into a textile basket piece.

Linen is my favourite fabric; it is the best to touch and feel. I love to dye it with plant dyes and sew it together within my slow stitching projects. All botanically dyed fabrics sing together with their colours. They are so exquisite. I will fold and arrange, touch and just look at them—they are so perfect they don't even need to be made into anything. But I do!

BASKET TECHNIQUES

I use a few different basket-making techniques, but mostly coiling basketry, and within this there are many techniques: wrapping stitch, blanket stitch, spiral stitch and a random stitch, to name a few. I also use a coiling technique for my plant baskets but it's the plants that are the feature, not the stitch, and the materials are totally free.

STUDIO HOME

My studio is basically one-third of the house plus a large deck! It's a good thing I have an understanding husband. (Although he's been nagging me for some space to install his train set! That's a difficult one, as I wasn't going to give up my space—so I suggested that we put the train set in the lounge room. We're not getting visitors at the moment because of Covid and the lounge room is quite big.)

I have one room with my sewing machines and also a large workbench, which is covered in computer stuff and research papers for a basketry book I'm working on. There is also a corner where I film my workshops that has lovely northern light (which is the same as southern light if you live in the Northern Hemisphere). I have a long sunroom that houses all my samples, materials and dried plants, and then a deck where I dye raffia, and plant-dye my fabrics. I feel very lucky I have such a large space, but it does help when all the kids have flown the nest.

craftschooloz.com
@craftschooloz

KAMI-ITO AND SHIFU

Sabrina Sachiko Niebler

Some people are particularly drawn to the tactile. "There is a deep satisfaction in the basic handling of fibres," states artist Sabrina Sachiko Niebler. "I find as a maker, using this touch-activated sense is essential to my creative process. Not only this, but thread and cloth communicate intimately in their own language, and when you've spent enough time with them, or through the effort to make them, you begin to speak the language, too. Colour, fibre, consistency, weight, structure and how the threads interact, all tell a story. I've also always loved thinking about the potential for handmade thread and cloth to hold energy. I love thinking about the energy I am putting into it and the energy someone will get from it by way of touch and sense. Thread and cloth are alive."

Sabrina's personal journey with hand-spun paper came through many little decisions and discoveries. "I started weaving with paper in a tapestry class during my undergrad at the Alberta University of the Arts (Calgary, Alberta, Canada)." Looking for a way to embed text into woven cloth, Sabrina turned to paper and discovered an art that was, unbeknownst to her at the time, part of her heritage.

"After my first piece, a woven portrait of my obaachan (grandmother), I fell in love with weaving paper and it never stopped being a source of material pleasure and intrigue for me. It wasn't until years later that I discovered there is a Japanese practice of creating paper thread (kami-ito) and weaving it into cloth (shifu). This connected me to part of my heritage in an unexpected way, and filled me with a desire to learn more. Since then, I have been learning this method and practicing it with a pretty singular focus." The process is steady and slow, but feels familiar—"somehow innate to my hands and material sensitivity."

"I am definitely a minimalist. I like the space that simplicity can create and the focus that can arise with subtlety. There is also more potential to notice all the details and the quiet texture of the materials."

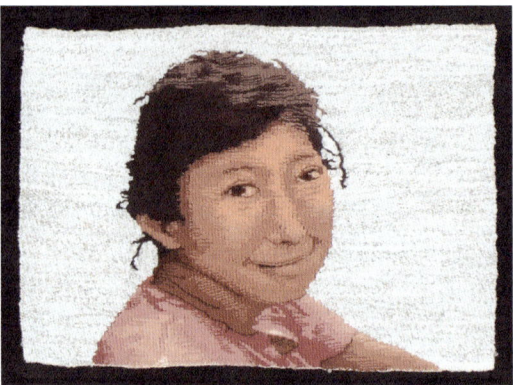

KAMI-ITO AND SHIFU

My particular area of interest is in making kami-ito and shifu using techniques originating in Japan. The origins of this craft are based in practicality, turning used paper into cloth and clothing, based on necessity. In later years it evolved into a highly refined cloth. I tend to make kami-ito and shifu that is of a finer weight for show and wear, and I aspire to the high quality of my mentors' work. The paper I use is handmade in Japan using fibre from the quickly growing mulberry tree (kozo). This paper is strong and already a beautiful creation in itself. Both the art of hand-making paper like this and making fine shifu are left to very few people these days. I like to do what I can within my practice to support artisans who are hand-making quality paper that is suitable to use in shifu, and also to keep the narrative of kami-ito and shifu alive for future generations.

Sabrina describes the process: "It starts with an idea that usually comes to me in moments of quiet contemplation. I get excited about it, think it through (practically and conceptually) and make a calculated plan. This plan provides the bones of which I can move around and make intuitive decisions within as I continue along with a project. Next, I start on making the kami-ito. This involves choosing the washi (Japanese paper), folding it, cutting it (usually into two millimetre widths), rolling the cut sheets on cement blocks, separating the strips into one long thread, spinning/twisting these threads and finally boiling the spun kami-ito. As I mentioned, these are all Japanese techniques that I have learned and now practice. If my project calls for it, I proceed to dye the threads using natural dyes. Good quality kami-ito is strong and can withstand dyeing and washing. From here, I proceed to warp my loom and then weave with the kami-ito. Oftentimes I use a different fibre for the warp—usually linen or cotton, but I am excited to use kami-ito as the weft and the warp in some of my next projects."

Sabrina cites shifu artisan Susan Byrd for being a supportive and generous mentor. "I would not be where I am today without her. There are also the generations of people in Japan who created and passed on this craft—I make it part of my practice to think about and give thanks to them as well." ✻

"Thread and cloth are both longtime companions for me."

FAVOURITE FIBRE?

Well paper of course! I'm not sure why, but something about the texture and feel of kami-ito and shifu makes me happy. To me it embodies the expression of light and beauty, with a resounding wisdom. One of my favourite aspects of kami-ito or a piece of shifu are the little "slubs" that run along the thread. These are actually the joins or "seeds" in the kami-ito which are a result of the way the paper is cut and separated. These little points of connection are enchanting.

"I put a lot of value on the process of determining your way in life by the way your heart beats for something. Why I continue to make room for my creative practice is because it is me and it fosters vitality in my life. My heart beats for this. As it evolves, I evolve, and vice versa. It helps me to process and move through experiences. It always keeps me learning and challenging myself. It is a space I can always count on."

@sabrinasachiko

HOME STUDIO

For the last seven years, my studio space has been in my home. Most of the time, that has meant it's a small room or section of a room full of materials, tools and inspiration. Often while I work, my studio naturally seeps into other parts of my home, too. My workspace has lots of sunlight and it feels good to be in there. If I'm in the middle of a project or stage in the process, my space is probably in major disarray, as I'm too excited to stop and tidy along the way. I work alone, apart from having some wonderful mentors in my life and art practice. I have many tools but the ones I primarily rely on would have to be my itoguruma (Japanese spinning wheel) and my 45-inch counterbalance floor loom, which is over 100 years old.

Sayan Chanda

Sayan Chanda grew up in Kolkata, India. "Surrounded by the starched, wispy muslin jamdani saris and dhotis, I always had an inclination towards textiles," he says. "Hence, working with textiles as a designer and now as an artist has been a natural progression for me." Sayan is fascinated by how intrinsic textiles can be to a people's identity and is drawn to the intimacy of the medium. "It's a critical marker in the broader context of visual and material culture."

Living and working in London now, Sayan completed design school in 2013. "I have been working closely with handloom craft clusters and co-creating with artisans across India." Partnering with WomenWeave, an organization in India that helps women weavers earn sustainable livelihoods through textile production, and other grassroots organizations, Sayan has made enduring connections with weavers, spinners, dyers and embroiderers. "While I wish to continue this work, my transition to art has been motivated by the limitations I faced while communicating exclusively through wearable textiles," he says. "Looking at textiles in a fine art context has broadened the scope for me, but the transition has also been a steep learning curve. To me, my work organically moved towards art, but the shift also meant I was entering a completely new world. Understanding the practical aspects of functioning as an independent artist is something I am still working on. But it has definitely been rewarding, allowing me more freedom to investigate, make and communicate."

The past few years have seen Sayan making a shift towards his independent studio practice in London. "I would describe my pieces as a personal take on indigenous votive objects. In short, I make

"I draw from indigenous traditions and work intuitively with cloth—weaving it, stitching it, piercing it, deconstructing it, creating a palimpsest of personal experiences, narratives and memories. I use mark-making and repetition as tools to signify change, the passage of time and the retention and rejection of memory."

FAVOURITE FIBRES

I have always gravitated towards natural fibres. But the cotton yarn hand spun by the women artisans of WomenWeave, an important organization in Central India, is my staple. The hand spinning renders the yarn a quality that cannot be replicated by any mill-spun yarn. The natural colour, the impurities, the texture makes it an absolute joy to work with. Hand-spun coarse wild silks from East India is another favourite. Textile woven using hand-spun undyed yarns have such a strong character that I often prefer not to dye them.

objects. These could take the form of wall-based pieces or soft sculptures. These objects are imbued with my personal history and experiences with local culture, traditions and faith-based practices. For my woven pieces I use hand-spun and hand-dyed cotton from India. For my other work I use vintage used quilts, khadi cotton from India, natural dyes as well as inks and acrylics."

The use of authentic cultural cloth within his art context is important. "And indigenous worldview is often marginalized and dismissed as archaic and irrelevant," states Sayan. "It's surprising to me that folk traditions and indigenous practices rarely feature in contemporary art. Through exploring personal and community history I intend to demystify and contextualize such living traditions. I would like to mention here that my work has nothing to do with the popular idea of religion. In fact, I focus on folk practices of Bengal because they represent the last vestiges of

syncretism unadulterated by organized religious influences."

His work initiates a dialogue between a lineage of makers and the art's viewer. "Through making, my attempt is to highlight and elevate native practices, narratives and history, which are often forgotten or excluded. I consider my work successful if it is able to spark a conversation about these and give my audience something new to ponder over."

Sayan finds himself increasingly drawn to research and conceptual work. "I have noticed that when I am working within a rigid framework of a technique and its application, I try to control every related aspect, and that often leads to self-doubt. Therefore in my recent projects, I am taking a more instinctive organic approach. As for my medium, textile is and will always be a big part of my work, be it as a material, a process, a philosophy or a metaphor." ✣

"I am drawn towards brave, evocative, often seemingly unmodern and deeply personal work that defies trends, and stays relevant for a very long time. I find it interesting when artists draw from unpopular or obscure references. I am influenced by the work of folk and outsider artists. Observing artisans at work or locals performing rituals have left lasting impressions on me."

ITINERANT

This series investigates deep-seated connotations and assumptions about craft processes through kantha, a Bengali quilting tradition.

Used vintage quilts have been rubbed, torn, cut, aged and embroidered with hand-spun cotton yarn to unravel the layered narratives that lie at the heart of craft-based practices.

SAYAN CHANDA

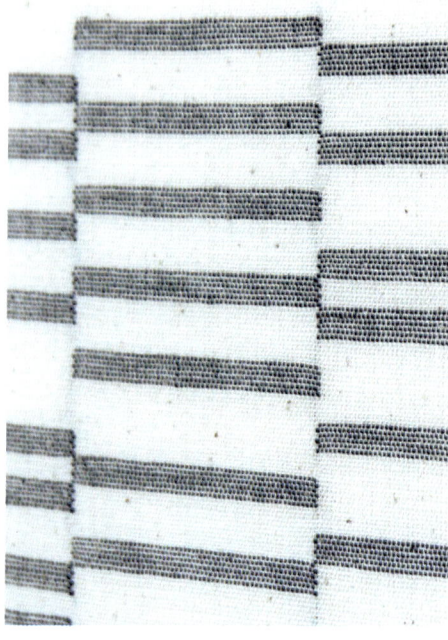

REPETITION

During my visits to craft clusters, the stories, legends and rituals surrounding the practice and its makers always fascinated me. From the practice of worshipping indigo vats to aniconic representation of local deities to a sect in rural Bengal which defies religious compartmentalization, such anecdotes have always been significant for me. The narrative quality and anthropological clues embedded in votive objects and related hyperlocal customs are potent references for me. My work is an ongoing exercise exploring meditative repetitive systems in such rituals, through techniques like weaving, stitching, deconstructing, etc. To give an example, while documenting a very fine reed mat craft in Bengal, I often noticed how the weavers would never want to pause weaving at an odd pick but would always pause, when needed, at an even pick. I formulate my own systems based on such obscure practices. Even though some pieces, like my woven work, may look precise and calculated, I don't always plan them extensively. I look into my own experiences of ritualistic processes and interpret them using material, space and form. At the same time, my work is material-led, so the fibres and their inherent characteristics also guide the process of making.

HOME AND GARDEN

I have converted a part of my home in North London into my workspace. I like to have everything within reach so my loom is right beside my work desk. I try to keep the loom warped at all times since I might intuitively want to test out an idea. My sewing machine and embroidery tools are around as well. I use a soft board and my sketchbooks to record ideas spontaneously. Even though my work process is instinctive and organic, I keep my workplace extremely organized and structured. I feel much calmer and settled when my physical surroundings are in order. When the weather is right I wind the warp and set up the loom in my garden.

sayanchanda.com
@sayanchanda

MARK HEFFLEY

Second Ascent Designs

Before becoming an artist—in his "previous life"—Mark Heffley was a personal trainer with a bachelor's in health science. "I got into training to help people," he explains. "I'm a rock climber who happened to have old rock climbing rope laying around, wanting to hold on to the memories of these first life-saving devices."

Initially, Mark wanted to make a rug, but the common methods of rug making didn't work with the climbing rope. "After a few experiments, I quickly realized that if you apply superglue in the right way you can go way beyond a rug." Even though it was a tedious process, Mark found it fun to create solid structures out of rope. "The engineering and forethought that was needed at each stage, along with serious problem solving, was just amazing!" It reminded him of playing with Lego as a child.

"Before my learning (tinkering? experimentation? journey?) began, I had no interest in art. If I couldn't see the skill or the function of something, I couldn't care less. That was until I found myself an artist and I started to learn. I've got a long way to go. I'm sure my style will change along the way, but one thing will always be true: it will always have a purpose. And sometimes that's just to be."

Climbing rope allows for certain structural possibilities because of the cord's layered strength. "If one was to dissect a rock climbing rope," Mark explains, "you'd first encounter the outer kernmantle sheathing (think finger trap, but for string). The next stage would reveal 8 to 15 tri-coiled and twisted threads—it's the coiling (a spring in reverse) of these threads that gives the rope the dynamic nature that allows one to fall over 30 feet and walk away thinking they were on a really fast elevator." Mark guesses that if you continued decoiling, each would have around 25 strands of nylon about the thickness of a human hair. "They run uninterrupted the length of the rope, typically 60 to 70 metres. When all of these parts are added together you get one 8- to 11-millimetre cord that can save a life."

Nylon is plastic, so reusing climbing rope is also about reducing waste. "Rock climbing is one of the fastest-growing sports year after year, which means more and more waste. The ropes the gyms use last only a few months, and the ropes we climbers use last a few years at best. There is far more retired rope in the world than I alone could ever deal with. Even with the constant expansion of other rope artists, none of us are really making a dent in this horribly wasteful aspect of a sport I love so much." That being said, Mark estimates that he has used nearly five miles of upcycled rope to date.

Using his own heat-welding technique and glue, he makes furniture and wall-hangings, as well as utilitarian items like dog leads, chess boards, wine racks and holders. "The bond created is strong enough for me to create functional furniture, oftentimes with no internal structure; think carbon fibre, just with rope."

As much as possible, Mark builds without internal supports. "Always partially failing is one of the reasons my work changes so much from piece to piece." ✳

"My learning journey is frequently present in my work. You probably won't have to look all that hard to see what I was studying at any given moment."

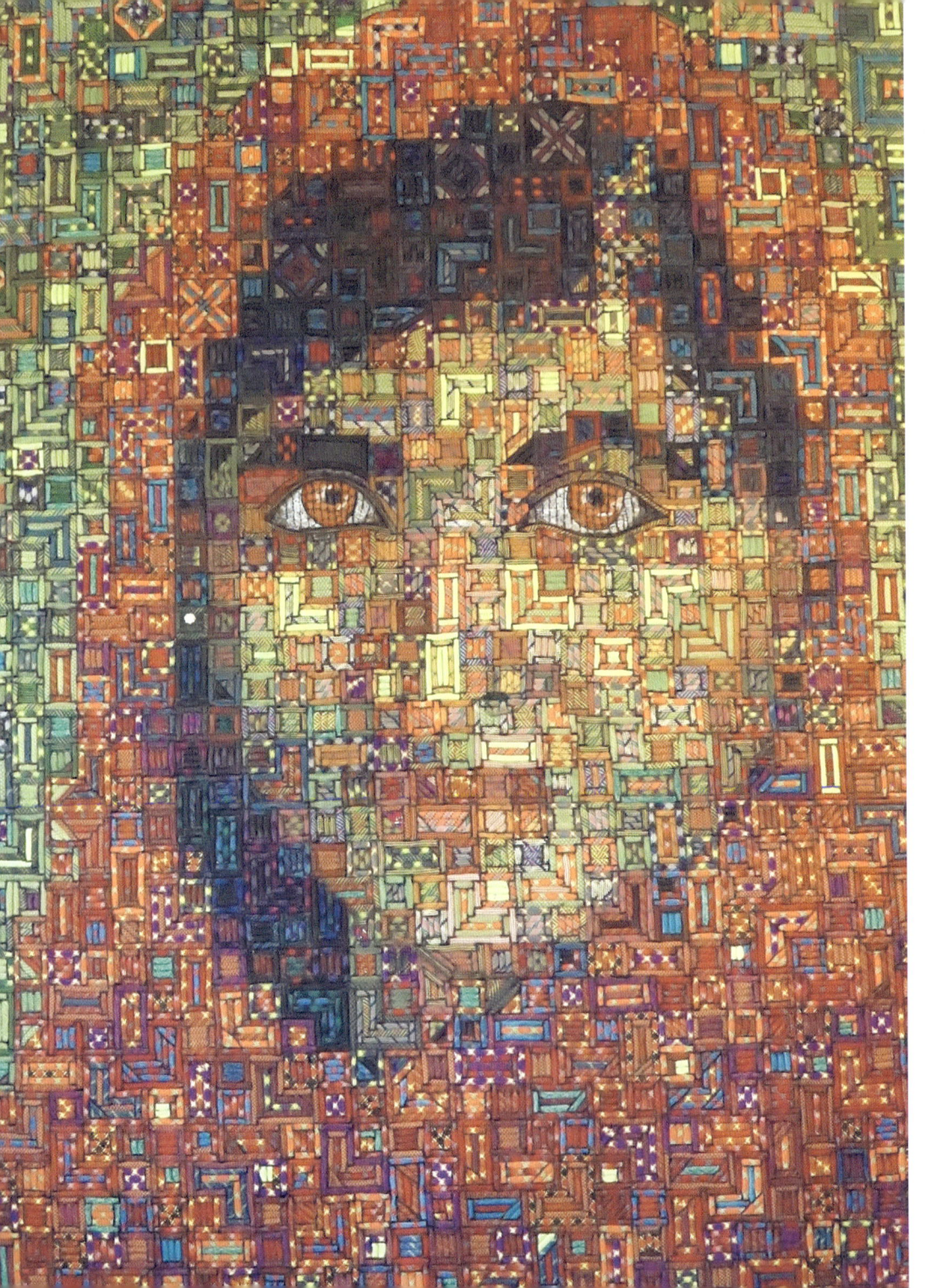

HOME MADE

I have a 1,000-square-foot, two-bedroom apartment. The second bedroom makes up my studio, which cnoom passes two folding tables: one for my stuff, and one for my work. My stuff includes a butane torch and extra butane, a couple pairs of scissors, a bunch of different glues, some measuring devices, tape, clamps and an air purifier. Other things in the studio bedroom include a desk and computer, along with a TV for the long days.

secondascentdesign.com
@secondascentdesigns

SECOND ASCENT DESIGNS

MEGAN BORG

Secret Wool Society

Megan Borg is a Calgary, Alberta-based fibre artist focusing on tapestry weaving and floor loom weaving (with the caveat: "I'm pretty obsessed with anything fibre-related"). Originally self-taught, along with taking classes through a local weavers' guild, Megan bought a vintage loom from the 1970s and has since begun her certification as a master weaver.

"I've been incorporating clay into my fibre pieces the last couple of years—I took up pottery to challenge myself. I'm most proud of my woven wool and clay wall clouds."

WOOL LOVE

My absolute favourite fibre has to be wool, not just because of my business name. When I first began weaving, wool was the first thing that I was drawn to because it's just so beautiful and authentic. I'm actually drawn to the super rustic wools that still look and feel like sheep. I love the hand of wool with a bit of oil and vegetable matter (like hay) still in it. I love the smell of it (even when it gets wet and smells like a soggy dog). And I love it even more when it's undyed. There's something so natural about wool with minimal processing. I also love the texture it has when it is woven, and I love the way it softens up so much after an aggressive washing. Mostly, I love the warmth it gives off when you wrap it around your neck in a woven scarf.

Megan remembers fondly making friendship bracelets as a kid: "I could keep my hands busy while making something beautiful." There was a gap in her crafting between high school and college graduation, but she eventually found her way to knitting. "I immediately felt the way I did as a kid making friendship bracelets. There is something so meditative about working with fibre, and I think that's exactly what brought me to weaving. Weaving is a whole-body experience, from the excitement of planning out your project to standing for hours measuring out each individual string, to setting up the loom and then double- and triple-checking that you haven't made an error, to sitting at the loom and throwing the shuttle back and forth while pressing the treadles with your feet, to the satisfaction of cutting your finished pieces off of the loom, to proudly sharing your accomplishments with your loved ones."

"I feel like this will ring true for a lot of people, but when I started weaving, it was on a small tapestry loom and the only thing I made was wall hangings," Megan says. After giving wall hangings to friends and family, the natural progression was to sell her work, on Etsy. "I realized I loved making wall hangings so much that maybe I eventually wanted to try making a career out of weaving, so I expanded to selling in a couple of local shops and participating in a few handmade markets." Beyond her wall hangings, Megan has been expanding into functional wovens like tea towels, face cloths and scarves. While concentrating on her master weaver certificate, she has necessarily had to limit selling her work to a select few times a year. "I still get excited when someone wants to buy one of my pieces, so I don't see myself giving this up anytime soon."

"I think my style reflects landscapes that make me feel the most comfortable and where I grew up—like a dense woodland. I love animals as well, so I like my pieces to sometimes look like an animal's coat by using undyed sheep's locks." ❋

"My main motivation is inner peace, meditation and a sense that I've made something beautiful. If someone else loves the thing I've made as much as I do, that's a plus. Having something that I love doing that brings me joy, peace and a clear head, while also providing a challenge and a problem to solve, is so amazing."

"My favourite part of weaving is sitting at the loom and thinking. There isn't a problem in my day that I can't work out at the loom. I make my biggest decisions at the loom."

WORK IN PROGRESS

My workspace has evolved so much over the years and is still a work in progress, as there never seems to be enough space for everything I want to do and I share a space with my partner, who operates a vintage clothing business. My weaving studio is in my home and includes two primary looms: Mira (a vintage floor loom) and Jane (a smaller portable loom that I've woven all of my master weaver assignments on). I keep all of my fibre in my basement, tucked away in storage containers, meticulously labelled, as I am a bit obsessed with being organized. I also have a little sewing station for hemming tea towels (or working on a little quilting project in my spare time), and I keep an old vintage kitchen table in the middle of the room where I can set up my warping mill for measuring threads, or to sit at to hand twist fringes on woven projects. I'm definitely an introvert, so I work alone in my weaving studio, usually listening to nostalgic '90s music from my teen years.

secretwoolsociety.etsy.com
@secretwoolsociety

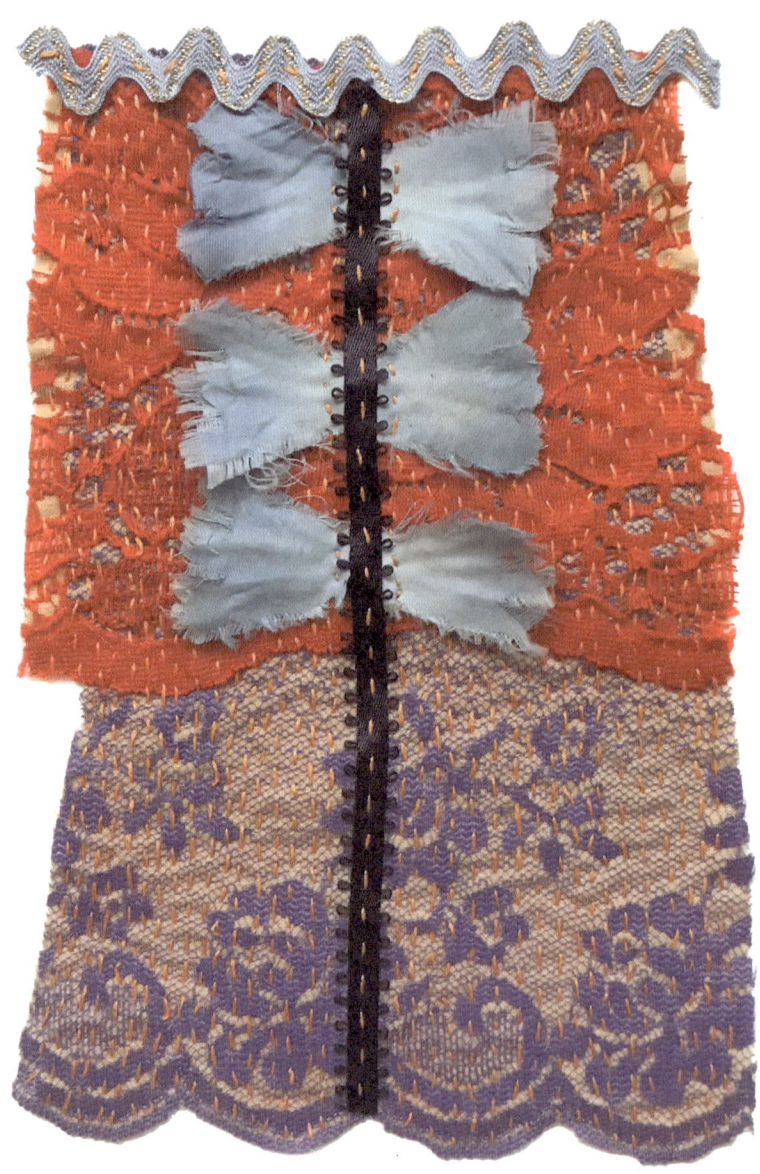

PAINTED PIECES

Shawn O'Hagan

Shawn O'Hagan was born in Toronto but has spent most of her life in Newfoundland. "I divide my time between my studio in Corner Brook on the west coast of the island and my off-the-grid cabin in the Bay of Islands." With childhood memories of making, colouring, painting, assembling and sewing, Shawn recalls becoming attached to the materials she was using and "the pure joy of touch." This love is apparent in her work.

"I hold a BFA, a BEd in art and an MFA. I have never settled on just one type of art making. Mostly I have been a painter, and my work has been exhibited across Canada in both public and commercial galleries and is held in many collections, including the Canada Council Art Bank. I have illustrated seven children's books. One of them was nominated for a Governor General's Award for illustration. For years I was the owner/operator of islandsweet, a hand-dyed/handspun yarn company, and I sold my yarn internationally in shops and online. And over the past 15 years, textiles have been my passion."

For the past couple of years, Shawn has been making small textile collages, to "loosen up" and get back to that wondrous tactile exploration that she loved as a child. The collage forms are nebulous, abstracted: "I am drawn more to the internal rather than the external world—inspiration coming from my unconscious. They are an external manifestation of my creative energy. They are about discovery—getting excited about how one colour, one texture, one pattern interacts with what lies beside it. I wanted to allow accidents to dictate the direction of the work, working only until it feels right."

She has made around 300 of these small collages thus far, using only repurposed, second-hand, gifted

"Working with textiles is visceral. It feeds my mind and soul and body."

and found materials. "Old textiles, with all their wear and tear, carry their histories and imperfections. As a maker who is also an environmental activist, I struggle with the idea of my adding more objects to the world. By using and reusing old materials, I make them new again—and keep them out of the landfill."

During the pandemic, Shawn also used these collages as a starting point for making paintings: "Beginning with the basic shape of the collage, then playing with the colours, the patterns, the textures. Floating them in a sensuous, undulating background. They reflect where my mind has been during the pandemic—the isolation, the fear, the anger and also the hope. The love."

These pieces do not have an intended audience, nor are they necessarily for sale. "I am making them for myself. It is a private investigation." ✽

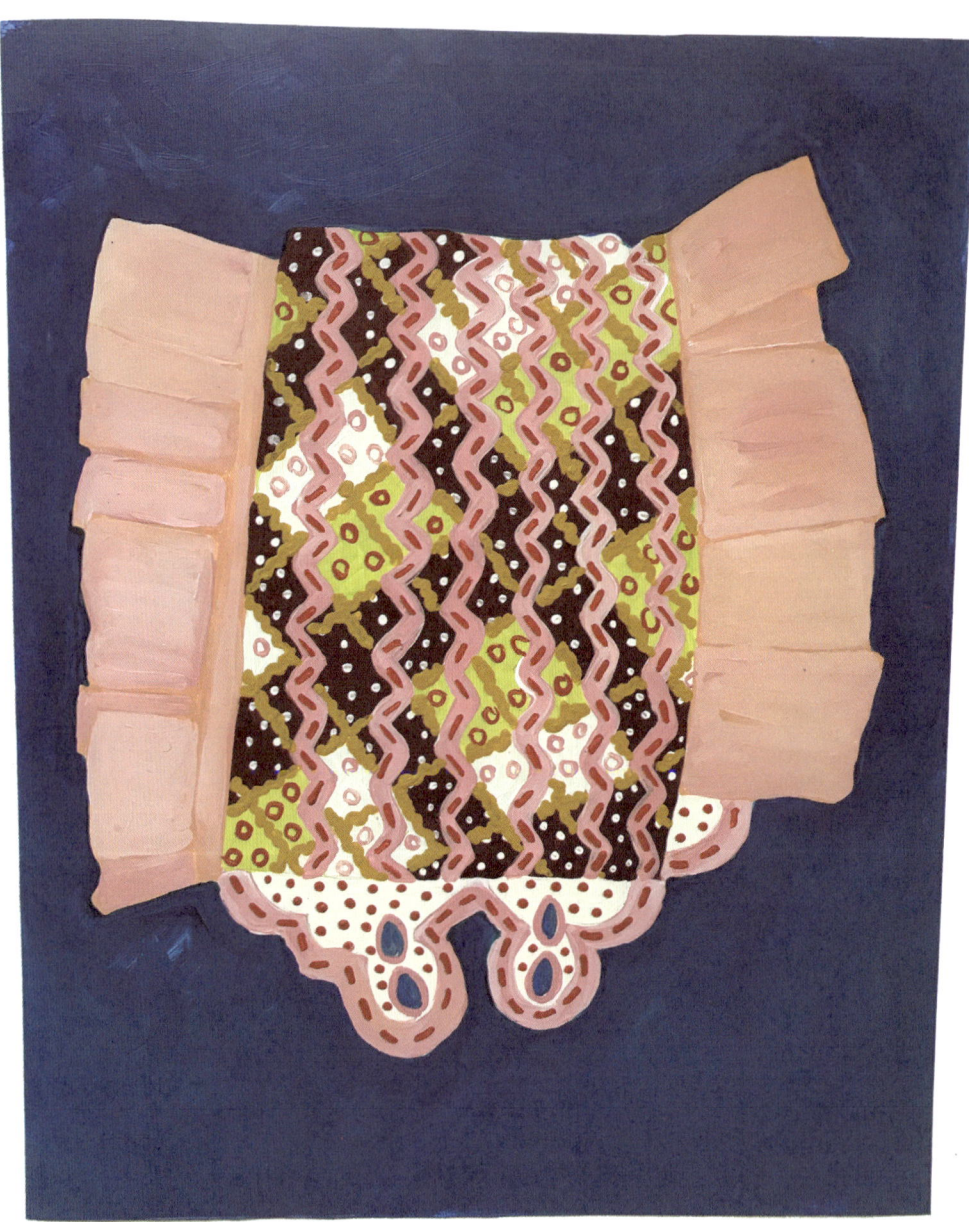

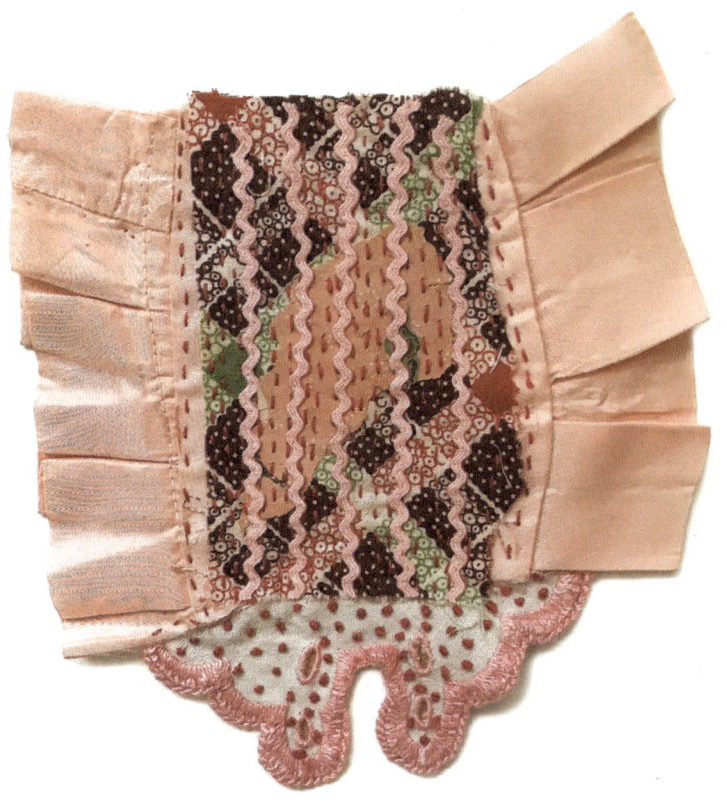

CREATIVE PROCESS

I begin with one scrap of material that catches my eye—its shape, its colour or texture. I pin it up and then try to empty my mind and allow the work to come to me. I feel my way into what comes next. It is all about how the work grows. It calls out for the next piece and then the next, until I know it is finished.

Once the work is pieced and pinned together, my hands take over. I fuse the work with slow hand stitching, embroidery and appliqué—again, feeling my way into the pieces. I spend time with the work. The more I manipulate the work, the more I breathe my life into it. I carry the whole history of my life, of my world, in my body and pour it into my work. These pieces are numbered, not titled. Although they are very personal, they are also universal. They come from a shared vocabulary.

HOME STUDIO

I always just want to be in my studio. Unless the weather is beautiful (which is kind of rare here in Newfoundland), and then I just want to be in my garden. My best kind of day is when I have nothing else planned and I can spend all day just making. Every day I am excited to be moving a piece along. Or better, starting something new.

My studio is fluid, changing when my materials change. I have large, custom-built shelves for wire baskets that hold my textiles and notions, which are separated according to types of materials— laces, silks, vintage doilies, ric rac and braid, etc. Often I dump a basket on the floor and something will jump out as a starting point for my next pieces.

Because I am now also painting, half the studio is devoted to that. I work flat on a large, custom-built table. It is near a big north-facing window that looks out on my garden. Right now there are apple blossoms and honeysuckle. Last week a young bull moose walked by my window as I worked…

shawnohagan.ca
@shawnkohagan

SHAWN O'HAGAN

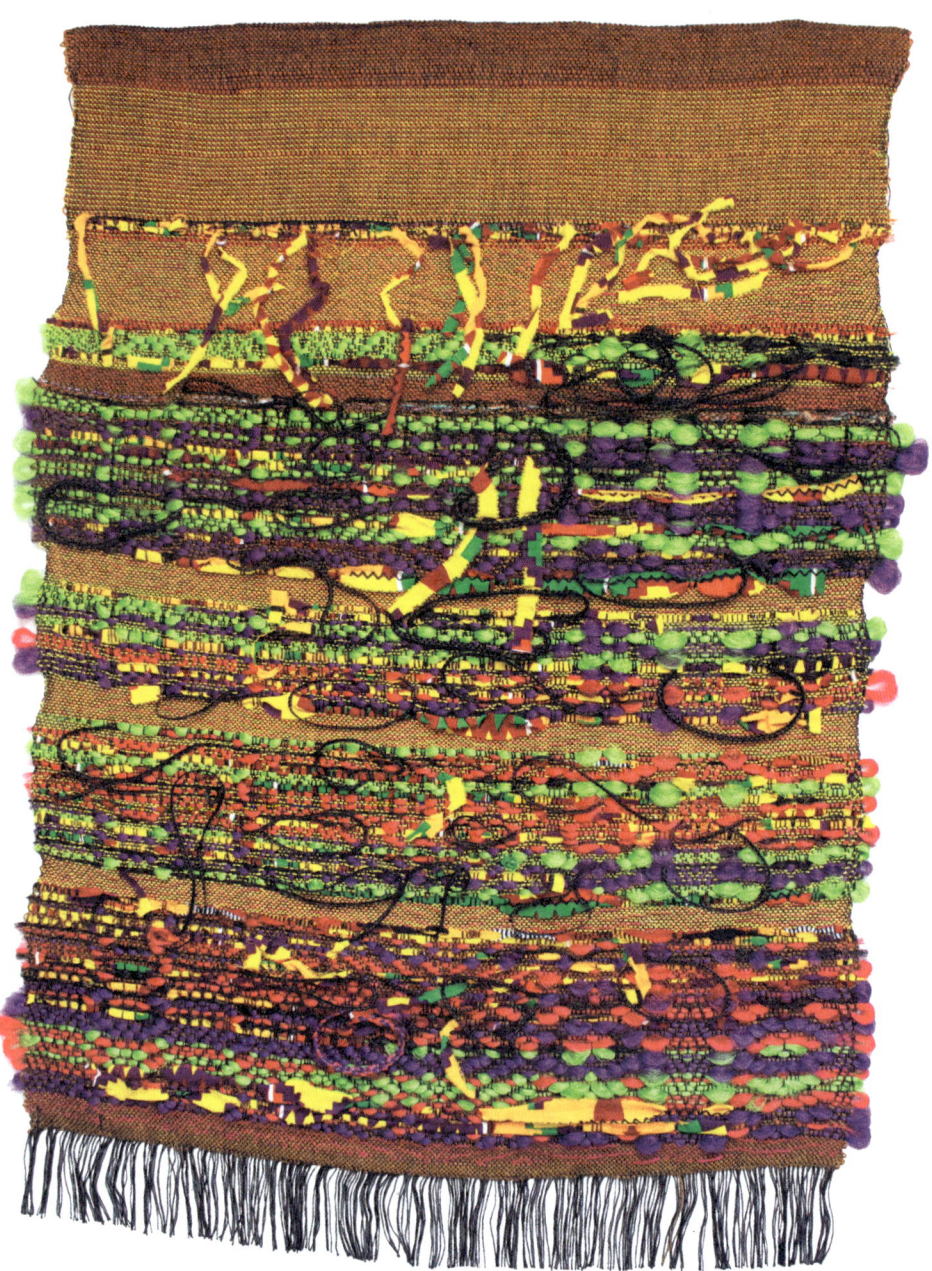

SHENEQUA

SHENEQUA's elementary school art teacher, Ms Hornstein, saw the young girl's aptitude for art and encouraged her to apply for a visual arts program. In high school, SHENEQUA showed her interest in adornment and yarn by hot gluing yarn onto old T-shirts to make dresses. "Thread and string have been love at first sight because of the endless possibilities that can be done with it, from adornment to holding something together, and decorative purposes," she says. "From there I wanted to explore deeper into how textiles are created just from yarn, thread and string. That's when I made it my mission to study fibres and found my passion for weaving." She earned her bachelor's in fibres/textiles at Kansas City Art Institute and a master's in design for fashion, body and garment at the School of the Art Institute of Chicago. "My passion and love for African textiles, especially Ghanian textiles, the black women in my life I love and care about, travelling, nature and conversations with others shaped my creative path."

Incorporating hair braiding techniques with weaving—combining the traditions of weaving on loom, weaving hair and her Afro-Caribbean roots—SHENEQUA creates what she terms "MAGIC"—an all-caps expression of the art she creates in various forms, from sculpture to wall hangings, garments, drawing, painting, performance and installation. "I weave with synthetic braiding hair, which I source from the beauty supply stores in my community," she says. "It can function as a work of art, a covering for the body or as an object in someone's home. My work celebrates life, memory, and Black/Caribbean women and African culture—shout out to Ghana, West Africa. It's for everyone, especially my Black and Caribbean girls, boys, women and men around the world."

"Working in fibre is a way for me to share my story, my magic with the world, and an access point for others to come together in celebration. It's a meticulous and engaging process to create and make what I've experienced, memories shared with those I love and care about, and my everyday life on this earth, to channel in a creative way and pass down to someone else to continue to share or cherish. I call it shining my light and love."

"I feel my personality is reflected in my pieces through the process of weaving with my hand. There are happy and intuitive surprises in my work."

SHENEQUA's work is one of a kind, both in materials and technique. At its heart, her weavings are a form of communication. "My motivations as a maker are conversations with others. When I talk with people, especially those I love and care about, new ideas begin to flow and spark other concepts that I thought of or haven't." Her work is a celebration of joy, Black women and identity. "I strive to be honest in the process of making my work and when I share it with the world. What I mean by being honest is showing up just the way I am. The way I look at life is different from others around me because we are all different. Yes, my work is Black, Caribbean, earth tone, motherland (Africa), strong, bold, royal, beautiful, dark, thought provoking, complex and detailed because I am or it's what interests me and what I want to talk about." ✣

"When I start to weave I have an understanding that the loom and I are having a conversation."

MATERIALS & PROCESS

I typically go through my sketchbook (which is filled with freewriting, ideas and inspiration) and images in my phone for concepts. Then I go to an overshot (a weave structure creating a plain-weave fabric with decorative weft floats) weaving book to source patterns that interest me. I collect about four to six patterns and create my custom pattern using weaving software.

I love black mercerized cotton (my warp) because it's a great background to work from, and I use various colours (my weft) because it pops a bit more on a solid background. Synthetic hair is my favourite fibre because of how it reminds me of sisterhood and womanhood, growing up in a black hair salon. I think of how I can turn a cheap material into something rich. When I do collages, I love using string or thread because of the various thicknesses and colours it comes in, to make more room for my inner child to play when making.

I choose my colours, calculate how much yarn I will need, dress the loom and begin weaving. I start by following the pattern that I created, then I add some flava (do what feels right) and incorporate various braiding techniques I grew up knowing in the black hair salon. Once I'm done weaving, I put the piece aside for a while and then come back to it and adorn, embellish and do what feels right again to do to finish the piece.

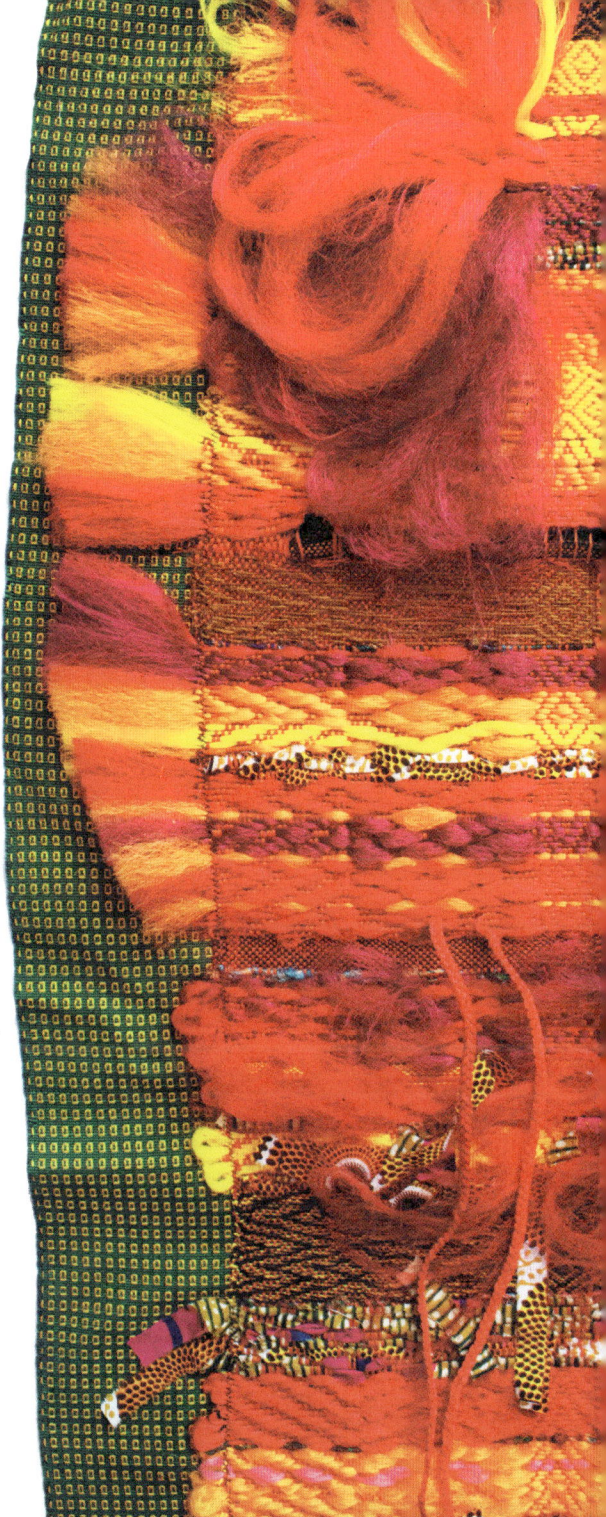

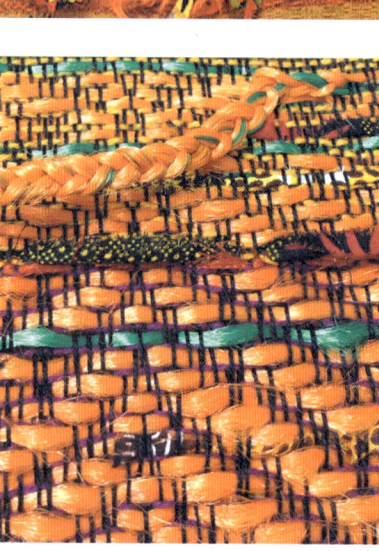

STUDIO

I work from home in my studio apartment. I have a table, a three-tier shelving unit that holds all of my various materials that I work with, from weavings to drawing, painting, collating, etc. I have my baby floor loom, and storage containers where I store my weavings.

shenequaabrooks.com
@she_ne_qua

SHENEQUA

Simone Elizabeth Saunders

Growing up in Canada, Simone Elizabeth Saunders has had many creative outlets: piano, dance, theatre and the visual arts. "I have a bachelor of fine arts from the University of Alberta in acting: exploring theatre arts, production and classical training. I spent a decade in the theatre arts, which took me to Toronto for many years. During my time there I segued into set design, which reignited my love for visual arts. I moved

"It is a gift to have the freedom to create, and to be paid for the work I create within my practice is what motivates and drives productivity. I will always find joy in making—and being able to do it as a living is a blessing."

home to the prairies and pursued another bachelor of fine arts, this time in fibre at the Alberta University of the Arts (formerly ACAD) in Calgary." For Simone, being creative is vital: "It's important for me to be creative; it's how I speak my truth and express my voice!"

A relationship with the fibre arts is relatively new in Simone's repertoire. She took to weaving immediately in college. "The gift for threads runs deep in my history," she says. "My Jamaican grandfather was an exceptional tailor." Though sewing has never been a passion, she discovered her own calling in working with a loom—from the mathematics of the setup to the artistry of making. During her final year of school, an instructor included a tufting gun in a slideshow and that was all that was needed to light a spark. "I spent my summer researching the tool and setting myself up for success. Punch needle and the tufting gun is such a satisfying craft. The vibrant array of bulky yarns, coming together on the stretched rug warp to create dynamic portraiture is a unique expression that has endless opportunities. As someone who enjoys drawing and painting, the ability to express myself through fibre is such a tactile experience."

"I am a biracial womxn of Jamaican and European descent," states Simone. "Weaving together a narrative that is embedded within cloth, mirrors the richness of my cultural heritage, of a Black history." Through her tufted portraits—in essence, they are paintings made with yarn—she portrays Black excellence in colourfully powerful ways. "Using my experiences of theatre, storytelling and research of my heritage, I am able to create portraits rendered from colourful yarn. I am constantly learning and challenging myself through my art, creating colourful, enigmatic textiles that I want to share with the world. They are timeless, highlighting Black womanhood, pop culture and mythological themes."

"Black women have been walked over for years. Realizing the psychology, for me, of using a rug-making tool to create portraits of Black excellence really fuels me. I continue to build up my heritage. I acknowledge the strength and wonderment of womanhood and of melanin magic."

FAVOURITE FIBRE

I use mostly acrylic yarn. It's accessible and vibrant—the cost is right. Its being affordable gives me permission to really play, as well as to go big!

"A strong accentuating line around the portrait, a vibrant, fluorescent or sparkling colour illuminating the character, has become a signature of mine."

Her work begins with deciding on the subject, whether a pop culture icon, a leader in the arts, sports, music or an advocate in public service. "I use influences from street culture, iconography from hip-hop and contemporary swag to embed in my textiles. I am influenced by the ornate patterns of Art Nouveau; the richness of style from this era is often referenced within my art. Having a theatre background, it is important to me that my textiles tell a story. Each character within the piece is depicted with cultural references and personal symbolism. This enriches each thread, intertwining to tell a story." She may include a predatory animal, talismans paired with Black figures "showing a kinship of power and survival." ✻

simoneelizabeth.ca
@simoneelizabethtextiles

AT HOME

I have a 70-inch by 70-inch tufting frame that my twin brother built for me. Behind it is a large shelf filled with vibrant bulky-weight yarn. I have a desk for drawing and writing, and a small cart with my painting, drawing and measuring supplies. It's a small studio, but mighty! My tufting gun sits on its own small table and my punch needle, scissors and measuring tape are always accessible on my desk. I do everything myself, although I sometimes rope my mom into help me with finishing. It's nice mother/daughter time.

STUDIO SIMONE POST

Simone Post

Simone Post grew up in a home with at least 10 sewing machines. They were her mother's machines—she hosted classes in their home sewing atelier. "I always love to be in this room, making things together with my mom," Simone says, reminiscing. From a young age, she believed that you could "make anything out of anything." As a teenager and young adult, fashion was her focus, until she discovered she was far more intrigued by the use of materials, not style or trends in themselves.

Simone is a 2015 honours graduate from the Design Academy Eindhoven in the Netherlands, and today runs an independent design studio built on "the

"For doing colour research I start with dyeing my own yarns or blending existing colours into each other—you always find more interesting colours than when you buy them ready-made in the shop."

principles of experimental research, sustainability and cultural heritage." She is particularly focused on the potential of materials and techniques, both new and innovative, as well as recycled and reimagined. She has collaborated with companies such as Vlisco, the Dutch textile manufacturer of high-end wax-printed fabrics that are mainly exported to Africa. Using their rejected fabrics, Simone turned the materials into new carpets. "I am cutting at the textiles in small strokes, somehow turning them into yarn again and coiling them up almost like a big bobbin, to turn them into a carpet. With endless possible colour combinations, a unique product is created each and every time. The design shields the original printed surfaces and potential flaws, while the resulting carpets still show off Vlisco's stunning colours with new and unexpected patterns."

She has collaborated with Kvadrat, the Danish commercial textile company, to design a 100% wool carpet. "This also started off with making my own yarns. It is based on how certain colours create a visual vibration when placed next to each other. Bold and vivid strings are created by hand-twining bundles of smaller yarns in five different colours. These twisted bundles are woven together with small single yarns using the same colours to create different levels of colour, mingling on the surface of the rug." The result is a pointillist effect, in which the detail and depth of the overall colour is revealed only at close proximity. "Twisted fringes in varying densities emphasize its lively and playful look."

Another project has been with Adidas, making new products out of ground-up used athletic shoes. She also collaborates with wood and plastic factories to turn their waste material into new products. "I do a lot of different things, from designed rugs to textile prints, wooden boards, chairs and throws. But somehow they all clearly show playful research into

materials and colours, and will you soon recognize it's done by me. Small details and repetitions and richness in colour are very important in this." For Simone, the raw material is always the starting point. "This can be of recycled yarns, or yarns I start twisting or making myself, and this will influence the entire output. So the material is the actual starting point and this will lead to the end product." Good design is also sustainable. "How can we reuse residual materials to create new things?" Simone asks. "For me, as a designer, it is the challenge to give new value to seemingly worthless materials—by embellishing it and giving it a new value. Beauty in this process is very important; with visual attraction, a product can make a connection with the user." In turn, this relationship encourages affection and care that goes beyond simply aesthetics. ✣

"I always start with the material and experiment with them, very hands-on, to see what the material is doing and how I can shape and change it into something unexpected."

TREND ALERT

I never look at trends. First of all, they don't interest me and I believe that when you try to follow certain trends you are always boring and behind. For example, a colour that is very trend-related mostly has a short lifespan. I often get my colour inspiration out of art—painters who have been studying colour for a long time and become real masters in it, like Matisse, Seurat and Hockney. I especially like the works in which different colours influence each other, which creates vibrating colour mélanges. This creates a very rich colourway. This playful way of working with colour, placing different colours next to each other and letting them vibrate with each other, is something which can be created in textile very well, because of its refined technique and all the different yarns and stitches you can use to place different colours next to each other.

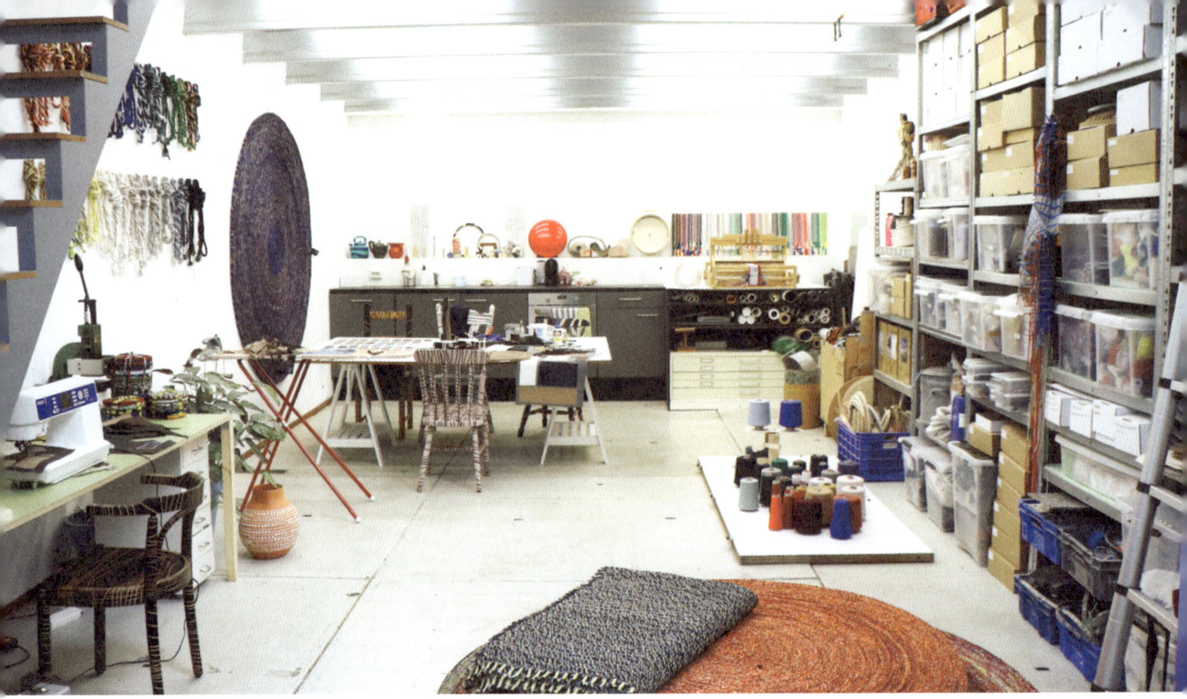

YARN·THREAD·STRING

WAREHOUSE STUDIO

My studio is in Rotterdam in an old warehouse next to the harbour. I have four different types of spaces. One is for clean work, such as drawing, computer work and reading. One is for making models, carpets, etc. There is a workshop where we have all kinds of woodworking machines to make bigger objects. And finally I have a bigger space for storage and for doing really big and "dirty" work, like making a big installation or working with ceramics. This is also where we produced the mats for Adidas out of recycled shoes. I work mostly alone, but I do have one assistant, which helps me with the organizational side of running a studio, and David van der Stel, who is also my partner and is a furniture maker, helps with construction work. Occasionally I have an intern.

simonepost.nl
@simone_post_

TEMARI BALLS AND NATURALLY DYED THREAD

Temaricious

Two Japanese women, Rika Abe and Naho Izumi, first met in Prague. After each had worked in Europe for a number of years, they returned home to Japan only to discover that they were working in the same Tokyo neighbourhood. Their friend Mary Fidler tells their story: "Over shared weekly lunches, ideas churned and developed as each woman in her own way looked for a way to enjoy life and work differently by creating something worth sharing with others, and spreading a little colourful happiness with the world."

While in Europe, Rika realized that she didn't know much about traditional Japanese handcrafting culture and vowed she would learn when she returned to Japan. Once home, she began exploring temari, folk art hand balls decorated with intertwined threads in creative geometric patterns. Her teacher encouraged her to dye her own threads to suit Rika's desired colour palettes. And so Rika started dyeing cotton threads using plants in her tiny Tokyo garden.

Her friend Naho brought some of Rika's temari balls and dyed threads to Paris and London, where she was working at the time. Following that trip, the pair received an order of naturally hand-dyed threads from Loop Knitting in London. That was the beginning of Temaricious, in 2014.

The threads are made from American cotton, spun in Indonesia and dyed locally. "Our threads are dyed with plants that are found in the corners of our everyday life," says Rika. "The plants or weeds are collected in various locations in Japan." They forage for dyes, too, with neighbourhood restaurants providing leftover coffee grounds and avocados. "The natural colours help us to express our temari the way we like—traditional patterns with a modern twist." Rika

"Our mission is to make people happy with our temari and threads!"

TEMARICIOUS 401

describes their temari as "Japanese but different from the typical style," which she attributes to their love of cross-cultures and memories of Europe, where they each spent their twenties. Temaricious thread is beautiful for temari but also for an array of thread crafts. Carefully packaged by hand, the threads are bundled and presented in a distinct way. They outsource this task: "Packaging is mainly done by Japanese women who cannot work full time due to nursing smaller kids, or older women who want to work at home."

Although they started dyeing in Rika's kitchen, they set up a new dyeing studio in August 2020 in their retail and workshop venue. At 15 square metres, it has six stoves for big pots. "We used to dye by ourselves, but currently our main dyeing craft man, Keisuke, is working for us."

"By making their own dyes from foraged plants and weeds in nearby parks and neighbourhoods around Japan, Rika and Naho have developed a very local colour palette unique to temari and have enlivened an art for a whole new demographic in Japan and around the world through in-person workshops, online videos and the sale of their thread both online and on location in their adorable atelier/shop in west Tokyo," says their friend Mary. ✻

"We sell opportunities, in a way, for customers from all over the world to learn about the culture of Japan through our products. We often run workshops in foreign countries and teach Japanese culture, and learn about foreign cultures. We hope we inspire everyone to make life more creative."

NATURALLY YOU

Naturally dyed thread colours are not even, might fade out and will change more quickly than colours from chemical dyes. But we think that is a rule of nature. Flowers in the garden have their own colours. People are all different and each one has their own personal colours. We would like to respect individuals and our biggest wish is that all the customers, students and staff who work for Temaricious stay just as they are.

Our threads and handmade temari balls are a symbol of being who you are, and might be the tool to help you believe that you can be.

temaricious.com
@temaricious

KELLY PHENICIE & ELLEN SAVILLE

The Endery

Ellen Saville and Kelly Phenicie have a vision for waste, and their brand, The Endery, creates statement fashion knits from "the ends" of other brands' production process—in essence, the leftovers. "The deadstock yarns, used for each knit, are sourced mainly from yarn mills and knitwear exporters in Peru," Ellen explains. "Manufacturing and producing on a large scale always has a margin of error, including human error. In managing a lot of different styles, a small mistake in consumption can have a big impact when multiplied by hundreds or thousands of units, and paired with the yarn suppliers who stipulate that they can give us up to 8% extra." Even the most sustainably minded manufacturers end up with extra materials, and so The Endery attempts to build a flexible system in its own design and production. From full cones to little odds and ends, these leftovers become new items.

"The Endery brand DNA is based on the idea of colour," says Ellen. "Essentially most leftover yarns are last year's Pantone trends." Since they can't plan for available colour quantities, they incorporate spontaneity into the design of their apparel—"swapping shades and the idea of unruly colour that didn't behave as it should. Stripes lend themselves well to this." The results are eclectic, vibrant combinations and bold swatches of colour.

Having successfully launched two collections, one in alpaca and the second in pima cotton, they are also focussed on mending and darning as ways of extending the lifespan of garments and promoting a circular fashion system. "The brand's vision is to really explore textile industry waste and find creative ways to inject it back into the fashion cycle in a usable way."

"The Endery uses deadstock yarns in their knits to communicate issues surrounding waste, circularity, recycling and craft communities to build a brand that speaks to consumers about the big hows and whys regarding the clothing they buy. Environmentally, they work to only use existing materials. Socially, they run a knitting workshop in Lima, Peru. The wider social context in Peru and the high rates of poverty mean that knitting gives workers an income and promotes the conservation of the craft."

"The Endery sees deadstock as a gigantic issue in the textile and fashion industry and we are just scratching the surface. We aim to develop a real process to approach deadstock more effectively and efficiently that allows other brands to do the same, and even create a deadstock sourcing platform for brands. The Endery is passionate about creating an innovative system to tackle waste, and aims to start moving into new product categories in the future. And we hope to inspire others to join the exploration of waste—how to reuse what we make and also make things that last longer." ✻

CREATIVE PARTNERS

Kelly was born in France, grew up in Oklahoma, then lived in London, Texas and New York City. Right after college she came to Peru and ended up marrying a Peruvian and has been living in Lima ever since. She started out in human rights research and translating, and later stumbled into textiles and manufacturing and finally hand knits. Now she owns and runs a company called Green Design Link that specializes in producing hand knits on a large scale for sustainable clothing brands. There aren't a lot of manufacturers willing to get into handmade items in the quantity and quality that Green Design Link does, but there is a lot of interest from consumers. She believes this is due to a huge shift in consumer attitudes, desiring more sustainable items, and she is inspired by the knitting jobs this demand creates.

Ellen has also moved around a lot prior to Peru. Originally from the UK, she fell in love with the people and the culture—the textiles are some of the oldest in the world and the fibres are incredible. She has done a lot of work with remote artisan groups of the continent and is a creative consultant. Ellen met Kelly through Green Design Link as a consultant before they decided to launch The Endery.

theendery.com
@the.endery

MINDY SUE WITTOCK & JENNA FREIMUTH

The Wondermakers Collective

The Wondermakers Collective is a long-distance embroidery collaboration between Mindy Sue Wittock of Cedarburg, Wisconsin, and Jenna Freimuth of Minneapolis, Minnesota. "We attended the same college at different times, connected on social media, and now mail abstract embroideries back and forth between Wisconsin and Minnesota," they say. "While pursuing our undergraduate art degrees at the University of Wisconsin–Green Bay, we both found our peers and professors mentioning that we had similarities and would benefit from knowing one another. Through social media, we became fast friends, admired each other's work and wondered what we could make together."

Determining that embroidery and embellishment was something that could be easily mailed, they send the same embroidery back and forth, each contributing stitches with every pass. "A new hoop always begins with one of us stretching a piece of felt and beginning to stitch. Often we will both start a new piece at the same time so we can swap in the mail and always have something to work on. Every hoop is buildable and we stitch knowing that some of our work may be layered or covered up, but the beginning is about establishing a base and trusting that our efforts contribute to the final piece." It is up to each artist to make individual decisions about what comes next: Does the fabric need more appliqué? What colour story is developing? Are there gestures in the thread to follow or challenge?

"We like how our work represents the art of disruption, when you have to stop, let go and allow someone else to contribute," says the pair. "Without hesitation, we both make space for the other to stitch and add what feels good, knowing that there will always

"This collaboration wouldn't be possible without the mutual respect and commitment we share for one another and this project. We take pride in building a collection of work that represents our growing friendship, the roots of our shared undergraduate education and the power of wonder."

be room for more. It can be difficult to stop what we are stitching to mail, and challenging to pick up what was sent, but the interruption creates opportunities to stretch ourselves. We often recognize how our particular pen-pal process affects our individual contributions to the collaboration and there is a mutual respect to add and build without erasing. We allow our embroideries to form from spontaneity and we navigate building a collaboration without the fear that our individual work will disappear, because time and time again our finished pieces show us how together we can arrive somewhere new and surprising." ✶

"We are collectively motivated by how well we continue to push each other to discover the boundaries of what a hoop can hold. Every finished piece is an example of how we learn what marks we both enjoy using, which visual elements to apply further and where we could expand our process. There is always a wonder for what the next piece could be, both in size and density."

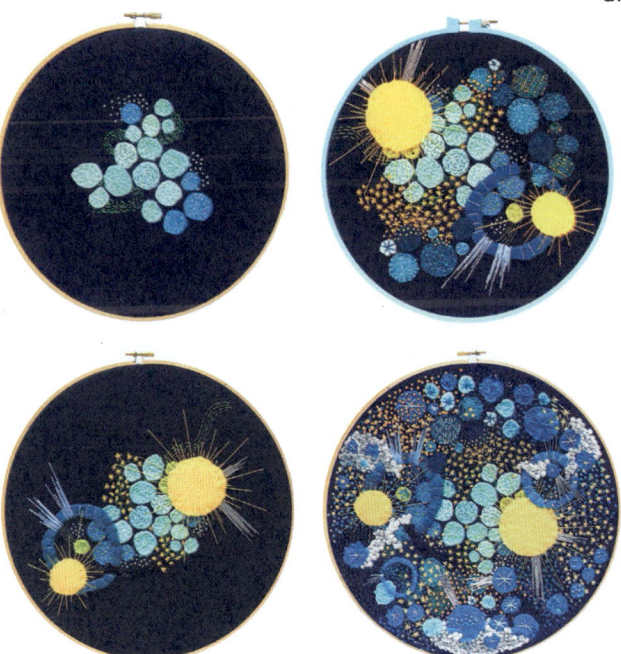

EXTRAS

Embellishments are a prominent technique in our finished work and we often turn to the use of sequins, beads and French knots to construct depth and add variety. There is an intuition to our work, and finished pieces are complete when we feel like we have pushed the boundaries of what the fabric can hold and have found balance in the visual elements.

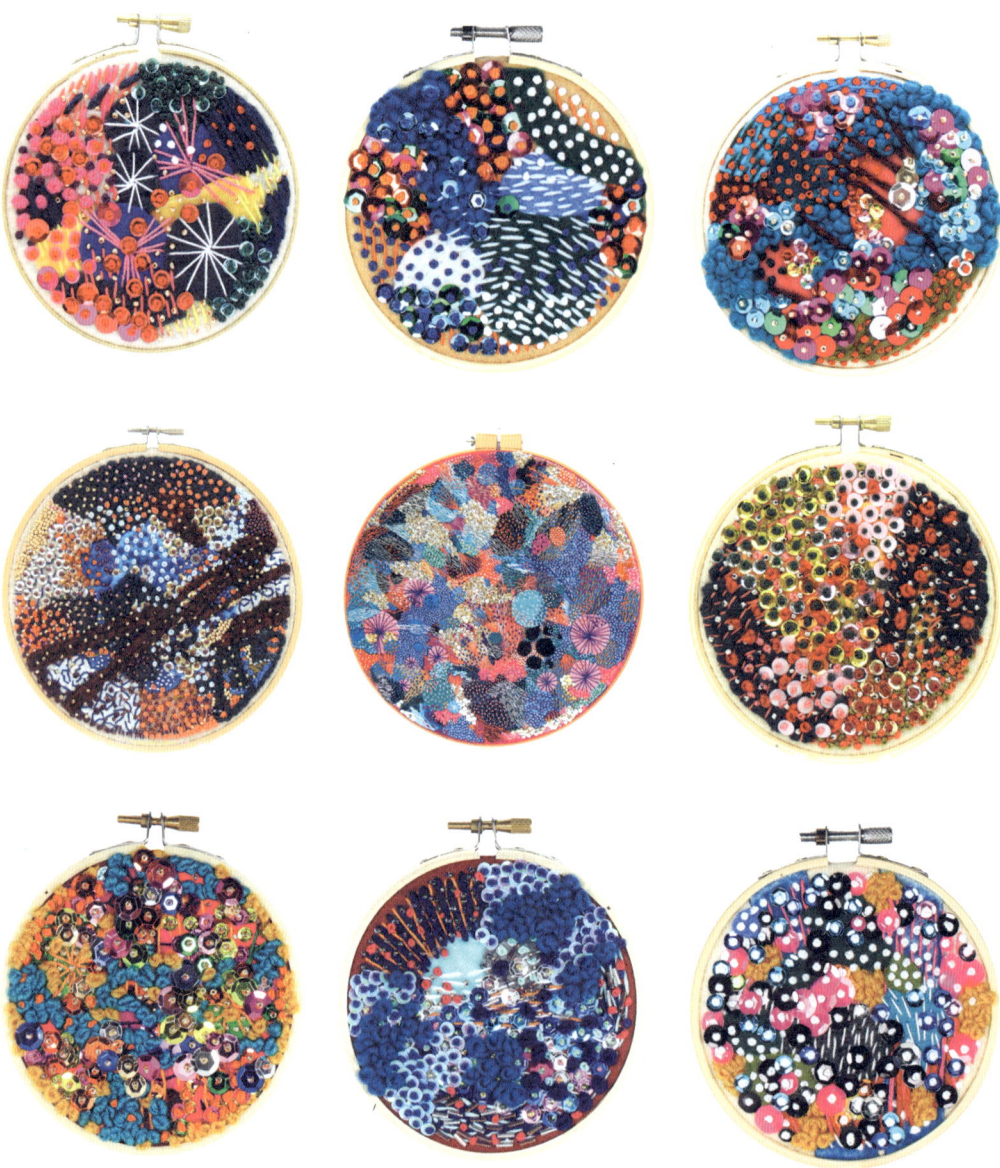

THE WONDERMAKERS COLLECTIVE

THREADS AND ADORNMENTS

We love to work with felt as our stitching matrix. It can hold a lot of weight and there's something great about stitching into a fibre that's pressed and not woven. Our favourite embroidery floss is DMC, as we can always rely on the colours and smooth grain of the thread. We adore sequins and beads for adding all kinds of textures and shine to our pieces, and yarn has become an essential material for us to explore different visual weight and depth. Occasionally, we enjoy working with velvet, spandex or other woven textiles as a source of appliqué.

ONLINE AND OFF

Mindy: I work in a home studio space at the top of our stairs in my family's townhouse. I have a window with New Kids on the Block curtains and my space is lit with large, colourful Christmas lights. I made my studio feel like a fort for art making and it's my favourite place to be.

Jenna: My workspace is a bedroom in my apartment, where I toggle between my drawing desk and my computer. All of my Wondermaking materials are stored in cubbies below a peg board wall, where I hang works in progress.

Together: While the majority of stitching happens in our individual studios, the heavy lifting of our collaboration is online. We connect regularly through video chats and texting to talk about ideas, manage admin, populate our online portfolio, sell hoops and organize our collection. When possible, we enjoy working side by side a few times a year, visiting each other's studios or finding quaint little rentals between our two locations for a Wondermaker art retreat.

thewondermakerscollective.com
@thewondermakers

TUFT THE WORLD

Tim Eads

Philadelphia-based artist and designer Tim Eads has an MFA from Cranbrook Academy of Art and regularly teaches at the Penland School of Craft and Tyler School of Art. Tim can follow the threads of his creative path back to his childhood, growing up on a family-run Texas ranch. "Before and after work and school my brothers and I tended animals, worked the ranch and made constant repairs," Tim recalls. "Ranch maintenance is stressful—windmills break down in bad weather and fences are randomly destroyed by marauding cattle that then have to be rounded up in the dead of night. Managing it all was a family affair, with aunts, uncles, cousins and grandparents pulling together."

His father also worked full-time in the West Texas oil fields. "To make ends meet my mother became a floral designer, baker, balloon specialist and professional clown—all from a shop in our house so she could stay home with us." At eight, Tim taught himself to juggle and by age 10 he was working with his mother as a clown. "I loved the surprise and excitement on peoples' faces as they were presented with magic tricks and balloon animals." He fondly remembers how his normally shy mother transformed into a boisterous character who loved to make folks happy.

Years later, you can see these influences in Tim's work through his humour, wild colours and work ethic: "I couldn't see the results of these experiences in my life for years—the creativity in constantly building and maintaining a ranch, the sense of accomplishment from hard work, the delight that comes from artistry combined with play."

Tim has used numerous media and techniques in his art-making, from screen printing and sewing to

"The materials I use change all the time. Experimentation and tinkering are foundational to making for me. I find endless inspiration in changing materials, techniques, scale or concepts."

> **"My foremost ambition is to elicit joy in people through my work and to enable them to share in that making process."**

ceramics and sculpture. He was making canvas bags from hand-printed yardage when he was introduced to yarn tufting. After raiding his wife's knitting stash, Tim quickly discovered that rugmaking requires very different fibre than sweaters.

Initially, Tim planned on incorporating tufted textures on his canvas bags, but instead he kept making "bigger and weirder rugs." He became obsessed with the process of tufting, which allowed him to create unique, dimensional textiles. "Electric tufting guns allow you to create beautiful projects in half the amount of time compared to traditional fibre processes like needle punching, hand tufting and hand knotting," explains Tim.

Tufting uses a lot of yarn, so he needed to source durable yarn that he could get in bulk at a reasonable price. This, combined with the popularity of his posts on Instagram, led him to sell tufting guns and supplies online.

"It did so well I closed my bag business to focus on tufting," he says. "It's really a better fit for me. There's so much I love in teaching people and watching them explode with creativity and ideas. I love sourcing yarns, and getting to support other folks in the fibre world."

Selling fibre also takes Tim back to his roots: his grandparents raised angora goats for mohair and his grandmother experimented with hand dying, sourcing local berries and plants as colourants. "There was a strong strain of creativity in my family, often in practical crafts like iron working and quilting—we all slept under homemade quilts and wore home-forged spurs." ✣

FIBRE FAVOURITES

It's more like a favourite of the week or of the day. Each material works better under different applications. For a while, I was obsessed with cutting discarded polyester into strips to reuse as yarn. Another time I got really into mop yarn. There's something magical about playing with something new and finding out how it can be adapted, what new texture it will produce, where it will shine. So I am always experimenting and have a new favourite probably on every project.

"I love mixing bright colours and layering geometric patterns. I surround myself with that look throughout my life—my work, my clothes, home decorating, everything. I think it's a kind of sharp-edged maximalism. I love things that feel surprising or playful."

PRODUCTION PROCESS

To make a tufted wall piece I start with a design made in Illustrator and projected onto the loom for tracing. This is when I plan the colours and pile heights for each section. Seeing the real yarn colours and textures makes a big difference. After marking everything out on the fabric it's time to tuft. I use a few different machines when tufting; my favourite machine is the AK-III industrial. It can tuft super deep shag from 18 to 60 millimetres in cut pile or in loops.

After the piece is tufted I'll spend a fair amount of time trimming the fibres. Sometimes I like to carve into the pile height with an electric trimmer to create neat edges and dimensionality. Once I'm finished I spread a layer of glue on the back that holds all the fibres in place and then I apply a backing cloth. At this point, it can either be a rug or wall tapestry, but I tend to be more drawn to putting the pieces on the wall. They get mounted to wood for easy hanging. This really puts them more in the realm of a painting than a floor piece, which is something I prefer.

"Making things has always given me relief from the stress and chaos of everyday life. And trying out a new process or material, learning and testing its limits, is captivating. It's very much a playful exploration that keeps me making things."

@tuft_the_world
thisistimeads.com

STUDIO

My wife and I share a home studio in West Philly that was a small neighbourhood church for 35 years. The main floor of the house had been converted to a large open room and now it holds a sewing studio, screenprint space, ceramic studio, wash out room and storage.

I love any machine that can increase my efficiency when I am working. As a consequence, my studio is full of industrial sewing machines, cutters, a felting machine, tufting machines and yarn-coning machines. I also have a six-yard fabric printing table with a screen-printing setup as well as a woodshop in case I need to build something.

Generally, my work is well organized once it's finished, but until then it's chaos. Piles of partially finished projects lie all around, waiting to be finished or discarded. And fibre is everywhere—rolls of felt, batting, fabric and always cones and cones of yarn. My working yarn is stored on floor-to-ceiling shelves in the studio, organized by colour, and the yarn for sale is in a nearby warehouse. I often have more than 5,000 pounds (2,270 kilograms) ready to be rolled onto cones and shipped out.

CROCHETED IMAGINATION

Tuija Heikkinen

Textile artist and educator Tuija Heikkinen lives close to the Arctic Circle in Rovaniemi, Finland. As a child, she drew a lot, and by her teens, she was sewing her own clothes. "I have always had a need to think, solve and do things in my own way and by my own hands," she says.

"My education is as a fashion and textile designer. My working life is divided: I work as a teacher, but also as a textile artist and designer-entrepreneur." Tuija teaches at a local arts and crafts school, to teenagers and adults. "I teach with hard and soft materials—wood, concrete, mosaic, textile printing, felting, dyeing and more." She considers her role as an "inspirator"—to both encourage and inspire her students rather than simply just conveying information and how-to instructions.

In her own company, she focuses on printed textiles and recycled vintage fabrics. "I do all of it by myself: design, print and sew. I have a basic range of products, but also an opportunity to test and try out small, unique series. I have no online sales, but a couple of retailers in Finland." As an outlet for her experimental and artistic side, she creates crocheted and embroidered works, available for viewing on Instagram.

She calls herself a late bloomer when it comes to yarn works, since her main fibre activity was with printed fabrics. "About five years ago I found crocheting. I started with granny squares," says Tuija. But she was missing out on something that would distinguish the crochet as her own, so she decided to pursue crocheting but without any instructions or particular goals—crocheting freestyle, if you will: "I don't use patterns or instructions, just a few yarns, some colour and a totally open mind."

"Although almost everything has been invented in the world, creativity always offers new challenges and questions."

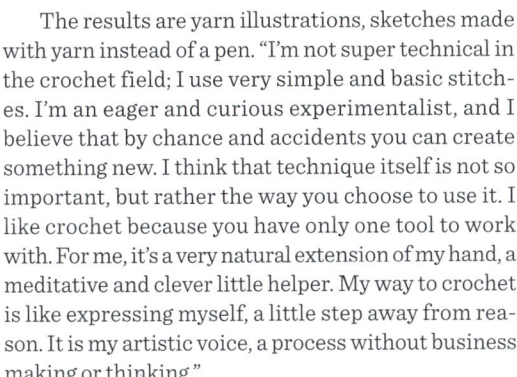

The results are yarn illustrations, sketches made with yarn instead of a pen. "I'm not super technical in the crochet field; I use very simple and basic stitches. I'm an eager and curious experimentalist, and I believe that by chance and accidents you can create something new. I think that technique itself is not so important, but rather the way you choose to use it. I like crochet because you have only one tool to work with. For me, it's a very natural extension of my hand, a meditative and clever little helper. My way to crochet is like expressing myself, a little step away from reason. It is my artistic voice, a process without business making or thinking."

Not only is it artistically freeing, making in this way is also good for the soul. "As a teacher and as an artist I see the craft area as part of well-being," she says. "I believe it has the power to rehabilitate and improve the quality of life. By thinking through your hands you can improve, structure and understand the world. And maybe bring some delight to the world." ✼

PROCESS

My crochet projects start very spontaneously. In the beginning, I have a very tiny idea of what I'm going to do, but the work takes shape, it transforms during the process. I barely make any notes or count stitches. That is the best part of the process, unpredictability—you don't know where you'll find yourself in the end. My works are like little notes from my diary, little stories, feelings about everyday life. I build my works piece by piece, take some work-in-progress photos, think about arrangements, balance, colours, backgrounds. Usually, I have several projects going on at the same time. Some are ready instantly; some take a longer time to get ready.

I'm very spontaneous and curious. I love to experiment, and the red thread in my work is an open mind, and what comes by accident and chance. I follow and get inspired from all the creative fields: art, design, fashion, crafts, history and so on. Also nature, of course. In northern Finland we have (still) four distinctive seasons, which offer a lot to work with. Colours, silence, frost, northern lights, darkness, lightness—the extremes feed the imagination and inspire. A big idea can be found from the forest or from the fridge. Sometimes it's a colour combination on the horizon or a captivating atmosphere in a old photograph.

STYLE

I describe my style as joyful, cheerful and a little bit childlike. My style is made of bright colours, simple shapes and graphic, abstract items, as well as free botanical forms.

Colours are a really important part of my work. I pay close attention to colours, picking up interesting colour combinations from my surroundings.

I have also a passion for the mid-20th-century-modern style. I collect vintage fabrics and I use them often as part of my work. That style is also visible in my designs. And those influences are often present in the way I dress or decorate my home.

"I think that an incomplete circle is more interesting than a perfect circle."

YARNS OF ALL KINDS

The range of yarns is so large. Basically, I'm inspired and curious about all kinds of yarns. I use cotton and wool ones, but I also use recycled materials as raw material. I make rag (scrappy fabric yarn) from old fabrics and textiles, and reuse them for weaving rugs. This is very typical and deep in the history of Scandinavian culture.

Luckily through my position as a teacher, I have learned something about "hard yarns," too. Tin yarn is a typical yarn material from the Sámi people (the Indigenous people living in Lapland). They make traditional yarn products by weaving and embroidering with tin (pewter) yarn.

My absolute favourite hard yarn is wire—it is flexible and graphic, and it endlessly feeds the imagination.

@tuijaheikkinen

STUDIO AT HOME

I have my own studio at home. It's small, compact, busy and full of projects. I run my small company there, from design to manufacturing. It's also my test laboratory for the experiments and prototypes for my company, and my teaching work. I have a variety of equipment, from a sewing machine to saws and drills.

My yarny life happens basically everywhere else. Yarns are stored in my studio, but crocheting and embroidering projects take place in my cozy armchair in my living room. I have a very large selection of all kinds of yarns. I also search for them and buy them from flea markets.

I also collect all kinds of old sewing supplies, old craft and fashion magazines, and books. So, all of my space is used thoroughly, from floor to roof. My wool yarns are stored in colour-coded boxes. Embroidery and the other extra yarns are stored in vintage-style boxes and containers.

I work alone in my studio. Teaching takes most of my week, but I have weekends and long holidays.

BREAKING TRADITION

Ulla-Stina Wikander

With many years of study—a total of seven years of art education—Ulla-Stina Wikander has a practical foundation in painting and sculpture, but that doesn't mean there isn't room for playful experimentation. She works as a prop designer a the Opera House of Gothenburg in her native Sweden, a job that requires her to frequent flea markets and vintage shops. "15 years ago I started to collect cross-stitch and midpoint embroideries. I did not know what to do with them and I had mixed feelings about them—they were both beautiful and regarded as kitsch." In those early years, there was plenty of needlework available for sale and her collection grew to hundreds of canvasses. "I do not have a history with yarn because I work with vintage embroideries, but I love these embroideries more than anything else."

With a growing collection, Ulla-Stina looked to create a use for them and she started by covering some mirror frames and chairs with the embroideries. The items were unique and popular and easy to sell. "One day in 2012, my vacuum cleaner broke down and instead of throwing it away, I had this idea that perhaps I should cover it with some of my embroideries. How would it look and what would I do with the object once completed? The vacuum cleaner was transformed into something else—a kind of art object. It caught my interest and I started to cover ordinary household objects from the seventies, such as sewing machines, electric mixers, typewriters and other forgotten things, typically thought of as a woman's domain of everyday labour."

"I find it interesting to see how these objects transform in a new context—the obsolete, the things we do not want any longer, the old and forgotten things. They

"I like to call my works mixed-media and some might call them kitsch. I like to see my work as a commentary on the current situation with recycling but also women's everyday work."

become artifacts from a bygone era, disguised, camouflaged and dressed. I give them a second life, and although I cut the embroideries into pieces, I think they look very beautiful when they have been dressed up."

At first, Ulla-Stina felt guilty about taking apart the needlework, but she is meticulous in her planning by first making a pattern in calico and ensuring that nothing is wasted. "The objects must be as perfect as possible," she says. "That is my tribute to the women who made the embroideries. I start to cover by sewing and glueing; everything has to fit and be sustainable. After that, I dye the rickrack ribbons in the right colour and cover cords if there are some with lycra in the same colour."

Ulla-Stina's work is sold at exhibitions and art fairs, and customers also request specific objects to be

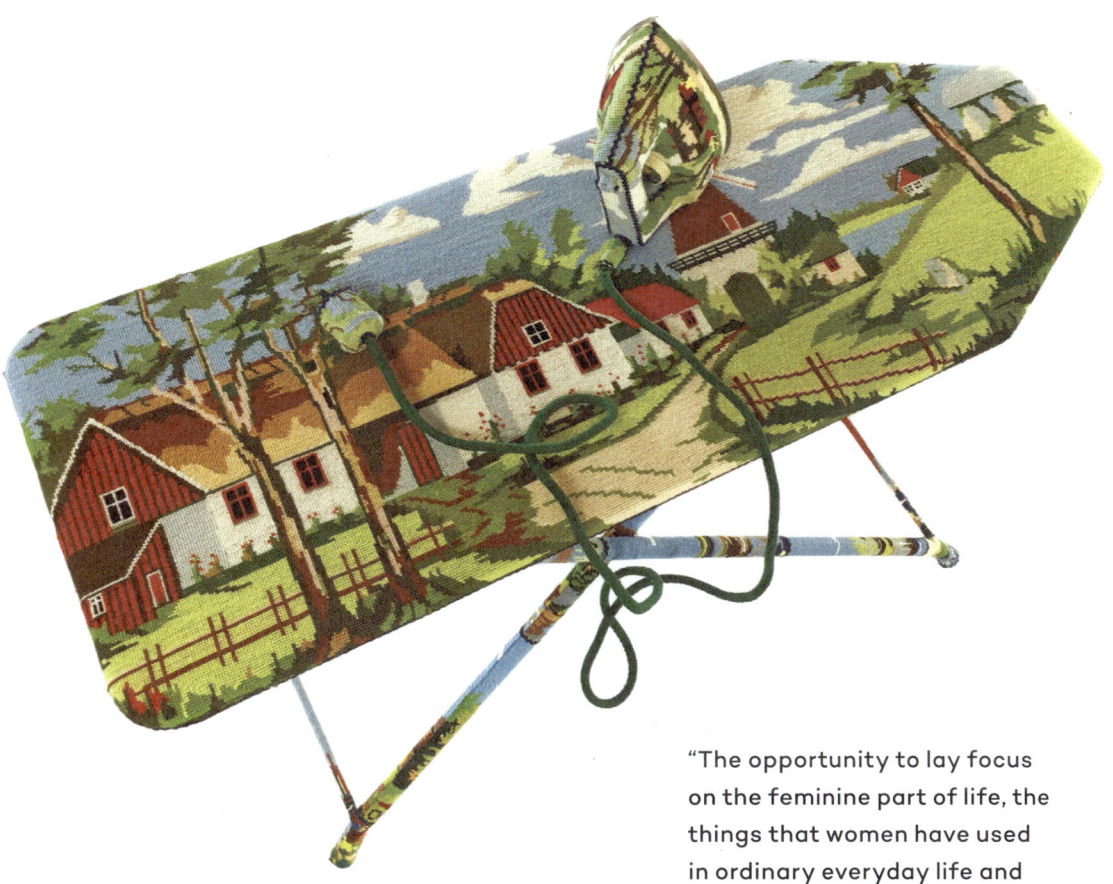

dressed in needlework, a challenge that creates new ideas. "I find new objects all the time that I would love to cover," Ulla-Stina says. "I also find it inspiring that you can see a growing interest in needlework among young people, and that is really encouraging." She still identifies as primarily being a painter, and wonders about her inclusion in the realm of textile arts, since her art involves "destroying" the handiwork of others. "My interest is not primarily what material I use; it's more to show the unexpected in the meeting of different expressions."

Eventually, she would like to cover an entire interior workplace or living room: "Something big and spectacular." ✣

"The opportunity to lay focus on the feminine part of life, the things that women have used in ordinary everyday life and still do, really interests me, but also the recycling idea appeals to me. My objects or small sculptures have no function, but they had back in the day. I use household objects that still function and I cover them with embroideries."

"Some of the small objects, like an iron or a phone, take me a day or two to make, but the bigger installations take weeks to finish."

HOME STUDIO

My studio is in a part of my house, so I don't have to travel to go there. That is both good and bad because I have a tendency to work all the time, but then to work is what I like the best. Sometimes I have hired an assistant for some weeks when I have had too much to do. My equipment is scissors, needles, pins, pliers, glue and colours. All my embroidery is stored in plastic boxes with different titles such as Flowers, Moose, Red Cottages with Birches and 17th Century, so I know where to look for a specific embroidery.

ullastinawikander.com
@uskonst

YARN FROM T-SHIRTS

Unravelled Yarns

"Unravelled aims to create high-quality T-shirt yarn that provides a third way to process waste textiles (after off-shoring and landfilling) that is truly sustainable and keeps waste on-shore."

Companies often print too many branded T-shirts for an event, or perhaps they go out of business, leaving branded inventory. Unravelled began as a student project by Diana Grant-Richmond and Ashika Thaker in Mount Royal University, in Calgary, Alberta, Canada. "Unravelled was created with the goal of finding a way to create truly upcycled T-shirt yarn that was comfortable and easy to use, and used 100% postproduction materials," explains Diana. "I had seen many other T-shirt yarns in the market and was disappointed to find out that most of it was new material, and often difficult to work with."

Today, Diana runs Unravelled from her home, releasing new colours as they become available. "T-shirts are sourced from companies that have over-printed branded materials and are storing them because they can't figure out what to do with the T-shirts. We help save the company money in storage costs and promise logo destruction so the branding is never misused. We have no control over the colours of T-shirts we receive for recycling, so colours are usually a surprise and highly limited. We do employ some dyeing techniques when we receive too much of a certain colour or a less popular colour, and we're looking forward to exploring and expanding on those techniques in the near future."

The T-shirts are washed to remove the sizing, then cut underneath the arms, cut again in a specific way, then stretched to form the yarn. "T-shirt yarn or rag yarn has been made for decades and has come in and out of fashion. It has never really been commercially available and has never used waste T-shirts as the raw material before," explains Diana. "To be able to

"The major impact of the business is the creation of a new form of upcycling and waste diversion, but the ultimate goal is to contribute to increased textile recycling and spread the story of how to be zero waste in all our deeds."

make the yarn in a repeatable, reliable and economic way, new templating technology was designed."

"Unravelled was formed with a minimalist aesthetic in mind, in order to emphasize the unique look and texture of the yarn. The edges are a bit distressed and we leave sections of heat-printed or silk-screened logos in the yarn, giving the yarn a really different look from other T-shirt yarns on the market. When made into a textile, you can sometimes see the shadow of the screen printing through sections of the yarn." This is an important part of the story, as it shows how creative upcycling can have a positive impact on something previously thought to be waste. ✻

UNRAVELLED YARNS

WHITNEY CRUTCHFIELD

WE GATHER

Crafting and making have always been important for Whitney Crutchfield. "Creating things by hand has accompanied me through almost every phase of life so far," she says, recalling her upbringing in a small town in Michigan. "I dabbled in almost any craft you could imagine, gradually claiming more and more drawers and kitchen cabinets for my art supply arsenal." Her mother taught her how to sew, she learned to knit using garage-sale yarns and she remembers weaving a scarf on a tiny rigid heddle loom. "I found myself making gifts for friends and family, and constantly picking up new creative hobbies."

Her father owned a small business in their rural hometown and Whitney says she had the itch to be a business owner from a young age. "I had the opportunity to witness both the good and the bad aspects of business ownership firsthand, and I was very much enchanted by the flexibility and satisfaction reaped from such a pursuit."

During college, Whitney began to follow her urge to explore materials and techniques in the fibre department. "That's where I began to believe that these skills might really be able to become a career path, in large part because of a very supportive and encouraging professor," she says. "I fell hard for the math and organization of weaving, for the function that can come from beautiful forms and for the purely aesthetic pleasure. I decided to enroll in an MFA program in fibres at Colorado State University and spent three years developing my screenprinting and dyeing techniques, using weaving as a means to relax in between academic projects."

After grad school, Whitney headed to New York City for an artist residency at the Textile Arts Center

"WE GATHER celebrates the threads that connect us, bringing you into the world of textiles through hands-on experiences and handmade goods that last. I aim to foster a more creative, less wasteful world."

in Brooklyn and an unpaid internship in the crafts department at *Martha Stewart Living*. "I thought that I might stay in the city for four to five months and then have to find some other alternative, but those two experiences proved to be formative and opened up two really vital networks of talented and thoughtful people," says Whitney. She landed what she thought was her dream job—textile designer for a major fashion brand—and while she adored working with colour and pattern on a daily basis, there was a lack on hands-on creativity. She was also concerned about the amount of waste in the fashion industry. With the desire for her own business still strong, and with over a year of planning and preparation, she left her day job to launch WE GATHER out of her studio—which at that time, was really just the tiny second bedroom in her Brooklyn apartment. Hand dyeing was done in the bathtub.

As her business has grown, Whitney has found a studio space outside of her home, for hosting workshops on weaving and dyeing, creating product kits and making her own art. "WE GATHER is a very small business," she says. "For most of its five-year history, I have been the only employee. However, it has come into being only through the efforts and support of a community of people, whether they be friends and family who have cheered me along, fellow textile entrepreneurs who have shared their perspectives, or customers-turned-friends who have inspired me to create better, more welcoming products and workshops. I am finding that the small scale of WE GATHER may be its largest asset—its impact is intimate, and I have no grandiose plans for wild growth. WE GATHER lives within its means."

Whitney thinks about her business as three different branches: DIY kits, in-person workshops and custom textile art. While the pandemic has made the physical aspect of gathering impossible for a time, WE GATHER's craft kits are prepared and packed in the studio. "The Frame Loom Weaving Kit is one of the

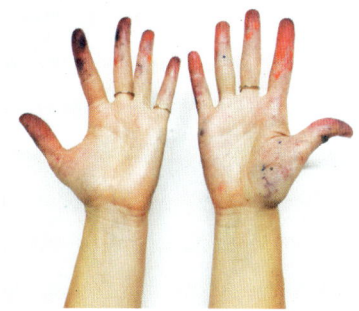

BALANCE

WE GATHER's signature is balance in all things. I apply that to the workshops that I teach, offering expert instruction with a compassionate and flexible approach. I do my best to offer balance in the kits I create, including really thoughtful and high-quality materials, without expecting you to invest your entire paycheck in a new, untested pursuit. There is physical balance in the textile techniques that I celebrate—weaving from side to side, stitching down and up, landing on just the right dye recipe. An emphasis on balance allows WE GATHER to remove the mystery of making while emphasizing how empowering it can be.

most popular products, and it is completely designed and packed right here in Brooklyn, with every component tested by my own weaving hands. The wooden parts of the loom come from a woodworker in Colorado. Once those arrive, I dust every single piece and power sand a few of the tools to work them into just the right shape for weaving. I wind each warp yarn holder individually with enough yarn for two projects. Then I select a collection of natural fibre yarns from the studio and wind kit-sized bundles of each of the six yarns. The organic cotton project bags are each stamped with the WE GATHER logo and left to dry. Then the loom and all of the wooden tools, metal needle, instruction booklet and yarn collection are all packed into the bag, ready and waiting for their new owner!"

Each order is packed with a handwritten note, a small touch that communicates a lot about creating personal connections. "The guiding value of WE GATHER is to build and support the community while honouring history and traditions," says Whitney. "That means that I always work toward learning experiences that welcome anyone and everyone, that our collective making histories are acknowledged and valued, and that we are able to create connection through cloth, even when we have nothing else in common." ✷

RESPECTING TRADITION

My processes are entirely rooted in tradition. There is no single textile technique that would exist today without the ingenuity, the skill and often the sacrifice of women and men around the world and over the course of millennia, and because of that, there is unending complexity and depth in the textile world. There are countless histories captured in our threads. I weave on looms that are not that much different from the looms used in Egypt 3,000 years ago. The linen and wool yarns that I run through my hands find their origins in the hands of people who lived 20,000 year ago. As a white woman privileged to make this my work today, I owe everything I know to generations of non-white experts who came long before me.

"Through WE GATHER, I embrace a holistic story of textiles, what they mean to us and the ways in which they touch every person on the planet."

wegathergoods.com
@wegather

STUDIO

I work out of a small studio space in a complex called Industry City, located in the neighbourhood of Sunset Park in Brooklyn, New York. I feel so fortunate to have a private space just for this business. It is bright with natural light and I'm surrounded by lots of other creative business people. There is a central table for workshops and big projects, and I've created a small shipping space and a "kitchen," as well as an area dedicated to dyeing supplies. My two main floor looms—Ruby and Lindy—reside here, too. I use these for commission weavings and for weaving samples for workshops and lessons.

WE GATHER

RACHEL SNACK

Weaver House

Rachel Snack began her creative studies with painting and making ceramics, but when she enrolled in an introduction to textiles class, her path changed. "There was a kinship I felt the first time I attempted to weave cloth," she says. "I saw weaving as a tangible way to form identity—I embodied the loom." Rachel describes the first loom she ever wove on: "It was a four-harness tabletop loom, which meant I had yet to be introduced to foot treadling. I was tasked to create a small sample and instead sat at the loom for several hours, embracing the way my body and the loom worked together in motion. I was quickly hooked and immediately enrolled in an introduction to weaving course."

Rachel received bachelor of fine art in fibre and material studies from the School of the Art Institute of Chicago and a master of science in textile design from Philadelphia University. For Rachel, weaving is a practice that pays homage to craft tradition and it is also a spiritual activity. The act of weaving creates a dialogue between the maker and the loom.

"My practice is grounded in the idea of growing a tangible language, by themes of weaving, the grid, body, place, land, sacred space, stillness, line, vessel and memory. My weavings celebrate the quiet and often missed moments in life, the sacred space of the loom, the concept of weaving in infinity and the tactile vessel. They are made on the loom in connection to the grid, to craft a relationship with the body and create a religion of space apart from the loom."

Her own identity as a person and a maker is preserved in the fabric she weaves. "They are a preservation of my place in the non-relational matrix, creating material evidence, bearing witness. They are my identity, my routine, my rite of passage."

"My practice is intuitive, responsive and anchored in textile history. I see the loom as an instrument, and as a maker I push the boundaries of this tool, finding new ways to approach textile making."

In our contemporary mass-produced culture, creating uniquely by hand, employing a traditional method that takes considerable time and uses natural materials, makes a statement. "Making thoughtfully and consciously is important not only to my practice, but also in the way I interact with our consumer-driven culture as an individual," says Rachel. "The idea of purchasing something that is produced in conditions that are inhumane, with unnatural and environmentally damaging materials—seen in fast fashion and large textile retailers—is an affront on humankind. I believe we all must take an active role in considering the way in which we invest our time and resources, on a small and large scale."

Furthering her art education with real-world experience, Rachel attended an artist residency in Peru, working with women weavers. "It was my first opportunity to immerse myself in another culture

"Woven structure formulates the grid, offering a basis and mode for development in areas reaching far past the loom. Subsequently, woven structure is also the interlacing of space, technically and conceptually, at the loom. Through methods of studying structure, I sketch and formulate a groundwork before responding instinctively while weaving."

and have some space from an American philosophy of living. When I returned to the US in 2014, I quickly realized I wanted to pursue a path that would allow me to weave often and spend a lot of time in the studio." She founded Weaver House at that time, at first as a passion project. It became a full-time business in the fall of 2019, encompassing a yarn shop, textile studio and weaving school. Rachel shares her philosophy of weaving with her students. "We teach mindfulness and mediation throughout all of our workshops and believe that weaving can be therapeutic and healing. Our workshops include all levels of weaving and sometimes highlight other craft techniques like yarn and fabric dyeing, sewing, fibre sculpture, macramé and embroidery. Our shop is carefully curated with specialty fibres sourced from around the world, hand-selected textiles and goods, and weaving equipment." ✺

"I work on 4- to 12-harness floor looms, using techniques such as pick up, supplemental weft, double cloth and ikat resist dyeing. I gravitate towards natural materials, and work mainly with cotton, linen and wool. Occasionally I will also work with mohair, bamboo, chenille and rope."

weaverhouseco.com
@weaverhouseco

STUDIO/SCHOOL

My studio is shared with Weaver House, the weaving school I own and operate. It comprises many floor looms, a large working table, a yarn wall and weaving equipment crammed into every corner. I appreciate having so many looms at my disposal, so I can have a few projects going at once and float between warps. I also have a loom at home that I weave on in the evenings.

Because of the nature of my practice, I tend to work alone. However, I find other ways of engaging with artists and makers — by teaching and through collaborative projects.

NIC CORRIGAN

Whitehall Studio

Nic Corrigan is a knitwear designer and maker based in Yorkshire, England. "I arrived at this fairly late in life," says Nic, who returned to university to study fashion design after an established career in marketing. It was a long-held dream that she had sacrificed to focus on a more "academic route." Working as a high street fashion knitwear designer seemed glamorous as first, with trips to the Far East and shopping trips to Paris and New York. "But the shine soon wore off and I became very disillusioned about the industry. I had risen to become a design manager and spent all of my time in meetings or working on costings or delivery schedules. All the creativity I had loved at uni had gone and the nastiness of the industry was soul destroying."

In 2014, Nic looked back to her creative dream and decided to launch Whitehall Studio, as a home for her own knitwear designs. "I now get to spend my days creating well-designed, machine-knitted garments in a slow, sustainable way as well as encouraging and supporting anybody who wants to do the same."

"I particularly wanted to promote the art of machine knitting, which is often seen as old-fashioned, unfashionable and not really a true craft. Many people think that because you are using a machine, you are cheating, and that anything you make is inferior to hand knitting. But there is still a huge amount of hand work involved and nobody ever tells a seamstress that using a sewing machine is cheating! There are a lot of incredibly talented designers around now who use knitting machines to design things that blow your mind."

By teaching others, Nic encourages others to give machine knitting a chance. "I am motivated by

"For me, the absolute joy of designing knitwear is starting with just a cone of yarn and ending up with something you can use or wear. Whilst I love all fashion design, with knitting you have total control because you are making the fabric at the same time as shaping the garment. There really is no limit apart from your imagination."

"I love the circular concept of knitting with wool, where you can take a sheep's fleece, process it and then knit something that is unique to you. It is the total antithesis of fast fashion and mass production."

a desire to try and reinvigorate the field of machine knitting. The heyday for knitting machines was in the 1970s and 80s, and so unfortunately a lot of the resources available date from that era and can be incredibly outmoded," she admits. "The machines can be a bit daunting for beginners and many try and then give up, which is such a shame. I really want to support and encourage others, as I know personally how rewarding it is to make and design your own clothes."

Nic is enamoured with the process. "When I get a new cone of yarn, the first thing I do is to jump on a machine and knit a few swatches." Using her expertise and knowledge, she typically has a starting point: "But sometimes ideas appear once I've started knitting, and tweaks and experiments can produce some really interesting swatches. This is one of the things I love about the immediacy of machine knitting—a small swatch will take you 10 minutes and after a couple of happy hours I have a heap of swatches to play and design with."

"Taking something that starts as just a germ of an idea in your head or on paper and realizing it into a 3D object takes you through all the emotions, from fear, frustration, confusion, curiosity, exploration and eventually to satisfaction," explains Nic. "The ability to be able to say, 'I made that,' and know that it would never have existed without your input is very affirming." ✻

PROVENANCE

I create garments and accessories using wool and cashmere. The majority of my work uses yarn from the oldest remaining spinning mill in Scotland, which has been in work since 1798! I love using their yarn, as it's high quality and available in a beautiful selection of colours. Normally I order a delivery but I have visited the mill twice and it's an amazing place: a small stone-built building at the end of a tiny lane in the middle of nowhere. You feel immediately as if you are stepping back in time. Even though it's small, they are highly successful and supply to many of the catwalk labels. The other yarn I use is from the opposite end of the spectrum and comes from a hobby farmer, Jo, who lives less than 10 miles from my studio. She has a small flock of pet Ryeland sheep (who all have names!). When they are sheared she gets the yarn processed and I receive cones of undyed yarn, which I use for a range of scarves and wrist warmers. All in all, from sheep to finished product, there is a journey of about 100 miles. This is an area I am keen to develop, as a local, circular economy is going to be an important asset in the future.

FAIR ISLE KNITTING

One of the techniques I love to use in my work is Fair Isle knitting, which uses punchcards to produce two-colour patterns. My most well-known design is called "Hebden Houses" and is based on the houses in my local town, which are quite distinctive, as they are built into the steep hillsides on either side of the valley. I use this pattern on socks, scarves and hats, and they are extremely popular. They have even been featured on the final episode of the *Great British Bake Off* TV program, when worn by one of the judges.

Place is an important element of my work and I feel very rooted to the landscape where I live and work. All my garments are named after local landmarks, and my "Calderisle" sweater is a modern Fair Isle pattern based on cups of tea, Yorkshire phrases and the weather!

Because of the nature of Fair Isle, each design has to work in a 24-stitch pattern repeat and so needs to be simplistic in style, and I get a lot of fun from sitting with square paper and marking out designs. I also love the colourwork aspect to it and spend time knitting swatches of multiple colour combinations.

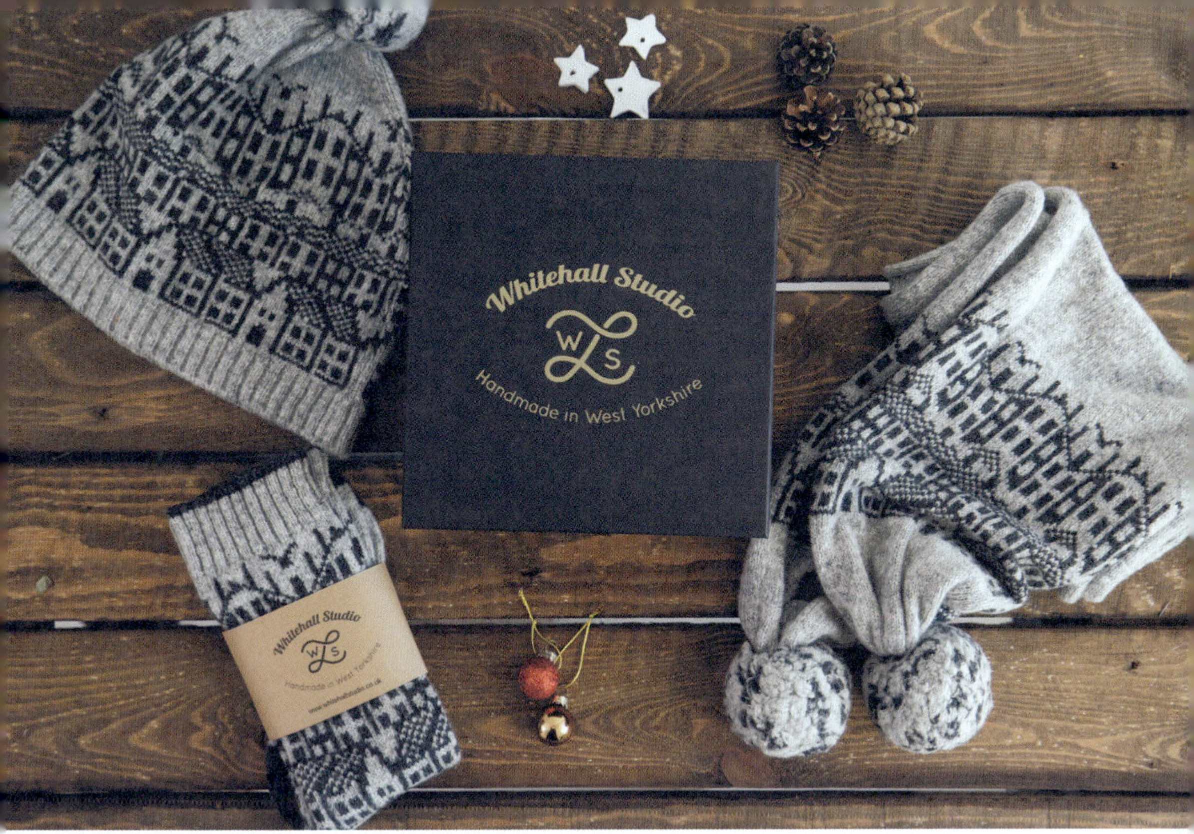
Whitehall Studio
Handmade in West Yorkshire
Whitehall Studio
Handmade in West Yorkshire

Whitehall Studio
Whitehall Studio

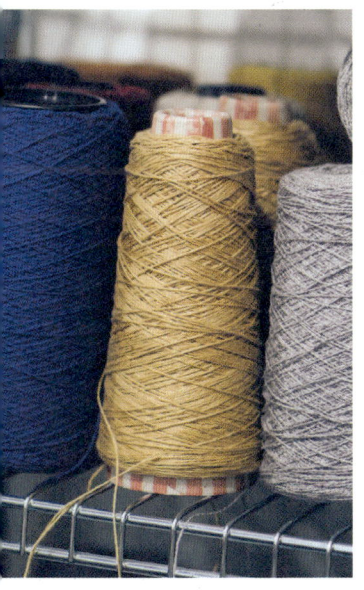

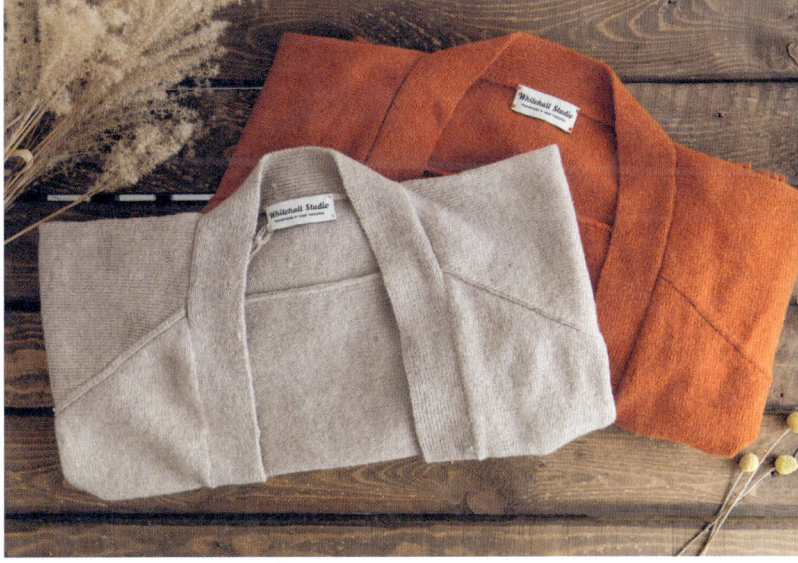

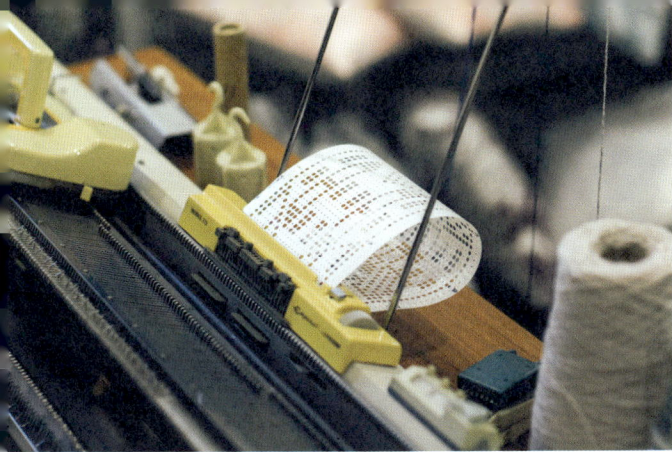

whitehallstudio.co.uk
@whitehall_studio

STUDIO

Since receiving my first knitting machine 15 years ago, I have now managed to amass more than 10 machines. I have a range of gauges so that I can knit all types of fabric, from really delicate to chunkier knits more akin to hand knitting. The majority of my machines are vintage from the 1970s but recently I invested in my first ever brand new machines. These give me the ability to link them to a laptop for designing patterns. I resisted this for a long time, as I liked the ethos of using pre-loved machines and the restrictions that designing in pattern repeats enforced. But I've had to admit that the range of patterns I can now design freely has opened up a whole new world to my work.

I work from a small studio at the top of my house, which is a 300-year-old converted barn in a small village that used to be a centre for weaving in the 18th century. I am surrounded by my machines and yarns, and I love the fact that as soon as I have an idea, I can jump on a machine and see how it will turn out.

SPINNER, PANGONG CRAFT CENTER, INDIA

LINDA CORTRIGHT

Wild Fibers

Linda Cortright is a writer, photographer, world traveller, publisher, entrepreneur and farmer, and likely has other vocations, talents and professions to add to this list. "I moved to the mountains of Maine from suburban Philadelphia in 1995 to begin raising cashmere goats," Linda says. "Prior to then, I had a 'tossed salad' of jobs, including working in television, dog grooming and nuclear training. My two passions from childhood had always been farming and writing. My move to Maine satisfied the first, and my experience as a farmer ultimately led to fulfilling the second, with the launch of *Wild Fibers* in 2004."

The publication, currently released annually, is often described as "the *National Geographic* of the fibre world" for its global exploration and high-

"The 'shop local' mantra now extends beyond the food industry and has become an increasing mantle within the fibre world. My readers constantly comment on how amazed (and grateful) they are to know how many small producers are tucked away in some very remote corners of the world."

ABOVE: RACKA SHEEP, ROMANIA
BELOW: SPINNER, OMAN

quality photography, shot by Linda herself. The content educates readers about the impact fibre farming has on people, culture and the environment. "Unlike yarn manufacturers, our focus is on helping people make informed choices. Teaching them through the magazine's educational and entertaining format underscores the impact of their purchasing power, whether it is directly from a fibre farmer or the artisan. One of the greatest challenges is teaching fibre enthusiasts in Western cultures that knitting, spinning, weaving, etc., as a hobby or passion, is a luxury ill afforded by the very people who provide us with the materials we need. I would like to believe that after 17 years, *Wild Fibers* has helped to change consumer's understanding of the natural fibre world."

Linda leads tours while gathering experiences to publish in the magazine, going to India's High Himalayas, the Falkland Islands, South Africa, Swaziland, Antarctica, South Georgia, Alaska and the Russian Arctic. "When I began leading tours, it was with the

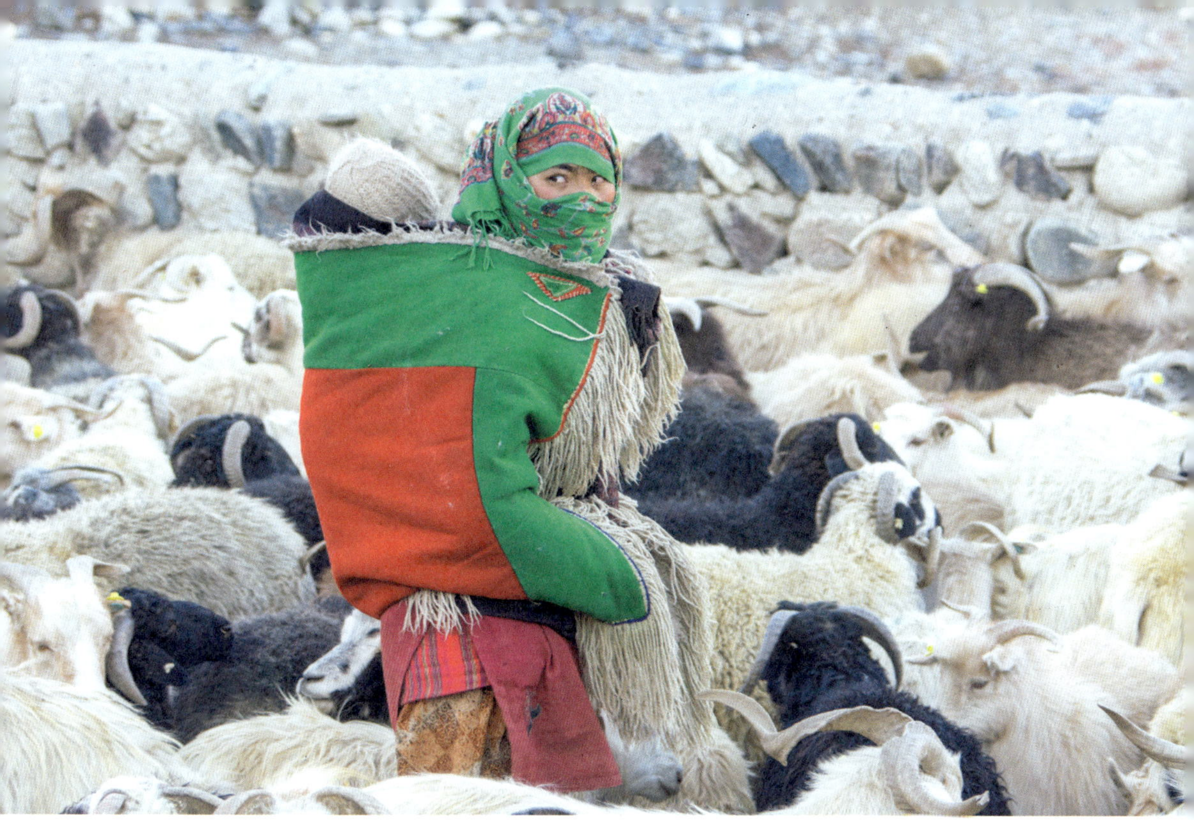

hope that I could directly share the extraordinary experiences I have had around the world, all because of my love of fibre. Beyond the impact of the magazine, there is no doubt that those who have been on a Wild Fibers Tour come away with a once-in-a-lifetime experience that has reshaped their understanding not only of others but of themselves. I have the deepest gratitude for having the opportunity to affect someone's life at that level, and not just once, but repeatedly."

Linda has found a way to give back to a culture and community that she loves, with *Wild Fibers* opening the Pangong Craft Center in Phobrang village in India's High Himalayas. At an altitude of 14,650 feet, the Center provides a warm, well-lit space for semi-nomadic women to spin and weave cashmere from the goats they lovingly raise. "We are fortunate to have been able to put into action the very principles we believe in by demonstrating the importance of natural fibres and how they can support local communities," says Linda. ✻

ABOVE: NOMADIC SHEPHERDESS, HIGH HIMALAYAS, INDIA
BELOW: WEAVER, HIGH HIMALAYAS, INDIA

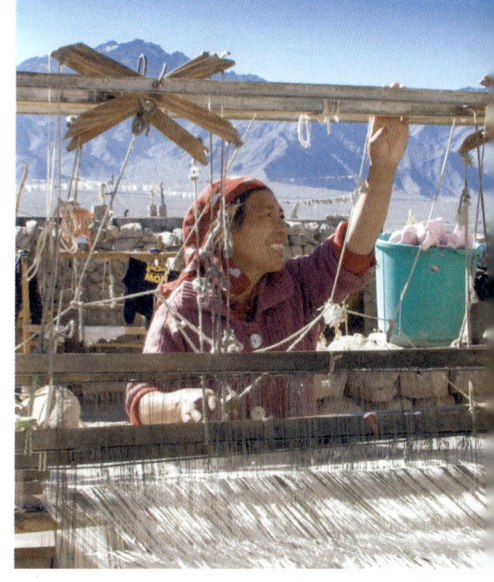

"Prior to becoming a farmer, I believed wool came in two flavors, itchy and super itchy. I had little understanding of alpacas beyond the shaggy ponchos friends brought back from Peru. And if you had shown me a picture of a musk ox, claiming its undercoat was softer than cashmere, I would have smote you with my knitting needle."

–FROM THE PREFACE OF *THE EYE OF FIBER*,
A PHOTOGRAPHY BOOK BY LINDA CORTRIGHT

PHOTO: CASHMERE GOATS, MONGOLIA

"In five short years, the Center has grown to more than 130 members, producing beautiful handspun yarn and other cashmere items. The women are deeply grateful for the opportunity to earn extra income, and for a communal space where they can socialize and bring their children."

PANGONG CRAFT CENTER CASHMERE

The Pangong Craft Center is heated by a special passive solar design, creating a greenhouse effect using a "greenhouse chamber" to heat the building. The bricks are made from locally sourced rammed earth and the ceiling is insulated with cashmere "waste" fibre from the mill.

Historically, the nomadic women of Ladakh do not spin cashmere; they would sell it to the traders who would then take it to Kashmir. However, they have always used spinning technology for their own needs, from clothing to tents, using a combination of sheep and yak wool. The Pangong Craft Center is vertically integrated, whereby the people who raise the animals are also responsible for all stages of processing, including knitted and woven garments.

The Center now has more than 130 members. Through the Wild Fibers website, we sell scoured, organic cashmere from the Chang-pa (nomads) in India. We know the nomads who raise the goats. The mill in Leh, India, is owned and operated by a semi-nomadic cooperative, using all organic materials, including solar power for heating the water. The cashmere is then hand spun on either a support spindle or a traditional wheel at the Pangong Craft Center in the village by Pangong Lake, at 14,500 feet. No other cashmere yarn is processed in this way.

wildfibersmagazine.com
pangongcraftcenter.com

REBECCA GLAZIER

WildWestDye

After working in the garment industry for 20 years, Rebecca Glazier was disillusioned with fast fashion. Though she loved that it had brought her from her native United Kingdom to Sri Lanka—"I had a fantastic time in Sri Lanka," she says, "it's a beautiful, colourful, inspirational place to live"—she had spent the last few years there soul searching and wondering what to do next.

"Whilst in Sri Lanka I realized how much I loved encouraging others to be creative. I set up a monthly knitting group and dreamed of opening my own yarn and tea shop one day. I thought about selling yarn kits for colourwork but never did I think of dyeing my own yarn—that came later. After eight years in Sri Lanka, the time had come to move on. I had the opportunity to move to Canada, and went for it. The first thing I thought about was knitting a sweater!"

Once settled in her new home in Vancouver, Rebecca started a weekly knitting meetup called Knit1Tea1. "I started teaching knitting, something I love to do very much," she says. With the encouragement of her partner, she also started her business, WildWestDye. "Without his encouragement, I do not know if I would have ever taken the leap, and I am truly thankful for all the faith he has in me. I had been naturally dyeing and attending workshops for years, and after completing a week-long intensive workshop on natural dyeing, all the pieces fell into place."

Loving lacework, cables and colourwork, Rebecca believes that knitting techniques look best with solid and semi-solid colours, which she sells in CakeQuarters. "All my yarn is sold in 25-gram increments and wound into one cake—up to 300 grams. If you buy 10 CakeQuarters, you receive one 250-gram cake of yarn.

"I follow the techniques and guidelines of traditional recipes that date back hundreds of years and adjust them where needed to create my own palette and colourways. I also use modern guidelines to ensure no toxic ingredients are used."

I do this for a few reasons: one, because my yarn is a higher price point due to it being naturally dyed, and if you only need 75 grams to complete a project you don't need to purchase 100 grams to do this." Rebecca also loves knitwear designs that use multiple colours, and having the CakeQuarters in small increments allows her customers to more easily purchase multiple colours. "As a thrifty person myself, I have always struggled to justify buying so many balls of yarn," she says. "I do not want my yarn to end up in a stash for years! Not that there is anything wrong with a stash, I have a large one myself—however, I want my yarn to be created into something and not just sit around."

Her business is new and her work is done at home. "I dye in my tiny kitchen on my hob and one additional heater, my balcony is where all the indigo is dyed and my living room is now my yarn processing and storage area."

With a memorable cowboy boot as her logo—and a collection of boots that match her colourways (or is it vice versa?), WildWestDye is ready for the next steps. "Eventually," says Rebecca, "my ambition is to open my own yarn and tea/coffee shop, with a space for community meet-ups and teaching. Talking with creatives about what they are working on, what they want to work on next, what colours and fibres they want to try is pure joy for me." ✿

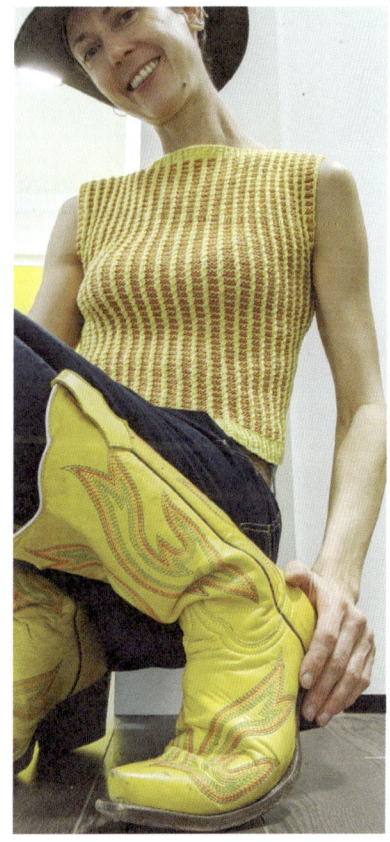

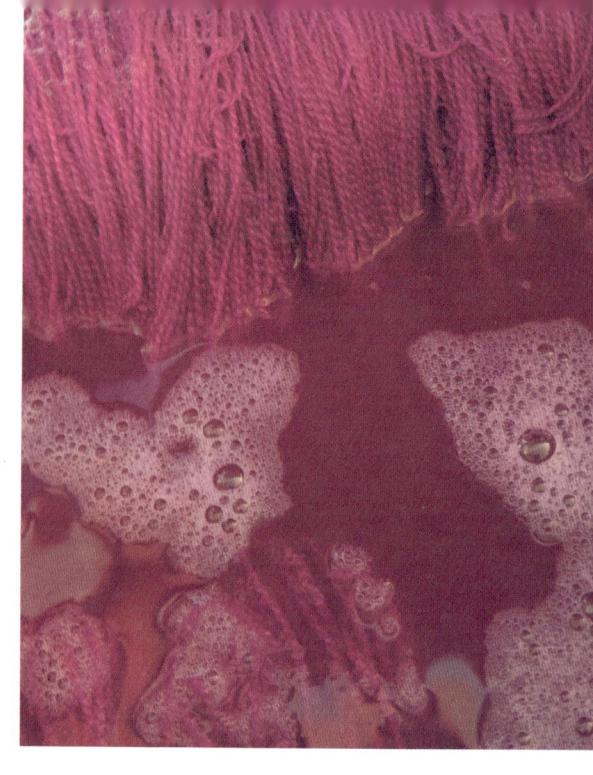

THE WILDWESTDYE PROCESS OF DYEING WOOL

YARN

My yarn is sourced from a Canadian mill, Elitespun—the first spinning mill in North America to be certified RWS (Responsible Wool Standard). The yarn is received on cones and wound into 300-gram skeins on a wooden vertical yarn swift. I dye in batches of 600 grams or 900 grams. The skeins are scoured (washed).

DYESTUFF

The dyestuff is sourced from Maiwa, a Vancouver family-owned business. Supporting local businesses means a lot to me.

If the particular recipe requires indigo as the first layer, the skeins are indigo dyed. Depending on how I want the indigo, depth and coverage will dictate the strength of the vat, how many times they are dipped in the vat, and whether they are agitated in the vat or squeezed and laid in the vat with little movement.

MORDANT

The next step is the mordant process. This is an application of alum (potassium alum sulfate). The skeins are brought up to a temperature of 90 degrees and held for an hour. They stay in the dye pot for 24 hours before proceeding with the next process.

COLOUR

Next is applying the colour—the fun part! The dye pot is brought to temperature and held for one hour. The skeins cool in the dye pot and rest in there for 24 hours. They are then rinsed, spun out to remove excess water and placed on a drying rack. After two weeks of resting, the skeins are washed with a pH-neutral soap and allowed to dry.

wildwestdye.com
@wildwestdye

PERSONALITY

One of the things I really love about natural dyeing is the many colours you can coax from the dyes. There is the colour in its "original" form, then blending colours and different dye ingredients together either by layering—dyeing one colour first (either indigo or a twisted skein low-immersion dye technique I use)—or by mixing two dyes in the same pot. I really love how using a shifter (such as cream of tartar or soda ash) and adjusting the pH level can change the outcome of the colour, I find this so interesting and such a joy to see how many colours you can get from one dye material using only shifters.

CAKES

Skeins remain as skeins until an order is placed. They are wound into one giant cake, and the order quantity is then wound off into the CakeQuarter quantity purchased, ready to knit.

THREADUCATION

WonderFil Specialty Threads

Beginning as a thread and yarn manufacturer founded in 1988 in Calgary, Alberta, Canada, WonderFil mainly supplied to industrial users. A dozen years into the business, the home sewing market caught the company's attention. Realizing that the thread variety available to sewers was limited, they saw an opportunity. "Instead of coming into the industry just as another brand, we decided to focus on specialty threads, and set up the WonderFil Specialty Threads division in the year 2000," says Andrew Ngai, president. "As a common purpose, of all our Specialty Threads must be able to help elevate the sewn quality and expressiveness of every single project. Our product development work is extremely application driven."

"Today we've expanded our selection to 36 specialty thread lines, ranging from 100 weight to 3 weight in cotton, wool, rayon, polyester and metallic materials,

"We're proud to be one of the very few thread companies that manufactures every single thread line ourselves. This means that every time you pick up a spool of WonderFil-brand thread, you'll know that we took the time to source the materials it was spun from, manufactured the thread in our own facilities and did all the checks to control the quality ourselves."

proudly allowing us to offer a versatile thread selection for every project. With our global team of designers, marketers and production workers, we take pride in sourcing and manufacturing each thread line ourselves so that we can guarantee the quality and consistency expected by professional and hobby sewists."

Their vision has always been to inspire and educate their retailers and their customers, and for that purpose, they have coined the term "threaducation." "We have strived to make our brand accessible to quilters, embroiderers and sewists of all levels," Andrew says. "Not just for professionals, but also for newer and younger generations. Our focus is to provide educational blogs, tips, free patterns and tutorials on our active YouTube channel, as well as Instagram, Facebook and a weekly newsletter. We stay on trend with the newest inspirations and keep active on our online platforms to threaducate the sewing community."

Customer satisfaction is important to the company, and with more education available to their customers—resulting in successful projects both large and small—the happier they are.

"With our devotion and determination in threaducating the industry, we have seen increased awareness and creativity in all walks of sewing projects since the launch of WonderFil Specialty Threads a couple of decades ago," Andrew says.

To maintain their quality standards, the company oversees all aspects of the production of their products, from sourcing the raw materials through manufacturing to marketing.

"Our vision from the very first day has been to inspire and educate our retailers and sewers across the globe," says Andrew, "giving them the right tools to create beautiful pieces that can be treasured. The most incredible part for us is seeing our threads in the hands of quilters, embroiderers and sewists. We absolutely adore seeing the beautiful and inspirational projects being made all around the world, and it brings us great joy to see them stitched in everything from award-winning quilts to a new grandson's baby blanket, or even a graduate's prom dress."

"We want to bring sewists something special that they can rely on and use to create memorable projects and quilts that will be passed down through generations." ✢

QUILTING BY DEBBIE BROWN

wonderfil.ca
@wonderfilspecialtythread

MAKING THREAD

PROCUREMENT

Our quality assurance starts at sourcing and procuring raw materials. Amongst the best origins of materials, we still scrutinize for the grade and category that best suit the manufacture of thread. To name a few, the fibres we adopt for our production include merino wool from Australia, Giza cotton from Egypt, anodized film from Japan and polyester chips from Germany.

SPINNING, TWISTING AND WRAPPING

There are typically three main processes in single-yarn production: they are spinning for staple fibre, twisting for filament and wrapping for core yarn. After the single yarn is made, the plying process follows, turning the yarn into thread in its greige form, which consists of two single yarns or more. With the greige yarn there are a number of different proprietary processes they may undergo for various purposes. The processed greige thread is then sent for dyeing and finishing, and subsequently spooling and packaging.

Our Konfetti line, for instance, is a spun yarn with Giza cotton from Egypt. There are various grades of Giza cotton—the one we adopt is Giza 88, characterized by longer, finer, more uniform, better-strength fibres.

Besides the inherent quality of the fibre, the following two processes have a direct effect on the quality of the finished cotton thread. However, these processes may not be adopted by every brand, for economic considerations.

MERCERIZATION

This finishing treatment enhances the dye uptake of the fibre to give a more saturated colour, increases the overall breaking strength by about 5% and reduces shrinkage.

GASSING

This manufacturing process reduces the amount of lint on the cotton thread by running the thread through a ring of flame at a controlled speed. At WonderFil, this process is carried out twice to eliminate as much lint as possible, and we have given it a unique term: "double gassed."

ENCYCLOPEDIA OF INSPIRATION

UPPERCASE

A multi-volume book series released in whimsical (non-alphabetical) order on all manner of intriguing and creative topics.

- C — CERAMICS
- Q — QUILTED
- V — VINTAGE LIFE
- E — EPHEMERA
- P — PRINT/MAKER
- B — BOTANICA
- S — STITCH-ILLO
- F — FEED SACKS

@uppercasemag
uppercasemagazine.com
encyclopediaofinspiration.com